IR
IN
P

IRELAND IN YOUR POCKET

COMPILED BY ANTONY SHAW

GILL & MACMILLAN

Published in Ireland by
Gill & Macmillan Ltd
Hume Avenue, Park West
Dublin 12
with associated companies throughout the world
www.gillmacmillan.ie
0 7171 3579 9

Published by arrangement with Salamander Books Ltd, London

Printed in China

A CIP catalogue record for this book is available from the British Library.

For All My Family

Credits
Consultant: Dr Mark Waugh
Editor: Michael Washburn
Art Director: John Heritage
Cover Design: Cara Hamilton
Interior Design: Heather Moore (twelveotwo)
Picture Research: Antony Shaw
Indexer: Chris Bernstein
Production: Don Campaniello
Colour Reproduction: Anorax Ltd

Contents

Introduction 6
Basic Facts 8
Getting to Ireland 15
Geography 17
Physical Extremities 20
Ireland's Weather 27
A Brief History 28
Key Dates 78
Irish Lives 99
The Irish Diaspora 134
A County Guide 144
Ireland's Cities 184
Place Names 194
Ireland's Landmarks 204
Family Names 224
Irish First Names 264
The Irish Language 282
Simple Irish Phrases 288
Literary Ireland 296
Authors and Poets 304
Music 318
Arts and Crafts 325
Round Towers 330
Sacred Ireland 336
Ireland's Saints 342
St. Patrick 350
Prayers and Blessings 358
Folklore 362
Irish Dancing 369
Quotes and Sayings 372
Toasts 377
Wedding Traditions 381
Sport 384
Flora and Fauna 389
The Peat Bogs 395
Native Dog Breeds 402
Ireland's Islands 411
Food and Drink 428
Favorite Dishes 446

Index 472
Acknowledgements 480

INTRODUCTION

◆ ◆ ◆

From dramatic mountains to elegant Georgian houses, Ireland is a land of contrast and beauty.

◆ ◆ ◆

Ireland is an experience different for every person, a place where one can enjoy some of Europe's finest unspoiled scenery, architectural gems, sacred sites, and greatest bars!

The island of Ireland is steeped in history, legend, and tradition. Today the island has a flourishing economy, a prosperous population, and a dynamic cultural life. Ireland's sons and daughters have had a huge impact on the arts, academia, religion, politics, and sport. Those who left Ireland have enriched their adopted homelands across the world.

Ireland's counties have a fantastic range of countryside and attractions. The cities and towns, although relatively contained compared to other European centers, have plenty to interest the visitor.

Ireland is idyllically and intrinsically green. The unspoiled landscape has many interesting features. The country is rich in natural produce. This book explores the many features of this unique and enchanting land.

LEFT: *The still waters of Killary Harbor, near Leenane in County Galway.*

Basic Facts

◆ ◆ ◆

Bunreacht na hÉireann, the Constitution of Ireland, provides in Article 4 that the name of the State is Éire, or in the English language, Ireland.

◆ ◆ ◆

Government type: Republic

Capital: Republic of Ireland: Dublin
Northern Ireland: Belfast

Administrative divisions:
Ireland consists of four provinces which are broken down into 32 counties:

Ulster: Cavan, Donegal, Monaghan (all in the Republic), Antrim, Armagh, Derry, Down, Fermanagh, and Tyrone (all in Northern Ireland).

Leinster: Carlow, Dublin, Kildare, Kilkenny, Laois, Longford, Louth, Meath, Offaly, Westmeath, Wexford, and Wicklow.

LEFT: *Government Buildings, in the heart of Dublin, was originally the Royal College of Science.*

Munster: Clare, Cork, Kerry, Limerick, Tipperary, and Waterford.

Connacht: Sligo, Mayo, Galway, Roscommon, and Leitrim.

Independence:
December 6, 1921 (from UK)

National holiday:
St. Patrick's Day, March 17

Constitution:
December 29, 1937; adopted July 1, 1937 by plebiscite

Legal system:
Based on English common law, substantially modified by indigenous concepts; judicial review of legislative acts in Supreme Court; has not accepted compulsory ICJ jurisdiction.

Voting:
18 years of age; universal

Executive branch:
Head of state: President Mary McAleese (since November 11, 1997)

Head of government: Taoiseach (Prime Minister) Bertie Ahern (since June 26, 1997).

Cabinet: Cabinet appointed by the President with previous nomination by the Taoiseach and approval of the House of Representatives.

Elections: President elected by popular vote for a seven-year term; Taoiseach nominated by the House of Representatives and appointed by the President.

Legislative branch:
The Republic of Ireland's bicameral legislature was established in 1949. The national parliament (*Oireachtas*) consists of the President and two Houses. The *Dáil* or Lower House is comprised of 166 members elected every five years. A member's official Irish title is *Teachta Dála* (Deputy to the *Dáil*) or TD. The Senate or Upper House (*Seanad Éireann*) consists of 49 elected members and 11 political appointees.

Elections:
Dáil (parliamentary) elections occur at least every five years; an election for the *Seanad* takes place not later than 90 days after a dissolution of *Dáil Éireann*.
Northern Ireland has 12 representatives in the British

House of Commons, although under the terms of the Government of Ireland Act in 1920, it had a semi-autonomous government. In 1972, however, after three years of sectarian violence between Protestants and Catholics, Britain suspended the Ulster Parliament. The Ulster counties became governed directly from London.

In 1998 an agreement created a new 108-seat Provincial Assembly for Northern Ireland, which replaced the direct rule of the province by the British Government. Northern Ireland also elects three members to the European Parliament. The First Minister is David Trimble.

Judicial branch: Supreme Court: judges appointed by the President on the advice of the government (Taoiseach and Cabinet).

Major political parties in Ireland: *Fianna Fáil*; Labour Party; *Fine Gael*; Progressive Democrats.

Major political parties in Northern Ireland: Ulster Unionist Party; Sinn Féin; Social and Democratic Labour Party; Democratic Unionist Party.

Population
The population of the Republic of Ireland is 3,744,700

(1999 estimate). Over one million people live in the greater Dublin area. The country has a young population, with 44 per cent of the population being under 25.

The 1999 population estimate is the highest on record since 1881. As a consequence of improved economic performance in recent years, there has been a significant increase in net migration. Latest projections of population growth suggest that in spite of falling fertility levels, the population could reach 4.2 million by 2011.

The total fertility rate for Ireland in 1999 was 1.89, below the theoretical population replacement level of 2.1. There were 53,354 births in 1999. This compares with a peak of 74,064 births recorded in 1980.

The population of Northern Ireland is 1.6 million.

Religions:
Roman Catholic 91.6 per cent
Church of Ireland 2.5 per cent
others 5.9 per cent (1998)

Northern Ireland: In the 1991 census, approximately 38.4 per cent of the population regard themselves as Catholic, 50.6 per cent as Protestant, while 3.8 per cent professed

no religion and 7.3 per cent refused to say.

Languages:
English is the language generally used; Irish is spoken mainly in areas located along the western seaboard.

Literacy: (definition: age 15 and over can read and write)
total population: 98 per cent

Time Zone information:
From late October to March the country is on GMT (five hours ahead of US Eastern time).

From late March to October the country is on GMT +1 (six hours ahead of US Eastern time).

Ireland goes to daylight saving time two weeks ahead of the United States.

GETTING TO IRELAND

◆ ◆ ◆

Ireland can be reached by air from Britain, continental Europe or North America. There are also ferry services from the west coast of Britain to Ireland.

◆ ◆ ◆

Airports

Dublin Airport is the Republic of Ireland's main international airport. Shannon Airport, near Limerick, also has sizable international facilities. Scheduled non-stop flights operate from Britain, continental Europe, and North America to Dublin and Shannon. There is also a good non-stop service from Britain and continental Europe to Cork Airport.

Other airports with non-stop scheduled flights from Britain are Kerry Airport near Killarney, Waterford Airport, and Knock International Airport, County Mayo. The airports in Galway, Sligo, and Donegal are all served by connecting domestic flights from Dublin.

Aer Lingus is the national airline, with non-stop flights to mainland Britain, continental Europe, and the United States. Ryanair, the second-largest Irish airline, offers no-frills flights to Britain and continental Europe.

Belfast International Airport is Northern Ireland's main

airport. There are flights to Belfast from Shannon, Britain, continental Europe, and the United States. Belfast City Airport is more convenient for the city center itself. It has non-stop scheduled services to British cities, as does Derry Airport.

Seaports

Various ferry and fast boat services operate from Britain to Ireland. These operate from England, Scotland, Wales, and the Isle of Man to both sides of the Irish border.
The main routes from mainland Britain to the Republic are:
Fishguard and Pembroke to Rosslare
Holyhead to Dublin and Dun Laoghaire
Liverpool and Mostyn to Dublin
Swansea to Cork

The main routes from Britain to the North are:
Heysham to Belfast
Liverpool to Belfast
Stranraer to Belfast
Troon to Belfast
Cairnryan to Belfast
Fleetwood to Larne

GEOGRAPHY

◆ ◆ ◆

The island of Ireland is situated in the extreme northwest of Europe between 51.5 and 55.5 degrees north latitude and between 5.5 and 10.5 degrees west longitude. The island of Ireland is just west of the United Kingdom and is the westernmost island in Europe.

The Irish Sea to the east, which separates Ireland from Britain, is from 17.6–192km (11–120 miles) wide and has a maximum depth of about 200m (650ft). Around the other coasts the shallow waters of the Continental Shelf are rather narrow and depths increase rapidly into the Atlantic Ocean.

The island of Ireland comprises a large central lowland of limestone with a relief of hills surrounded by a discontinuous border of coastal mountains which vary greatly in geological structure.

The mountain ridges of the south are composed of red sandstone separated by limestone river valleys. Granite predominates in the mountains of Counties Galway, Mayo, and Donegal in the west and northwest, and in Counties

Down, and Wicklow on the east coast, while a basalt plateau covers much of the northeast of the country.

The central plain, which is broken in places by low hills, is extensively covered with glacial deposits of clay and sand. It has considerable areas of bog and numerous lakes.

The island has seen at least two general glaciations and everywhere ice-smoothed rock, mountain lakes, glacial valleys and deposits of glacial sand, gravel, and clay mark the passage of the ice.

Size:
Width 275km (170 miles) at its widest point.

Length 486km (301 miles) at its longest.

Total coastline 3,172km (1,970 miles)

Area:
Total 84,421 sq km (32,595 sq miles)

The Republic of Ireland is 70,282 sq km (27,136 sq miles)

Northern Ireland is 14,139 sq km (5,459 sq miles)

Natural resources:
zinc, lead, natural gas, petroleum, barite, copper, gypsum, limestone, dolomite, peat, silver.

Land use:
Arable land: 14 per cent
Permanent crops: 0 per cent
Meadows and pastures: 71 per cent
Forest and woodland: 5 per cent
Other: 10 per cent

Environment: current issues:
water pollution, especially of lakes, from agricultural runoff.

PHYSICAL EXTREMITIES

◆ ◆ ◆

The Irish Republic comprises about five-sixths of the island of Ireland. The island's northeastern part constitutes Northern Ireland which is governed by Britain.

◆ ◆ ◆

The most northerly point is Inishtrahull Island, situated in the Atlantic Ocean, 7km (4.3 miles) north of Inishowen Peninsula, County Donegal. It lies at latitude 55.43 degrees north. The most northerly point of mainland Ireland is a headland 2km (1.2 miles) northeast of Malin Head, Inishowen Peninsula, County Donegal. It lies at latitude 55.38 degrees north.

The most easterly point is Big Bow Meel Island, which is a rock situated 900m (2,952ft) off the Ards Peninsula, County Down, at longitude 5.42 degrees west. The most easterly point of the mainland is Burr Point, Ards Peninsula, County Down, at longitude 5.43 degrees west. It is situated 2km (1.2 miles) southeast of the village of Ballyhalbert.

The most southerly point is Fastnet Rock, which lies in the Atlantic Ocean, 11.3km (7 miles) south of mainland County Cork. It lies at latitude 51.37 degrees north. The most southerly point of the mainland is Brow Head, County Cork, which lies 3.8km (2.3 miles) east of the marginally

more northerly Mizen Head. It lies at latitude 51.43 degrees north.

The most westerly point is Tearaght Island, which lies in the Atlantic Ocean, 7.7 miles (12.5km) west of Dingle Peninsula, County Kerry. It lies at longitude 10.70 degrees west. The most westerly point of the mainland is Garraun Point, Dingle Peninsula, County Kerry, which is 2.5km (1.5 miles) northwest of Slea Head. It lies at longitude 10.51 degrees west. The geographical center of Ireland is to be found in eastern County Roscommon, 3km (2 miles) south of Athlone town.

The summit of Mount Carrauntuohill, County Kerry, rises to 1,041m (3,414ft) above sea level. The second highest point is the summit of Mount Beenkeragh, County Kerry, which rises to 1,010m (3,314ft) above sea level.

The highest point in Northern Ireland is the summit of Slieve Donard, County Down, which rises to 852m (2,796ft) above sea level.

The sea cliffs at Croaghaun, Achill Island, off western Ireland, fall 668m (2,192ft) into the Atlantic Ocean. Slieve League in County Donegal has a drop of 601m (1,972ft) into the same ocean.

FOLLOWING PAGE: *Healy Pass joins Adrigole in County Cork with Lauragh in Kerry. Cork is Ireland's biggest county while Kerry has the highest point.*

The most heavily populated county is County Dublin, with 1,056,666 inhabitants at the last estimate. The next most heavily populated county is Antrim, with 566,400 inhabitants.

The most densely populated county is Dublin, with 1147.3 inhabitants per sq km (2,971.5 per sq mile) at the last estimate. The next most densely populated is county Antrim, with 199.2 inhabitants per sq km (516 per sq mile).

The county with the fewest inhabitants is Leitrim with just 25,032 inhabitants at the last estimate.

The most sparsely populated county in Ireland is Leitrim, with 15.8 inhabitants per square km (40.9 per sq mile) at the last estimate.

In terms of area, the largest county in Ireland is Cork at 7,457 sq km (19,318 sq miles). The next largest is County Galway at 6,148 sq km (15,927 sq miles). The largest county in Northern Ireland is Tyrone at 3,155 sq km (8,173 sq miles).

The smallest county in Ireland is Louth, which is just 820 sq km (2,124 sq miles) in area—nine times smaller than County Cork. The next smallest is County Carlow, which is 896 sq km (2,321 sq miles). The smallest county in Northern Ireland is Armagh, at 1,254 sq km (3,248 sq miles).

The largest city in Ireland is Dublin which at 859,976 inhabitants is home to almost one in five Irish people, and

more than one in four in the Irish Republic. The next nine largest settlements are Belfast (Counties Down and Antrim, 475,968), Cork (County Cork, 174,400), Limerick (County Limerick, 75,436) Derry (County Derry, 72,334), Newtownabbey (County Antrim, 56,811), Dún Laoghaire (County Dublin, 55,540), Bangor (County Down, 52,437), Galway (County Galway, 50,853) and Lisburn (County Antrim, 42,110).

The longest river in Ireland is the River Shannon whose source is Shannon Pot, County Cavan, and which enters the sea between Counties Clare and Limerick after a journey of 386 km (240 miles). It is, in fact, the longest river in the British Isles. The longest river within Northern Ireland is the River Bann, whose source is in the Mourne Mountains, County Down, and which enters the sea in County Londonderry after a journey of 122 km (76 miles).

Lough Neagh in Northern Ireland, which is 396 sq km (153 sq miles) in area, forms part of Counties Tyrone, Derry, Antrim, Down, and Armagh. It is the largest lake in the British Isles.

The closest point that Ireland comes to Britain is Torr Head, County Antrim, which is just 23 km (14 miles) from the Mull of Kintyre, Scotland.

The largest offshore island in Irish waters is Achill Island, County Mayo. The island covers an area of 148 sq km (57 sq miles).

LEFT: *Baled straw awaits collection on the Cooley Peninsula, County Louth. This county is the smallest one in Ireland.*

Ireland's tallest waterfall is Powerscourt Falls, County Wicklow, where the water drops 106m (350ft). It is the third tallest waterfall in the British Isles.

The town in Ireland which enjoys the most sunshine is Rosslare, County Wexford, which has over 1,600 hours of sunshine per year (4hrs 20mins per day).

The town in Ireland which receives the least sunshine is Omagh, County Tyrone, which has less than 1,200 hours of sunshine per year (3hrs 20mins per day).

The wettest place in Ireland is the area of the Maumturk and Partry Mountains of Counties Mayo and Galway, which receives annually over 2,400mm (94.4in) of rainfall.

The driest place in Ireland is Dublin city which receives less than 800mm (31.4in) of rain per year.

IRELAND'S WEATHER

◆ ◆ ◆

Ireland, known as the Emerald Isle, is so green because the land receives a lot of precipitation.

◆ ◆ ◆

The weather in Ireland is influenced by the Gulf Stream and the prevailing winds, predominantly from the southwest. The climate is equable and temperatures are fairly uniform over the whole country.

The coldest months in Ireland are January and February. In these months the mean daily air temperatures are between 39.2°F (4°C) and 44.6°F (7°C), while July and August are the warmest, 57.2°F (14°C) to 60.8°F (16°C). Extremes of air temperature, below 14°F (-10°C) or above 86°F (30°C), are extremely rare in the country.

May and June are the sunniest months, averaging five to seven hours of sunshine per day. In low-lying areas average annual rainfall is mostly between 800mm (31.4in) and 1,200mm (47.2in), but ranges from less than 750mm (29.5in) in some eastern areas to 1,500mm (59in) in parts of the west. In mountainous areas annual rainfall may exceed 2,000mm (78.7in). Rainfall is normally well distributed throughout the year, but about 60 per cent of the total falls between August and January.

A Brief History

◆ ◆ ◆

From the first inhabitants through to the formation of the Republic and beyond, Ireland has been formed by the tragic and glorious events that have given its people their unique character.

◆ ◆ ◆

Pre-Celtic Ireland

Ireland was first inhabited around 7500 B.C. by settlers who probably came from Scotland to what is now County Antrim. These early Mesolithic (Middle Stone Age) people were primitive hunters and fishermen. They settled the coasts and the bigger river valleys, especially in the northern half of the island, although archaeological remains of their settlements have been found as far south as County Cork. However, the most extraordinary Mesolithic site is at Mount Sandel, County Derry, which has been dated to 5935 B.C. Its excavated structures are the oldest discovered human habitations in Europe.

Around 3500 B.C. the Mesolithic peoples were superseded by a new wave of settlers. Once again, these Neolithic (New Stone Age) people probably came from Scotland, making the short sea crossing from Argyll. They brought a priceless new skill—agriculture. The ability to

cultivate land enabled them to outstrip the hunter-gatherers and establish permanent settlements. Their coming marks the beginning of civilized life in Ireland. Evidence for the existence of Neolithic agriculture may be found at numerous archaeological sites throughout the island, but none is more extensive or impressive as that at Belderg, County Mayo, which dates from the earliest period of Neolithic settlement. In addition, there are many surviving Neolithic burial sites that indicate the supreme importance these people attached to funerary ritual. They range from dolmens—two or three standing stones supporting a huge capstone—such as that at Poulnabrone in County Clare, to fully excavated passage graves, of which those in the Boyne Valley in County Meath are the most spectacular examples. The Boyne Valley is the pre-Celtic Ireland's Valley of the Kings, a site of obvious religious significance both then and in later times. It is here that we find the three most famous Neolithic passage graves, those at Dowth, Knowth, and Newgrange. The important Newgrange site dates from about 2500 B.C. Its archaeological excavation in the 1960s was an outstanding achievement which uncovered this sophisticated structure for the first time in almost four millennia.

Around 2000 B.C. the Bronze Age came to Ireland; many metal objects of great beauty still survive from this time. Irish Bronze Age metalwork was as fine as any in

PREVIOUS PAGE: *Dún Eoghanachta, located on Inishmore in the Aran Islands. This is a ring fort built during the last centuries B.C. The fort has marvellously preserved walls with sets of steps on the inside running up to the parapets.*

contemporary northern Europe, and was not confined simply to bronze. Gold was also popular and gold mining was an important economic activity. The Bronze Age was followed by the Iron Age, dating from about 250 B.C., and was carried to the island primarily by the latest and most significant of its many waves of settlers—the Celts.

The Celts

Ireland, even today, is still considered a Celtic country. The Celts, however, when they first arrived from Europe, were invaders just like the Mesolithic and Neolithic peoples before them.

The Celts came in waves, different tribal groups arriving at intervals over a period of centuries and settling in different parts of the country. The last of the major Celtic groups to invade Ireland were the Gaeil, who landed first in the southeast and gradually conquered the whole island, displacing earlier Celtic settlers. By A.D. 400 the Gaelic conquest was total. It was this people, with their culture and language, who were to dominate Irish history for almost a thousand years.

The Gaelic world was soon divided between two powerful tribal coalitions: the *Eoghanacht* based in the southern half of the country and the *Connachta* in the north. Of the Connachta tribes, by far the most powerful and influential was the *Uí Néill*. The *Uí Néill* were the ancestors of the modern O'Neills. By the end of the 6th Century, they dominated most of west Ulster and north Leinster. From their southern base at Tara, County Meath, they claimed the high kingship of the entire island. This claim was never universally accepted, least of all by the *Eoghanacht* in the south, although they were not in a position to challenge the dominance of the *Uí Néill*. Beneath these two powerful provincial tribal groups, there was a network of about 150 *tuatha* or minor kingdoms, whose rulers were subordinate to regional overlords, who in turn were subordinate to the provincial kings.

The Romans never thought Ireland worth conquering. The island missed out, therefore, on the great centralizing and civilizing effects of the Roman Empire. There were, however, compensations. Most notably, Ireland was a thoroughly Celtic culture from the center to the sea. It shared a common language, a common legal system, and a common currency based on the value of cattle. This cultural unity coexisted with an ever-present militarism, as various *tuatha* fought each other back and forth for petty advantage in land, cattle, and slaves. There was no strong political

center—the claims of the Uí Néill notwithstanding —which could hold the ring between the various warring factions. Gaelic Ireland was a culture without a state. It was a thoroughly stratified society, in which there were no less than 27 different classes of freemen. At the summit of the social scale, along with the petty kings, were the lawyers or brehons, the druids, and the *filí* or poets. Economically, Gaelic Ireland was a pastoral, cattle-rearing society based on yeoman farmers who, although not of the aristocracy, were freemen. Most significantly, it was a completely rural society—the Gaels built no towns.

This fascinating, remote and undisturbed culture was not totally isolated, however. Irish raiding parties regularly attacked the British coast and for a time there were even Irish settlements in Wales. It was through this cross-channel activity that Gaelic society unwittingly opened the door for the first great intrusion into its secular world—Christianity.

Christianity

St. Patrick, the patron saint of Ireland, was the most important of the country's 5th-Century Christian missionaries. Before his arrival, however, Palladius was sent by Pope Celestine in 431 "as the first bishop to the Irish who believe in Christ", which clearly suggests that Christians were on the island even at this early date. Significantly, Christianity was the state religion of the

Roman Empire and so Roman civilization at last reached Ireland. It did not overwhelm the Gaelic nation, however. Rather, it took on a protective local coloring, so that Irish Christianity soon diverged in a number of important respects from continental and Roman norms. The Irish Church, for example, was monastic rather than episcopal. There were no towns to act as foci for diocesan organization, so monasteries assumed a great importance as centers of Christian learning, scholarship, and discipline. But the effect of the new religion in the social sphere was more limited than in most other Christian countries.

There were many famous monasteries throughout Ireland, not least those at Glendalough, County Wicklow—founded by St. Kevin—and at Kells, County Meath. The chief treasure of the Kells monastery was the amazing illuminated manuscript version of the four Gospels, known as the *Book of Kells*. Irish monks were famed for their scholarship, especially in the Dark Ages following the collapse of the Roman Empire in the West. The monastic foundation at Clonmacnoise, County Offaly, was one of Europe's contemporary powerhouses of learning, justly earning early Christian Ireland the famous epithet of the "island of saints and scholars".

Irish Christianity also developed a hermitic tradition. There were many religious settlements in remote and inhospitable locations, such as Skellig rocks, off the County

Kerry coast. Here hermits renounced all material comfort and lived lives of heroic self-sacrifice in atonement for the sins of the world.

Most of all the early Irish Church was a missionary organization, reintroducing the faith to the continent after the Roman Empire's collapse. The Irish missionaries travelled everywhere, founding religious settlements across northern, central, and eastern Europe. The decline of Christianity had paralleled that of the Empire, so that even places like Italy needed to be re-evangelized. Germanic and Slav lands beyond the old imperial borders were brought within the Christian world for the first time. This was a staggering achievement.

The Vikings

Viking raiders first appeared off the Irish coast in 795. Irish monasteries, with their precious ornaments and vessels, offered tempting targets to these intrepid pirates. Gradually, the scale of the raids increased and the Norsemen built coastal bases from which they forayed deep into the heart of the island. Dublin, Wexford, Waterford, Cork, and Limerick all owe their origins to the Vikings.

The Vikings burst in upon a stable but also vulnerable world. They were militarily more advanced than the Gaelic kings in their mastery of the longboat, as complete on Irish rivers as on the high seas. This enabled them to move with

terrifying speed. Monasteries were almost defenceless before them. It was in an attempt to survive these raids that the distinctive round towers were developed at monastic sites. Their doorways were well above head height and were reached by ladders that could then be pulled up behind the fleeing monks.

These Scandinavian invaders were also traders. Their towns, especially Dublin which they founded in 841, became centers of commerce, trading in particular with other Norse settlements in Britain such as York.

In time, the Gaelic kings began to grapple with the Vikings on more equal terms, and none more so than *Mael Sechnaill*, king of southern *Uí Néill* at Tara. Yet he was not a national leader, for there was no Gaelic nation in the modern, political sense. Indeed, the pattern soon emerged of a constantly shifting series of alliances between Gaels and Vikings, many of them directed against *Mael Sechnaill*, who was feared by other Gaelic kings as a potentially overwhelming threat.

The Vikings were merciless and efficient fighting men. The Gaels soon learned their ways. This introduced a seriously destabilizing element into Ireland. Previously, the endemic wars between the *tuatha* had not disturbed the overall balance of Gaelic society or its political structures. Now, however, more effective and destructive military methods began to have that effect. As the Viking threat itself

was gradually contained from about 900 onwards, Gaelic warlords could use the lessons they had learned from the Norsemen to shatter the equilibrium of the old order.

The most spectacular winner in this game was a small *tuath* from east County Clare called *Dal Chais*. As the traditional *Eoghanacht* power in Munster declined, the kings of *Dal Chais* spread out from their ancestral heartland into *Eoghanacht* territory, while also reducing the Norse settlement of Limerick.

In 976 Brian Boru became king of *Dal Chais*. Two years later, he broke *Eoghanacht* power forever at the battle of *Belach Lechtna* in County Cork and became king of Munster. He then waged war against the southern *Uí Néill*, and by 1005 had done what no one had thought possible —gained effective control of the whole island by securing the submission of the *Uí Néill*, both the northern and southern branches. Brian was a revolutionary, but his revolution did not last. The Leinstermen and their Norse allies revolted against him and engaged him in battle at Clontarf, near Dublin, in 1014. Brian's army routed their enemy but at a price, for the High King himself was killed. With him died the possibility of a united Gaelic kingdom.

The Anglo-Normans

The battle at Clontarf was not a contest between Irish defenders and Viking intruders. It was part of the endless

series of conflicts between Irish warlords, in which the Norsemen of Dublin—plus some Viking mercenaries specially shipped in from the Isle of Man—were recruited on the side of the Leinstermen. The Munstermen's victory was a Pyrrhic one, for it both robbed them of their king and so weakened them that they could no longer aspire to that all-Ireland sovereignty which had been the essence of Brian Boru's claim to the high kingship. There was to be no strong political center in Gaelic Ireland. Instead, the old pattern resumed. The O'Briens (as the *Dal Chais* successors of Brian Boru now called themselves) fought for supremacy with the *Uí Néill*, although by the middle of the 12th Century both groups had been eclipsed by the rising power of the O'Conors of Connacht. Their claim to the high kingship, however, was little better than nominal, as events were soon to prove.

Everything was turned upside down by the arrival of the Anglo-Normans in 1169. The Normans were descendants of Viking marauders who had settled in Normandy; in 1066 they conquered England and gradually extended their supremacy over most of Britain. They were but one element of a vast imperial enterprise which carried the culture of Charlemagne's successors from its heartland between the Loire and the Rhine to places as far flung as Riga, Sicily—and Ireland. It was to the Norman, Henry II, that *Diarmuid MacMurrough*, the deposed king of Leinster,

turned for help in an attempt to recover his kingdom.

MacMurrough had first become king of Leinster around 1126. In 1152 he abducted the wife of a neighboring king, O'Rourke of Breffini (roughly modern-day County Cavan), and sparked the series of events that finally led to his defeat by Henry II.

Henry was too busy to bother about the squabbles of Irish sub-kings but the internal chaos of Ireland made it promising territory for further Norman expansion. Henry therefore gave Diarmuid permission to drum up support among the restless and aggressive Norman lords of the Welsh marches.

Diarmuid's principal recruit was Richard FitzGilbert de Clare, better known as Strongbow, under whose leadership the Norman invasion took place. The vastly superior military skills of the Normans swept aside initial opposition and soon they had possession of the east coast towns. In 1171 Henry II came over and received the submission not only of the new Norman colonist but most of the Gaelic kings as well. Thus began the long and fateful involvement of the English Crown in Ireland.

The Normans might as well have come from another world. They brought European feudalism, a legal system based on the alien concept of primogeniture, highly sophisticated construction techniques, and superior military expertise. The Gaels were swept aside, as often by honeyed

words as by the sword, for the Normans had no intention of honoring promises to uphold traditional Gaelic rights and liberties. They conquered vast tracts of land and established their leading men as lords, in defiance of Gaelic customs which they considered barbarous. They built magnificent military structures, like King John's Castle in Limerick, and Carrickfergus Castle in County Antrim. By 1250 the Normans had effectively accomplished that which the Vikings had never even attempted—the conquest and ownership of more than three-quarters of Ireland.

Medieval Ireland

In two generations, vast tracts of Irish land passed out of Gaelic control, leaving only scattered pockets, mainly in the west. The largest such pocket was in western Ulster, where the modern counties of Donegal and Tyrone remained in the hands of the O'Donnells and the O'Neills (the successors of the *Uí Néill*). The rest of Ireland comprised first an area around Dublin known as the Pale, which was adminstered by the Crown, and secondly the great liberties of the Norman feudal magnates who, although ultimately loyal to the Crown, resented any encroachment on their territories. Liberties were autonomous territories in which the magnates controlled the administration of justice, the collection of revenue, and the keeping of the peace. The King's writ was as unwelcome to them as the threat of

Gaelic resurgence.

That resurgence came at the start of the 14th Century. Gaelic chieftains pressed alike on the Pale and on the semi-independent Norman liberties. The Gaels had two great advantages: first, force of numbers, for the colonists were thin on the ground; also their laws of succession decreed that a king could be succeeded by any male relative who shared a common great-grandfather. This may

RIGHT: *Norman knights in chain mail armor shown on a tomb slab at the 12th-Century Jerpoint Abbey in County Kilkenny.*

have been responsible for many of the endemic quarrels in Gaelic society; but now it came to the rescue because of the wide range of people always available to succeed a fallen king. The Normans could defeat Gaelic kings; Gaelic kingdoms were a bit more durable. In addition, the Gaels learned Norman ways as they had once learned Norse ones. They became more sophisticated in military affairs and began importing mercenaries from Scotland.

By the middle of the 14th Century, all of Connacht except for the town of Galway had been recovered and all of Ulster except for Carrickfergus. The Pale had shrunk. Only the great Norman magnates of the south and east—the FitzGeralds of Kildare and Desmond and the Butlers of Ormond—were proof against the Gaelic resurgence, and many of these were themselves relatively "Gaelicized" through inter-marriage, and also through the adoption of the Irish language. This was especially true of the FitzGeralds of Desmond.

This Gaelic cultural infiltration of the Norman colony led to the passing of the Statutes of Kilkenny (1366), an attempt to forbid by legislation the wearing of Gaelic dress, the speaking of Irish, or the adoption of various other undesirable Gaelic attributes by the Anglo-Normans. These statutes were largely ignored.

The Gaelic resurgence became so pressing by the end of the century that King Richard II himself came over twice,

principally to defeat the Gaelic chieftain Art MacMurrough Kavanagh who had for years been attacking the southern borders of the Pale. Richard failed on both occasions, underlining the weakness of royal power in Ireland.

This weakness further accelerated the independence of the Norman magnates who, in the absence of effective royal power, were happy to look after themselves. The Fitzgerald family, based in Kildare, became the greatest magnate family of the period and dominated Ireland for two generations.

Geraldine Ireland

In the long series of English dynastic struggles known as the Wars of the Roses, both sides (York and Lancaster) were glad of support from the great Anglo-Norman families. Both branches of the Fitzgeralds, Desmond and Kildare, were Yorkists. The Butlers of Ormond were Lancastrians. By 1461 the Yorkists had triumphed in the person of King Edward IV. He first appointed the Earl of Desmond as chief governor of Ireland, but when the Earl proved to be too Gaelicized in his ways, the King had him summarily beheaded. The Butlers, as Lancastrian supporters, were obvious non-starters for governorship. That left the house of Kildare. It acquired the chief governorship in 1470, lost it briefly, then was threatened with having to share it with an Englishman. All these expeditions failed. By 1478 Gearóid Mór FitzGerald, 8th Earl of Kildare, was chief governor of

Ireland. He might more properly have been called king of Ireland, so total was his authority.

The FitzGeralds of Kildare were enormously rich and well connected. The rule of Gearóid Mór (the Great Earl) was the high-water mark of Anglo-Norman magnate power in Ireland. The central administration, far away in London, had not the resources, the military means, or the will to enforce direct rule. Even the return of the Lancastrians in 1485 in the shape of Henry VII, failed to shake the Great Earl's position. The King did manage to dismiss Kildare briefly in the 1490s, replacing him with an Englishman, Sir Edward Poynings. He was the author of Poynings' Law (1494) which made acts of the Irish Parliament subject to English approval, a provision which was less important at the time than it was to become later.

Henry VII, however, had no intention of maintaining Poynings and a costly army in Ireland indefinitely. In 1496 he was recalled, the Great Earl was restored and held the position until his death in 1513. He was succeeded by *Gearóid Óg*, his son. The 9th Earl remained in office until 1534. The Kildare ascendancy had meant that Ireland could be governed in the King's name without the King having to pay for it. The Earls of Kildare controlled the country through their own armies or those of their family allies; they received the revenues from taxation; they controlled patronage and jobs. It is interesting, however, that they

never took the fateful step of attempting to proclaim themselves kings of Ireland. For all their powers, the earls answered to England in the end. By the early 1500s, England was in the grip of a religious and constitutional revolution that would sweep their world away.

Tudor Ireland

The Tudor "revolution" in England began as a desperate search for a means to allow King Henry VIII to divorce his wife. It ended with the creation of a new kind of European state. To effect the divorce, the King renounced the spiritual authority of the pope and proclaimed himself head of the Protestant Church of England. In addition, he was determined to centralize power and reduce the influence of provincial magnates. This had obvious implications for Ireland. The English of the Pale were great enthusiasts for the new regime. They plotted against the Earl of Kildare, who was duly summoned to London. He left his son Lord Offaly (known as "Silken Thomas") in charge with instructions to make a show of force if he himself was dismissed from office. The Earl was dismissed and imprisoned in the Tower of London. Silken Thomas's show of force turned into rebellion after rumors circulated that

RIGHT: *Henry VIII of England formally became King of Ireland in 1541. His predecessors had only held the title, Lord of Ireland.*

his father had been executed. This uprising was crushed by the English, Kildare died in the Tower in 1536, and his son was executed in 1537. The power of the FitzGeralds was crushed by 1540.

Henry VIII was determined that his realm would be administered by a new, loyal English bureaucracy, judiciary, and clergy. He gained control of the Irish Church by dissolving the monasteries. Henry formally became King of Ireland in 1541. His predecessors had only held the title, Lord of Ireland. The Gaelic chieftains had to acknowledge his power by surrendering their lands. These were granted back but under English legal title.

Mary I, Henry's daughter and successor, encouraged colonization (plantation) in the midlands during the 1550s. Elizabeth, Mary's sister and successor, then began to enforce the Protestant faith that their father had never truly embraced. During the first three decades of Elizabeth's reign, new English settlers increasingly arrived, encroaching into Gaelic and Anglo-Norman areas. The earldom of Desmond, that supported the old Church and political system, was crushed.

The Nine Years' War

Elizabeth, although reluctant to engage in a costly expedition to conquer Ireland, could not avoid conflict. Since the 1540s there had been tensions between the new

English state and the Gaelic world. The destruction of the FitzGerald and Desmond dynasties had politically neutralized the Anglo-Normans (or "Old English") in Ireland. Elizabeth's "New English" regime was increasingly encroaching on Gaelic Ireland.

The forces of Gaelic Ireland made their last stand in Ulster. This was led by the Lord of Tyrone, Hugh O'Neill, and was opposed by Sir Henry Bagenal, a New English supporter of Elizabeth. Bagenal was responsible for replacing O'Neill's traditional administrative powers under Gaelic customs and enforcing Elizabeth's laws in Ulster.

Open rebellion by O'Neill began in 1595. He won two defensive engagements at Clontibret and Yellow Ford, but was unable to resist full-scale English offensives. In order to secure assistance, O'Neill turned to Catholic Spain to help fight their Protestant enemy. This fateful move drew Ireland into the European wars of religion. In 1601 Philip II of Spain sent an army to Kinsale, County Cork. O'Neill's men marched south from Ulster to meet them, but both forces were defeated at Kinsale. Gaelic Ireland was effectively crushed except for isolated opposition.

The Plantation of Ulster

By 1603 sporadic resistance had ceased, O'Neill had surrendered, and English law replaced traditional customs in the strongly Gaelic lands of Ulster. The "Flight of the Earls"

LEFT: *Queen Elizabeth I, the last of the Tudor monarchs, effectively completed the English conquest of Ireland.*

in 1607 saw O'Neill and the O'Donnells of Donegal depart for the continent, leaving Ulster under Dublin's administration. The vacated land was given to loyal English and Scottish Protestants. Over 809,000 hectares (2 million acres) of fertile land in west Ulster were occupied by these settlers. The Irish were left with under 404,000 hectares (1 million acres) of inferior uplands. Private plantations went ahead in east Ulster. Although other areas were planted, the island remained largely Catholic except for Ulster. English and Scottish planters dramatically modernized the agriculture and settlements of Ulster. The Ulster Protestants were technically and politically different to the Gaelic people. They came from a highly developed nation state rather than a decentralized land of diverging loyalties. The Ulster Plantation introduced colonial settlers with a sense of superiority over the displaced indigenous people. Assimilation did not occur and the foundation for future troubles was established.

Early Stuart Ireland

Elizabeth I died in 1603 leaving no children. The throne passed to James VI of Scotland, her cousin, who became James I of England. James was succeeded by his son

Charles I in 1625, who reigned until his execution in 1649 after his defeat in the English Civil War.

Scotland and England shared the same monarch but not the same religious doctrine. Both countries were Protestant, but the Church of England followed the teachings of Lutheranism, while Scottish Protestants followed Calvinism. The vast majority of New English settlers in Ireland followed Calvinism. The Old English elite, the tenants, and laborers in Ireland remained Catholic.

New English Protestants controlled the Dublin administration and the Irish Parliament. James I and Charles I tolerated Irish Catholic landowners in order to secure tax revenues from them. This paid for defenses against possible Spanish attack. In 1628 Charles I made a series of promises to the Old English known as the "Graces", including the confirmation of their land titles and to relieve New English pressure upon them. In return, the Old English would give £120,000 to King Charles I over two years. After a few years, when the Spanish threat subsided, Charles reneged on his pledges.

Thomas Wentworth, appointed governor to Ireland in 1633, was an Episcopalian like King Charles I. He disliked the New English Calvinism and the Old English Catholicism. The Episcopalian governor was recalled back to London after causing widespread antagonism by imposing heavy taxes on both these groups.

Crisis

Charles I's desire for Irish tax revenue arose from his desire for absolute monarchy, which he saw emerging in France and Spain. In pursuing this ambition he ruled without parliament from 1629–40, but could not raise revenue legally without their consent. The King had thus looked to Ireland for financial support.

The King was finally forced to recall parliament in order to meet the costs of suppressing a Scottish rebellion. This arose after Charles tried to enforce his Anglican beliefs on Scottish Calvinists. Most of Parliament, however, were Calvinists. Relations between King and Parliament had by this time seriously deteriorated and war erupted in 1642.

The Old Irish powers in Ulster had already exploited the turmoil in England by revolting against the Dublin administration. Old English and Gaelic landowners from Munster and Leinster joined them to form a quasi-parliamentary assembly (the Confederation of Kilkenny) in 1642.

In Ulster the indigenous population attacked the settlers. Massacres and church desecration followed. The main rebellion failed to seize the central administration at Dublin Castle, but had raised an army under Owen Roe O'Neill. In response, a Scottish Covenanter army, under General George Munro, was sent to Ireland. The country was now divided into three main groups: Ulster

Protestants, the royal administration in Dublin under James Butler (Earl, later Duke, of Ormond), and the Confederates.

O'Neill inflicted a major defeat on Munro at Benburb (1646), but could not seize Ulster. Neither side had the ability to secure a complete victory. Control would rest with the victor of the English Civil War. Parliament, led by Oliver Cromwell, won the war in 1649. They executed Charles I and sent an army to Ireland.

Cromwell

The experienced and disciplined troops of Cromwell's New Model Army were determined to avenge the Ulster massacres of 1641. The English Calvinists (now called Puritans), motivated by religious zeal, seized control of the eastern half of Ireland within two months. Garrisons at Drogheda and Wexford were massacred in the autumn. By the early 1650s the English were masters of Ireland.

Cromwell dispossessed every Catholic landowner in Ireland. There was no distinction between Gaelic and Old English landowners. The land was taken by those who had financially supported the Parliamentary army and soldiers. These settlers became known as the Protestant Ascendancy. This plantation was achieved through a remarkable mapping project, the Down Survey, supervised by Sir William Petty. It set the pattern for Irish land ownership until the early 20th Century. Cromwell, however,

died in 1658 and Charles II returned to rule the kingdom.

Restoration Ireland

Charles II was keen to keep his throne and thus avoid enemies. Unlike Charles I, he did not force the Scottish Presbyterians to accept Episcopalian doctrine. The Protestant Ascendancy in Ireland were allowed to retain their land, but James Butler, the Old English Earl, again took charge of royal administration in Dublin. Charles II, a moderate Anglican, left Irish Catholics alone, except for a brief persecution after the "Popish Plot" in England that led to the murder of St. Oliver Plunkett. After the death of Charles II (1685), the Crown passed to his brother James who was Catholic. James II gave Richard Talbot, an Old English noble, charge of the army in Ireland. Catholics were brought into the Irish administration. Talbot, now the Duke of Tyrconnell, was viewed with suspicion in England. Protestants in England supported a *coup* to prevent any Catholic succession. The Crown was taken by William of Orange, husband of James II's daughter Mary, in the "Glorious Revolution". James fled to Ireland supported by the Catholic Old Irish "patriot parliament".

Protestants in Ulster, Leinster, and Munster welcomed the Glorious Revolution. James II led forces into Ulster, surrounding the walled plantation towns of Derry and Enniskillen. Derry was besieged but resisted for 105 days

and Williamite forces were sent to relieve the town. This conflict had now become part of the War of the League of Augsburg involving the King of France against a coalition under William of Orange. French forces reinforced the Jacobites in Ireland in order to draw Anglo-Dutch forces away from continental Europe.

William of Orange landed at Carrickfergus, County Antrim, in 1690. At the Battle of the Boyne on July 1 he defeated King James who then fled to France.

Resistance, however, continued and Limerick was besieged by Williamite forces. Jacobite resistance was finally crushed at Aughrim, County Galway. They surrendered after a second short siege at Limerick and then signed a treaty. The Treaty of Limerick allowed the Jacobite officers to leave for continental Europe (the "Flight of the Wild Geese"). The civil articles promised religious toleration, but this was quickly overturned.

Ascendancy

King William and the English Parliament were willing to honor the civil articles of the Treaty of Limerick. The Irish

LEFT: *William of Orange and his wife Mary ascended the English throne in 1689. James II fled to Ireland seeking help to reclaim his throne. William defeated King James II at the Battle of the Boyne in 1690 but met Irish resistance until the Treaty of Limerick in 1691.*

Parliament, however, were insecure after previous uprisings and refused to honor them.

Ireland in the 18th Century had a Protestant Ascendancy of leading landowners who supported the Church of Ireland's Anglican doctrine but did embrace some Calvinist beliefs. Ulster Presbyterians (or Dissenters), however, were strict Calvinists and had no support from the Ascendancy.

Penal laws against Catholics and Dissenters were passed by the Ascendancy in the early 1700s. Restricting Catholic land ownership, which was just 10 per cent of the island, was a key objective. Catholics were banned from practising law, holding public office, or bearing arms.

During this period, however, the Roman Catholic Church retained its institutional structures; its members now formed a coherent group without any Gaelic or Old English distinctions. Penal laws were gradually relaxed but left feelings of dispossession among Catholics and led to some Dissenters migrating to Puritan New England in North America.

The Protestant Ascendancy became increasingly confident during the 1700s. They created fine Georgian streets that can still be seen today. Despite the architectural elegance of Ascendancy Ireland, the country was essentially a colony governed by an elite that differed in race and religion to the impoverished population.

18th-Century Reforms

The Irish Parliament, controlled by the Ascendancy, gained formal independence in 1782. Real power, however, lay with the royal administration in Dublin Castle. The administration's key figure from 1789 to 1802 was John Fitzgibbon. He resisted all concessions to Catholics during this period. This issue emerged in the 1860s after serious agrarian unrest over farming reforms. Liberal Ascendancy figures influenced by the European Enlightenment and the need to recruit Irish support to help fight various wars also created a desire to relax penal laws.

Restrictions on Catholic land ownership were relaxed through the 1778 Catholic Relief Act, passed by the Irish Parliament under pressure from London. In 1793 Catholics gained further rights amid fears of Irish unrest after war broke out with Revolutionary France. Reforms included allowing Catholics to enter the professions, join militias, and to vote on the same basis as Protestants. Despite these reforms there was widespread agrarian discontent. This had resulted in the growth of violent secret peasant societies. In Ulster these were sectarian: the Orange Order for Protestants and the Defenders for Catholics.

Revolution

Further instability was created by the French Revolution of 1789 that promoted liberty, democracy, and the rights of

man. Catholics hoped the French might send forces to liberate Ireland. Radical Ulster Presbyterians in the Society of United Irishmen were inspired to break with England and form a republic. The United Irish separatist Theobald Wolfe Tone persuaded France to send an invasion force to Ireland. The landing at Bantry Bay, County Cork, in 1796, however, was abandoned due to bad weather.

In May 1798 rebellion erupted in Leinster. The rebels were motivated by a combination of agrarian grievances, social injustice, French republican idealism, hatred of the military, and sectarian conflict. A peasant army was raised. Fighting erupted in Counties Wexford, Wicklow, and Kildare. The rebels, however, failed to spread the uprising to the midlands or Munster. They were crushed at Vinegar Hill. The United Irishmen also revolted in Counties Antrim and Down, but their forces were insignificant. In the west, a small French force landed at Killala, County Mayo, but was defeated. A second force was intercepted trying to land in Donegal. Wolfe Tone was among those captured. He committed suicide before being hanged for treason.

The Irish Parliament dissolved itself under the 1800 Act of Union. Ireland became a wholly integrated part of the United Kingdom. Rebellion again erupted in 1803 when

RIGHT: *A 1798 memorial in Tralee, County Kerry, to one of the ordinary soldiers, the "Croppy Boys" of the infamous rebellion.*

Robert Emmet, a United Irishman, sparked a riot in Dublin. This was quickly crushed and Emmet was hanged.

The Catholic Association

In 1823 Daniel O'Connell founded the Catholic Association. He was a lawyer who saw that political freedom was the key to the advancement of Catholics. The association introduced associate membership for a small fee and thereby generated mass support. Subscriptions were collected by the Catholic Church as its nationwide structure was ideal for membership administration. This united Catholicism with Irish nationalism.

O'Connell created a new, populist, functional style of politics in Ireland. In 1828 he stood in the Clare by-election although Catholics were barred from sitting in parliament. His opponent, Liberal Protestant William Vesey Fitzgerald, supported Catholic emancipation, but O'Connell won. In response to this victory and the mass movement behind it the British conceded Catholic emancipation. Catholics could sit as MPs without having to subscribe to the Oath of Supremacy and were eligible to hold key state appointments. The British Government, however, disenfranchised a large section of O'Connell's supporters known as the "Forty-Shilling Freeholders". Tenants with assets of at least 40 shillings (£2) who could vote had their franchise limit raised to £10.

Catholics remained a poor and marginalized social group ruled by a Protestant elite. Their only form of real protest had been the violent methods of the secret societies. The Catholic Association now gave them a new mass movement that defined Irish nationalism. This was essentially Catholic (with clerical support), strong on communal solidarity, populist, and local.

O'Connell's main aim was to repeal the Act of Union that joined Ireland to England. He also had short-term objectives and his work was assisted by getting his supporters into an alliance with the Whig Party. They were in government almost continuously between 1830 and 1841 but needed support after losing their parliamentary majority in 1835.

One major reform was the resolution of the tithes question in 1838. Catholics had bitterly opposed a forced charge to support the Church of Ireland. The "tithe war" of the 1830s saw widespread violence. O'Connell helped resolve this and other issues, but did not achieve the repeal of the Act of Union. Radical elements in the Repeal Association grew impatient with O'Connell and formed the Young Ireland movement. Although they generated considerable propaganda, they only succeeded in launching a bungled rebellion in 1848.

In 1841 O'Connell launched the Repeal of the Union movement and held "monster meetings" at various

locations. This did not, however, include Ulster where conservative Presbyterianism was becoming the dominant force. They were alarmed at the prospect of a Catholic dominated restored Irish Parliament. O'Connell's Repeal campaign failed, but he is still credited with being the creator of the modern Irish nation.

Famine

Most of Ireland's 8,175,124 inhabitants, recorded in the country's first truly reliable census in 1841, were from impoverished, rural families. Their staple diet was the potato whose high yields helped feed the dramatically increasing population. Most people were engaged in agriculture as there was little industrial work. In 1845 and 1846 the potato crop failed due to a new, unknown fungus. There was widespread starvation but the Whig government strongly believed in *laissez-faire*. They believed that market forces rather than state intervention would solve the problem. Parliament insisted that relief efforts were to be funded by local landlords. These landlords had to pay for this from their rents. Tenants who were unable to pay rent were evicted. Thousands of evicted and starving people roamed across Ireland.

Fevers then broke out, including typhus, dysentery, and scurvy. Potato yields were very low in 1847; they failed again in 1848, and finally recovered in 1849. Some one

million people died in the greatest subsistence crisis in Western Europe. Many more fled abroad. Despite the British Government being the world's greatest power, they had failed to stop the Famine. The Famine and hardships of rural life forced thousands to endure the dangers of a transatlantic voyage to North America aboard cramped, disease-ridden ships. Some 780,000 Irish people went to the United States in the 1840s. Others went to Britain, Canada, or Australia. The Irish in the United States remained particularly hostile to the British. Activists in the United States would become leading supporters of militant Irish nationalism, separatism, and republicanism.

Fenians and Men of Ulster

In 1858, James Stephens and John O'Mahony, both Young Irelanders, founded the Irish Republican Brotherhood. It was a transatlantic group, with O'Mahony based in New York and Stephens remaining in Ireland. They were nicknamed the Fenians after the legendary Celtic warriors called *Fianna*. They aimed to secure an Irish republic through force. The Fenians only managed to launch a futile rebellion in 1867 and the Catholic Church condemned their revolutionary conspiracies.

During this period the Industrial Revolution came to northeast Ulster. Manufacturing, engineering, and shipbuilding turned Belfast into a dynamic city. A large

working-class population of Protestants and Catholics emerged. This industrial advancement, however, was led by the Protestants and it reinforced their link with Britain and its economic powers.

Land Reform

Populist nationalism again emerged in the 1870s when Isaac Butt led a campaign to restore the Irish Parliament to control domestic affairs. He demanded Irish Home Rule within the United Kingdom. There were 56 "Home Rulers" in Westminster by the late 1870s. Charles Stewart Parnell replaced Butt as their leader and formed them into the Irish Parliamentary Party by the mid-1880s. This became a national organization and led on to the Irish National Land League. This was formed by Parnell and Michael Davitt in 1879. It demanded fair rent, fixity of tenure, and free sale of a tenant's interest in a property. These far-reaching land reforms were directly linked to the wider questions of who owned the land of Ireland and who governed the land.

The 1881 Land Act established the principle of the tenant's interest in his holding, and set up arbitration courts to settle rent and other disputes. The 1885 Act accelerated the process of actual land purchase by making loans available on easy terms to tenants who wished to buy. In the 1903 Land Act huge tracts of land were transferred from landlords to tenants. The Ascendancy estates were

replaced with small landowners.

The 1885 general election returned 85 IPP (or Nationalist) members and made Home Rule a key issue in Westminster. These MPs had the balance of power and Parnell forced Prime Minister William Gladstone to introduce a Home Rule bill in 1886. This split his Liberal Party, the bill was defeated, and the government fell.

Parnell was now the leading Irish nationalist and was called the "uncrowned king of Ireland". He led a formidable political organization, was responsible for major land reforms, and had the support of both the masses and the clergy. Protestant Ulster, however, resisted the nationalist movement. They saw the 1886 Home Rule bill as a major threat to the Union. In response, the Irish Unionist Party was formed.

In 1890 Irish nationalism was shaken by a scandal involving Parnell. For many years he had lived with Kitty O'Shea, the estranged wife of a philandering Nationalist Party colleague. When the couple began divorce proceedings, Parnell was cited as co-respondent.

In response, Gladstone began to distance himself from Parnell, who was considered an adulterer by the Irish Catholic hierarchy. The Irish Parliamentary Party MPs decided to remain loyal to the Liberal alliance and the influential Catholic clergy. Parnell lost his power and died in October 1891.

Cultural Revival

During the 1880s there was a widespread revival in Irish culture that contributed towards the birth of the Irish state some 40 years later. A movement to revive the Gaelic language began to develop, Irish literature flourished, and there was growing interest in the nation's history. In 1884 the Gaelic Athletic Association (GAA) was founded to promote indigenous sports, such as hurling. The organization had strong Fenian connections and middle-class nationalists distanced themselves from its aggressive nationalism.

The IPP, under John Redmond, became increasingly dominant in politics, although a small group called *Sinn Féin* was formed by Arthur Griffith in 1905. This organization wanted Irish MPs not to sit in Westminster, but instead form a constituent assembly in Dublin.

In 1910 the IPP held the balance of power in Westminster. In return for supporting the Liberal Government they were given the Home Rule bill in 1912. In response a "Solemn League and Covenant" against Home Rule was signed by over 400,000 Ulster Protestants. Ulstermen also planned a provisional government to defy the bill. British Conservative figures colluded with them,

RIGHT: *A World War I recruiting poster for the British Army. Many Irishmen fought and died on the Western Front and at Gallipoli.*

FOR THE GLORY OF IRELAND

BELGIUM

'WILL YOU GO OR MUST I'?

arms were imported, and army officers in County Kildare refused to move against the activists.

The Home Rule bill was passed in 1914, but its operation was suspended until after the end of the European war that had erupted. Catholics and Protestants alike then fought for Britain in World War I. Some 35,000 Irish soldiers died in the conflict.

The Easter Rising

John Redmond promised the British Government that nationalist Ireland would support the war effort after they were granted Home Rule. This decision, however, was not completely supported by a nationalist militia group called the Irish Volunteers. Those who supported Redmond called themselves National Volunteers, while those who disagreed retained the original title.

Within the Irish Volunteers was a hard-core Irish Republican Brotherhood (IRB) led by Thomas J. Clarke, Sean MacDermott, and Patrick Pearse. They planned an armed uprising, asked Germany for arms, and enlisted support from the small socialist Irish Citizen Army. This was all concealed from the official Irish Volunteer leadership.

On Easter Monday, April 24, 1916, the IRB seized several key public buildings in Dublin. Patrick Pearse proclaimed the Republic of Ireland from the General Post Office. The Easter Rising was heavily suppressed by the British within a

week and 16 leaders were executed. The executed rebels became martyrs in the eyes of the Irish public and increased nationalist fervor.

Revolt and Civil War

The British mistakenly blamed *Sinn Féin* for the rising. The rebel movement that emerged from the Easter Rising took this name, but the leadership changed from Arthur Griffith to Éamon de Valera (the senior surviving commandant from 1916). Irish nationalists were then united after the British attempted to introduce conscription in Ireland to provide manpower for World War I. The IPP, *Sinn Féin*, the GAA, the IRB, and the Roman Catholic Church all joined the anti-conscription campaign.

In the 1918 general election, *Sinn Féin* won 73 seats, the Nationalist Party won 6, and Ulster remained in Unionist hands. The Sinn Féin MPs constituted themselves as *Dáil Éireann* (the Assembly of Ireland) instead of going to Westminster, and met on January 21, 1919. The War of Independence began the same day. This involved Irish Volunteers (who now formed the Irish Republican Army or IRA) fighting a guerrilla campaign against the British for two and a half years. The IRA's director of organization and intelligence, Michael Collins, masterminded their operation. In response the notorious Black and Tans (British auxiliary police) were deployed. Many civilians were terrorized

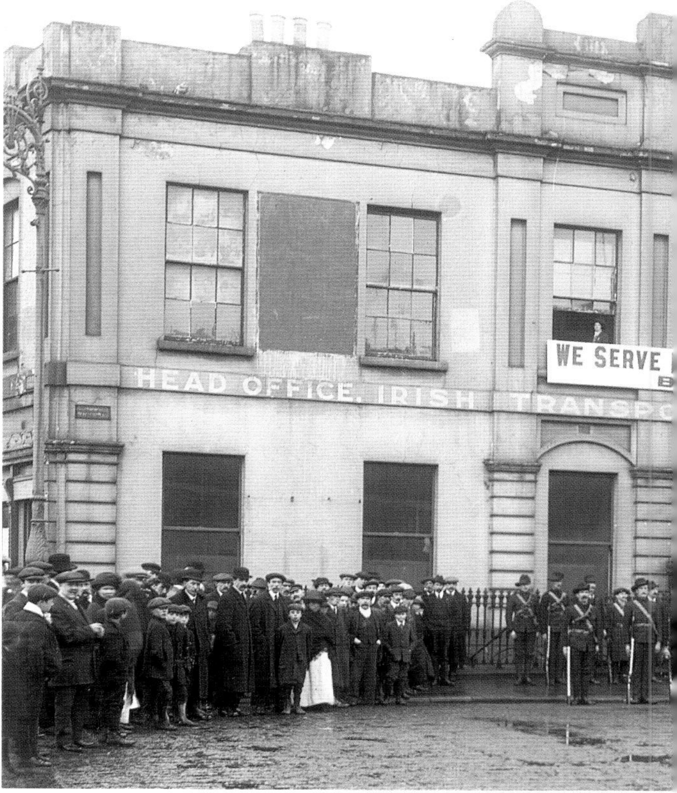

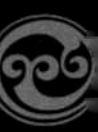

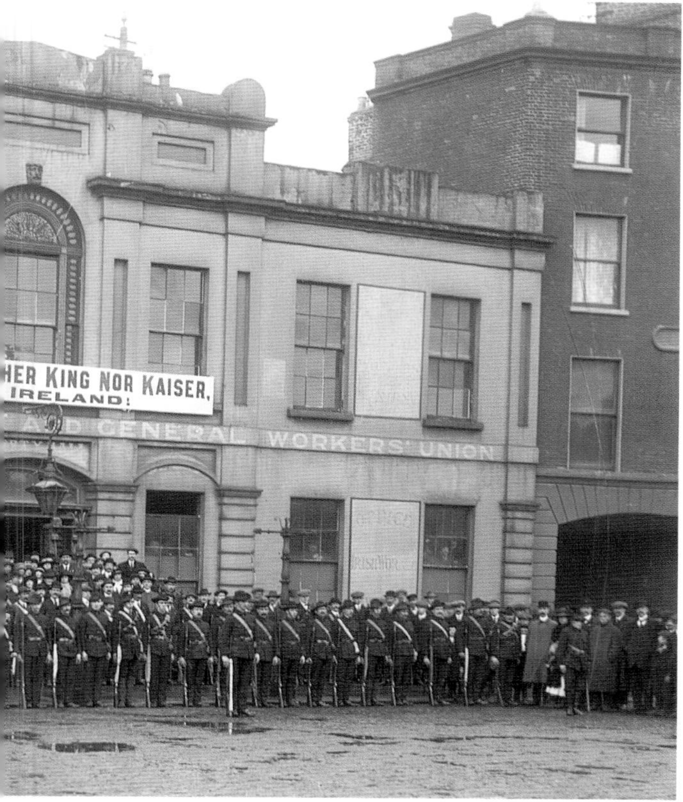
HER KING NOR KAISER,
IRELAND!
AND GENERAL WORKERS' UNION

PREVIOUS PAGE: *The Irish Citizen Army on parade. They united with the Irish Volunteers in order to launch the 1916 Rising.*

during the conflict.

During this period the island was partitioned. Home Rule was granted to the six most Protestant counties of the northeast. Northern nationalists were thus trapped by the "Orange" state. The Anglo-Irish Treaty of December 1921 ended the southern conflict. Arthur Griffith and Michael Collins represented the nationalists; de Valera would not participate as he wanted a republic, not the dominion status that was granted.

The *Dáil* and most of the people supported the treaty. *Sinn Féin* and the IRA split and a short war followed. Both Griffith and Collins died in the fighting. The pro-treaty side won and a new state was established.

States of Ireland

The Irish Free State corresponded to that part of the island which had remained Catholic at the Reformation. It finally became the Republic of Ireland in 1949. Political life was dominated by William Cosgrave, who succeeded Griffith and Collins, and Éamon de Valera from 1932. De Valera formed a national, populist party called *Fianna Fáil*. For the first 40 years the state was determined to express its differences from Britain and guarantee its independence.

This was manifested in Ireland's neutrality during World War II. De Valera's Ireland was largely rural and insulated from urban modernity. Ireland became protectionist and domestic enterprise was safeguarded by high import tariffs. This, however, led to economic inefficiency and financial crisis in the late 1950s.

The Republic of Ireland, despite its economic problems, remained politically stable. In Northern Ireland, however, there were deep social and political rifts. Catholics, comprising some 40 per cent of the territory, faced discrimination in jobs and public housing. As part of the United Kingdom, the North was economically more prosperous than its neighbor.

Modern Ireland

During the 1960s thousands left Ireland to escape economic hardship. In order to generate growth Ireland abandoned protectionism, embraced free trade, and joined the European Economic Community in 1972.

In Northern Ireland a new era of political unrest and violence erupted in October 1968. It began with a civil rights campaign by Catholics seeking fairer treatment in housing allocation, an end to electoral discrimination, and reforms to the state security structures that were considered oppressive. Most Protestants opposed any civil rights being granted. By the summer of 1969 violence was

spreading across the province and troops were deployed to keep the sides apart. The long dormant IRA was revived to protect the Catholics, but soon adopted an offensive terror campaign to drive out the British.

To stop the bloody sectarian conflict both Dublin and London have in recent years collaborated to create peace and justice in the troubled province. The 1985 Anglo-Irish Agreement aimed to promote better relations within the province and enhance cross-border cooperation. The 1993 Downing Street Declaration advanced these aims and the 1998 Good Friday Agreement introduced an elected assembly and secured pledges to decommission terrorist arms.

The European Union (EU) has provided a new focus for the Irish nation. Generous regional funding has helped modernize Ireland and stimulate the economic prosperity it enjoyed at the end of the 20th Century.

Ireland has embraced EU economic integration. European Union coins and notes have been the sole legal tender since 2002. Ireland has also been more outward looking on social issues. The Catholic Church has been challenged by liberal and secular trends.

Ireland has been a member of the United Nations since 1955, and has been active in efforts to maintain international peace and security in accordance with the Charter of the United Nations. The country has twice

served already on the Security Council, in 1962 and in 1981–82, and was elected to a non-permanent seat on the Council for the 2001–02 term. The Irish Defence Forces have served with distinction in many UN peace-keeping missions, such as the Lebanon, and a significant proportion of their personnel are deployed on UN service today around the world. Members of *An Garda Síochána* (the police force) have also served in UN peace-keeping operations in recent years.

Ireland entered the 21st Century as a confident and vibrant nation. Traditional and contemporary culture has flourished. Mary Robinson, Ireland's first woman president (1990–97), and other talented national figures have enhanced the country's international profile. It is hoped that peace and prosperity will eventually be enjoyed by all who inhabit the island of Ireland.

KEY DATES

◆ ◆ ◆

Ireland has experienced a long series of political, cultural, and religious changes from the Stone Age to the present day.

◆ ◆ ◆

c. 7500 B.C. Earliest settlers arrived in Ireland in the Mesolithic period. They crossed by land bridge from Scotland.

c. 3000 B.C. Colonists of the Neolithic period reached Ireland. These people were farmers. One of their monuments, a megalithic tomb at Newgrange in County Meath, has survived.

c. 2000 B.C. Prospectors and metalworkers arrived. Metal deposits were discovered, and soon bronze and gold objects were made.

c. 1200 B.C. More people reached Ireland, producing a greater variety of weapons and artifacts. A common dwelling of this period was the *crannóg*, an artificial island constructed in the middle of a lake.

LEFT: *The entrance to the passage grave at Newgrange, County Meath, is an extraordinary example of Neolithic architecture.*

c. 600 B.C.	Celts started arriving in Ireland from central Europe. They continued to arrive up to the time of Christianity. They soon began to dominate Ireland and the earliest settlers.
c. 200 B.C.	The Celtic culture of the La Téne civilization, named after a Celtic site in Switzerland, reached Ireland. Celtic Ireland was divided into about 150 miniature kingdoms, each called a *tuath*.
c. 100 B.C.	Arrival of the Gaels.
A.D. 200	Beginnings of High Kingship at Tara in County Meath.
c. 300	Ireland inhabited by tribes known as Scoti.
377–405	Niall of the Nine Hostages, High King.
428–63	Reign of King McNeill.
431	Pope Celestine I sent Palladius to the Irish as their first bishop. Palladius died soon after.
432	Arrival of St. Patrick to help convert pagan Gaelic kings to Christianity.
550	Irish monks started to re-Christianize Europe.

Time of Written History

461	St. Patrick died.
521	Birth of St. Columba at Gartan in Tyrconnell, County Donegal.
561	Battle of Culdremna.
563	St. Columba sailed to Iona, where he

Christianized Scotland and much of England.

597 St. Columba died.

800 Ireland attacked by Viking Norsemen, on Lambay Island, off Dublin

841 Vikings constructed a defended camp on the site of present-day Dublin

908 The *Eoghanachta* were defeated when they tried to subject Leinster to Cashel's rule. Their king, *Cormac MacCullenan*, was killed.

914 Vikings established settlements at Waterford.

920 Vikings established settlements at Limerick.

940 Brian Boru was born.

976 Brian succeeded his brother Mahon as king of *Dal Chais* until 1014.

978 Battle of *Belach Lechtna*.

1002 Brian Boru wins recognition as the High King of Ireland.

1014 High King Brian Boru killed at Battle of Clontarf.

1066 Norman invasion of England.

1156 Death of Turloch More O'Connor, king of Connacht, who had become High King in 1119, and who was the greatest of Brian Boru's successors.

1167–69 Norman invasion of Ireland commences.

1170 Arrival of Richard FitzGilbert de Clare, known

	as Strongbow.
1171	Strongbow crowned king of Leinster. Arrival of Henry II, end of the Milesian kings; thus began the political involvement of England in Ireland's affairs.
1166–75	Reign of Rory O'Connor, last native High King of Ireland.
1235	Richard de Burgo conquered Connacht.
1258	Gallowglasses (mercenary soldiers) from Scotland arrived in Ulster.
1264	Walter de Burgo was made Earl of Ulster.
1272	The English had now conquered Ulster, east of Lough Neagh, Meath, and most of Connacht and Munster.
1315	After the Battle of Bannockburn, Edward Bruce of Scotland invaded Ireland but failed in his attempt to overthrow Norman rule.
1318	Edward Bruce killed by the English near Dundalk, County Louth.
1361	An edict bans native men from becoming mayors, bailiffs, officers of the King or clerygmen, serving the English.
1366	The Statutes of Kilkenny forbade Irish/English marriages and prevented the English from using the Irish language, customs or laws.
1394	October: King Richard II landed at Waterford

	and marched up to Dublin.
1478	*Gearóid Mór FitzGerald*, 8th Earl of Kildare, assumed role of chief governor of Ireland.
1507	Accession of Henry VIII.
1515	Anarchy in Ireland.
1529–36	Henry VIII declares himself head of the Church in England.
1534	Kildare rebellion.
1541	Henry VIII declares himself King of Ireland.
1545–63	The Council of Trent.
1547	Henry VIII died and was succeeded by the boy king Edward VI. England and Ireland were ruled by the senior nobility of England.
1553	Accession of Mary I.
1558	Accession of Elizabeth I.
1562	Elizabethan wars in Ireland.
1588	Spanish Armada sent by Philip of Spain to conquer England.
1594	August: Hugh O'Neill defeated a small English force at the Ford of Biscuits near Enniskillen.
1595	Rebellion of Hugh O'Neill, Earl of Tyrone.
1598	O'Neill's great victory at Yellow Ford in Ulster.
1601	Defeat of O'Neill, O'Donnell, and Spaniards by Lord Mountjoy at Battle of Kinsale.
1603	Accession of James I. Surrender of Hugh O'Neill. Enforcement of English Law in Ireland.

LEFT: *Detail from the O'Conor wall memorial (1624) at Sligo Abbey, in honor of Sir Donogh O'Conor Sligo. The O'Conors were a warring clan and from the 14th to the 16th Century they were involved in continual warfare with the O'Donnells and the English. This ancient and princely family attained the zenith of their power in the 16th Century. After Sir Donogh O'Conor Sligo's death in 1609 the strength and power of the O'Conors began to decline and they lost all their possessions in the wake of the Cromwellian wars.*

1606	Settlement of Scots in Ards Peninsula. Land in six counties of Ulster confiscated by English.
1607	"The Flight of the Earls" (including O'Neill, Earl of Tyrone, and O'Donnell, Earl of Tyrconnell) to Spain.
1608	A government survey of confiscated Ulster lands is initiated.
1625	Accession of Charles I.
1628	Charles I granted 51 Graces for subsidies.
1632–38	Compilation of the *Annals of the Four Masters*.
1633	Thomas Wentworth appointed governor of Ireland.
1641	Great Catholic-Gaelic rebellion for return of lands; later joined by Old English Catholics in Ireland. Under leadership of Irish chieftain, Rory O'More, a conspiracy was formed to seize Dublin and expel the English. English settlers were driven out of Ulster.
1642	Confederation of Kilkenny met.
1647	Alliance between lords of the Pale and native Irishmen came to an end.
1649	Oliver Cromwell landed at Dublin. His troops killed 2,000 men. A great amount of land in

Right: *Oliver Cromwell obliterated any remaining sizable Catholic landholdings after landing in Ireland in 1649.*

	Munster, Leinster, and Ulster was confiscated and given to the English soldiers.
1650	Catholic landowners exiled to Connacht.
1656	Over 60,000 Irish Catholics had been sent as slaves to Barbados, and other islands in the Caribbean.
1658	The population of Ireland, estimated at 1,500,000 before Cromwell, was reduced to 500,000 at Cromwell's death in 1658.
1660	Accession of Charles II.
1661–68	The Duke of Ormond ruled Ireland as Viceroy.
1685	Accession of James II.
1688	James II deposed in England. Gates of Derry shut in face of James's troops.
1689	Siege and relief of Derry. James II's Parliament restored all lands confiscated since 1641.
1690	William of Orange (William III) lands at Carrickfergus and defeats James II at Battle of the Boyne. Flight of the "Wild Geese" to France.
1691	Catholic defeat at Aughrim and surrender at Limerick.
1692–1829	Exclusion of Catholics from Parliament and all professions.
1695	Anti-Catholic penal laws introduced.
1775	Henry Grattan becomes leader of Patriot Party.

1782	Legislative independence won from Britain by Irish Parliament.
1798	Arrest and death of Lord Edward Fitzgerald. Battle of Vinegar Hill. Battle of Antrim. French forces attempted to invade Ireland. Death of Theobald Wolfe Tone.
1798	Daniel O'Connell takes law degree at Trinity

ABOVE: *A memorial to Wolfe Tone at Collins Barracks, Dublin. Tone led the doomed 1798 Rising against the English.*

	College, and is admitted to the Bar.
1800	Act of Union passed (effective January 1, 1801).
1803	Robert Emmet's rebellion is crushed.
1823	Daniel O'Connell's Catholic Association founded.
1828	O'Connell elected for County Clare.
1829	Catholic emancipation passed. Tithe war began.
1837	Accession of Queen Victoria.
1839	January 6: The Night of the "Big Wind".
1840	O'Connell's Repeal Association founded.
1842	*The Nation* newspaper founded by Thomas Davis.
1843	O'Connell's "Monster Meetings" for the repeal of the Union.
1845	Blight in the potato harvest.
1845–49	Start of the Famine. Charles Trevelyan, permanent head of treasury. Sir Robert Peel, Prime Minister, imports Indian corn.
1846	April. Trevelyan opened depots for the sale of Indian corn, but closed them later in summer. Corn laws repealed.
1846	July: Lord John Russell replaced Peel as Prime Minister. August: Total failure of potato harvest. October: First deaths from starvation.
1847	Fever spreading. Trevelyan winds up Soup

Kitchen Act, and retires.

1848–49 Worst years of Famine. Ireland's population has decreased by more than two million people.

1848 Smith O'Brien (Young Ireland leader) arrested. James Stephens fled to France.

ABOVE: *William Smith O'Brien (seated) in Kilmainham Jail after his failed attempt to launch an uprising against the British in 1848.*

1856	Stephens returned from France.
1858	Irish Republican Brotherhood founded by Stephens.
	Fenian Brotherhood founded in America.
1863	*Irish People* newspaper founded.
1865	*Irish People* editorial board arrested.
	James Stephens arrested but escaped from Richmond Jail.
1867	February: Abortive raid on Chester Castle.
	March: Fenian rising in Ireland.
	December: Clerkenwell explosion.
1869	Gladstone, Prime Minister, dis-established Protestant Church in Ireland.
1870	Gladstone's first Land Act.
1875	Charles Stewart Parnell elected MP for County Meath.
1879	Threat of famine. Irish National League founded.
1879–82	Land War
1881	Gladstone's 2nd Land Act. Parnell imprisoned.
1884	Gaelic Athletic Association formed.
1885	"Ashbourne" Land Act.
1886	First Home Rule bill.
1891	Parnell loses three by-elections in Ireland. He dies in October.
1893	Second Home Rule bill. Gaelic League founded.
1903	Land Purchase Act (Wyndham Act).

1905	*Sinn Féin* formed.
1906	General election won by the Liberals.
1909	Land Purchase Act.
1914	Outbreak of World War I. Home Rule bill passed.
1916	Easter Rising in Dublin.
1917	East Clare by-election won by De Valera.
1918	November: End of World War I.
1919–21	Irish War of Independence against Britain.
1921	December: Anglo-Irish Treaty.
1922–23	Civil War.
1926	De Valera founds *Fianna Fáil*.
1927	General elections in Ireland. De Valera and *Fianna Fáil* enter *Dáil*.
1932	General election. *Fiánna Fail* victory.
1937	Constitution of Eire claims 32 counties.
1939	World War II begins.
1945	End of World War II.
1948	General election. *Fiánna Fáil* defeated.
1949	Repeal of External Relations Act. Ireland (26 counties) officially declared a republic and is no longer in the Commonwealth.
1951–62	IRA campaign in Northern Ireland.

FOLLOWING PAGE: *Irish nationalists defending the General Post Office against attack by British troops during the 1916 Rising.*

LEFT: *British troops were first sent on to the streets of Northern Ireland in 1969 as a result of increasing sectarian violence.*

1955	Ireland admitted into the United Nations.
1965	O'Neill-Lemass talks.
1967	Northern Ireland Civil Rights Association founded.
1968	August: First Civil Rights march. October: Derry Civil Rights march, banned by William Craig, Minister of Home Affairs; held but broken up by police.
1969	January: People's Democracy Belfast to Derry Civil Rights march. January 4: Marchers attacked at Burntollet Bridge. April: Resignation of O'Neill. Succeeded by Chichester Clark as the Northern Ireland Prime Minister. August 14: British troops ordered into Derry. October: Protestant riot in Belfast.
1970	Dublin Arms Trial.
1971	First British soldier killed by IRA in Belfast. Chichester Clark resigns, Faulkner Prime Minister. Unionist Government of Northern Ireland introduced internment without trial for suspected republicans.

1972	Ireland joined the European Economic Community.
1972	January 30: Bloody Sunday in Derry. British paratroopers shot 13 civilians during Civil Rights march. March: Stormont suspended.
1973	Sunningdale Agreement.
1974	Faulkner and the Assembly brought down by the Ulster Workers' Strike. Direct Rule is reimposed. Dublin and Monaghan bombed by loyalists.
1981-82	10 republicans died on hunger strike in the Maze Prison, Northern Ireland. Prisoner Bobby Sands elected to the British Parliament.
1993	Downing Street Declaration: British Government accepts the right of the people of Ireland to self-determination.
1994	Cease-fire declared by the IRA.
1996	Cease-fire ended after British Government refused to allow Sinn Féin to join all-party talks on Northern Ireland.
1997	IRA cease-fire resumed; talks started in Belfast between politicians from Dublin, Westminster, and Northern Ireland.
1998	Good Friday Agreement signed.
2002	Ireland puts the EU currency (IEP) into circulation and abolishes the Irish pound (IR£).

Irish Lives

Throughout history the Irish nation has produced a plethora of scholars, statesmen, warriors, and scientists. This list celebrates the diversity of Ireland's famous sons and daughters and their contribution, not only to the life of Ireland, but to the world.

Gerry Adams (1948–)

Northern Ireland politician. The dominant figure in the Republican movement since the early 1980s, he has played a central role in the gradual assertion of the importance of a political, as opposed to a military, strategy. Adams was interned in 1971 but released. He was arrested again in 1973 and held until 1977. He became *Sinn Féin's* leader in 1983 and was MP for West Belfast until 1992. In 1997 he regained the seat. Following the Good Friday Agreement, Adams was elected to the Northern Ireland Assembly.

Bertie Ahern (1951–)

Statesman who entered the *Dáil* in the *Fianna Fáil* landslide of 1977. Ahern was appointed as assistant government whip in 1980 and served as chief whip from March 1982 until the Haughey government fell in November. On the return of *Fianna*

Fáil to government in 1987 he became Minister for Labor. Ahern was a member of Dublin City Council (1979-91) and Lord Mayor (1986). He became Minister for Finance in 1991, leader of *Fianna Fáil* (1994), and finally *Taoiseach* (1997).

Harold Alexander, Earl of Tunis (1891–1969)
Military commander. Served with the Irish Guards in World War I and rose to the rank of major-general by the outbreak of World War II. Appointed Commander-in-Chief Middle East (1942) and then Commander-in-Chief 18th Army Group, North Africa. Alexander commanded the Allied forces in Italy (1943–44) and then was made field-marshal and Supreme Allied Commander in the Mediterranean theater until the end of the war. He also served as Governor-General of Canada (1946–52) and Minister of Defense (1952–54).

Francis Bacon (1909–92)
A self-taught artist whose works focus on shockingly grotesque and brutally satiric themes. From the 1950s onwards his images become increasingly distorted and abstract. Bacon lived in London but in 1998 his studio and its contents was gifted to the Hugh Lane Gallery, Dublin.

Michael William Balfe (1808–70)
Composer and singer. Of his many operas, very popular in

their time, the best known was *The Bohemian Girl* (1843).

Thomas John Barnardo (1845–1905)
Doctor and philanthropist. He went to London to study medicine and founded a home for destitute children in London (1867). He built a number of homes in Greater London and the organization he founded now flourishes under the name of Barnado. It is one of Britain's largest child-care charities.

John Barry (1745–1803)
US naval officer in the American Revolution. He went as a youth to the American colonies, where he was a trader and a shipmaster. In the Revolution he commanded the brig Lexington when she captured the British tender Edward (1776)—first British ship taken by a commissioned American ship. His renown as a naval hero of the revolution was second only to that of John Paul Jones.

George Berkeley (1685–1753)
Anglican bishop and philosopher. Berkeley was a fellow and tutor of Trinity College, Dublin, until 1713. He was Dean of Derry from 1724 and Bishop of Cloyne until 1752. His major works include *Essay towards a New Theory of Vision* (1709), *A Treatise concerning the Principles of Human Knowledge* (1710), and *Three Dialogues between Hylas and Philonous* (1713).

George Best (1946–)
Northern Ireland footballer. At 15 Best joined Manchester United then went back to Belfast because of homesickness, but was persuaded to return. He was always a prolific scorer and won League Championship medals in 1965 and 1967. He gave a masterly performance in United's victory in the European Cup in 1968, when he was also voted European Footballer of the Year. In his first season with Manchester United he also made his international début for Northern Ireland and went on to be awarded 37 caps. By the early 1970s, his career as a top-class player was over.

Robert "Danny" Blanchflower (1926–93)
Footballer, manager, and sports writer. Blanchflower left Belfast to play professional football in England. His genius became apparent at Tottenham Hotspur. He made 553 English League appearances, and was capped 56 times for Northern Ireland. He captained the Northern Ireland team in the 1958 World Cup and later served as manager.

Bono (Paul Hewson) (1960–)
Rock musician, singer and songwriter. Together with Larry Mullen, Adam Clayton, Dave Evans ("The Edge") and his brother Dick, he formed the group Feedback, later to become The Hype and then U2 (without Dick Evans). Their first release, the EP *U23* was made in 1979. In 1980 they

released their first single *11 O'Clock Tick Tock* the following month and their first album, *Boy*. Their 1987 album *The Joshua Tree* reached No.1 in Britain, the USA, and 20 other countries and confirmed U2 as the world's biggest rock band. U2 have sold close to 100 million albums worldwide in the last 20 years.

Brian Boru *(Brian Boroimhe)* (c. 940–1014)
King of Ireland. Brian subjugated all Munster, then extended his power over all of southern Ireland. In 1005 he became High King of Ireland by right of conquest. As his power increased, relations with the Norse rulers on the Irish coast grew steadily worse. Sitric, king of the Dublin Norse, formed a coalition of the Norse of Ireland, the Hebrides, the Orkneys, and Iceland as well as Brian's Irish enemies to overthrow him. In 1014, Brian's forces annihilated the allies at Clontarf, near Dublin. Soon afterwards he was killed. Norse power was broken by Brian's victory, but the country fell into anarchy.

Charles Boycott (1832–97)
The practice of concerted economic or social ostracism of an individual, group, or nation to express disapproval or coerce change was named after Charles Boycott (1880). He was an English land agent in Ireland whose ruthlessness in evicting tenants led his employees to refuse all cooperation

with him and his family. In the United States the boycott has been used chiefly in labor disputes; consumer and business groups have also resorted to the method.

Robert Boyle (1627–91)
Chemist and physicist noted for his pioneering experiments on the properties of gases and his advocacy of a corpuscular view of matter that was a forerunner of the modern theory of chemical elements. He formulated the law of physics that bears his name (Boyle's law). He is often referred to as the father of modern chemistry; he separated chemistry from alchemy and gave the first precise definitions of a chemical element, a chemical reaction, and chemical analysis. He also made studies of the calcination of metals, combustion, acids and bases, the nature of colors, and the propagation of sound. Boyle also contributed to physical theory, supporting an early form of the atomic theory of matter, which he called the corpuscular philosophy.

Edmund Burke (1729–97)
Political writer and statesman. Burke's political career began in 1765 when he became private secretary to the Marquess of Rockingham, then prime minister. He entered Parliament in 1765. At a time when political allegiances were based on patronage and political opposition was generally regarded

as factionalism, Burke became the first political philosopher to argue the value of political parties. His writings on British political thought had far-reaching influence in America and France.

John Burke (1787–1848)

Irish genealogist who issued *A Genealogical and Heraldic Dictionary of the Peerage and Baronetage of the United Kingdom* (1826). He published the guide irregularly until 1847, after which it became an annual, commonly called *Burke's Peerage*.

Robert O'Hara Burke (1820–61)

Explorer of Australia. In 1860, with W. J. Wills and eight other whites, he left Menindee, on the Darling River, to cross the continent. Dissensions broke up the party, but the leaders reached the estuary of the Flinders River, in the Gulf of Carpentaria. On the return journey both Burke and Wills died from hunger and exposure.

Isaac Butt (1813–79)

Politician and nationalist leader. A member of the Irish and English bar, he was a noted Conservative lawyer. After the Irish Famine, however, he became increasingly Liberal, defended participants in the abortive Young Ireland revolt (1848), and entered parliament (1852). As a Liberal-

Conservative he continually urged land tenure reform, defended the Fenian leaders, and founded the Home Rule Society (1870).

Gabriel (Gay) Byrne (1934–)
Broadcaster. He joined *Radio Éireann* in 1958. He also worked with Granada TV in England and with the BBC. Byrne joined *Telefís Éireann* (later RTÉ) in 1961 and presented various successful shows. He produced and presented the first *Late Late Show* on July 6, 1962 and it was to go on to become the world's longest-running live television talk show. It was a pacesetter for public opinion and raised many controversial topics. He retired in 1999, the same year he left his popular morning radio show.

Sir Roger David Casement (1864–1916)
Revolutionary and British consular official. Although an Ulster Protestant, Casement became an ardent Irish nationalist. After the outbreak of World War I he went first to the United States and then to Germany to secure aid for an Irish uprising. He returned to Ireland in April 1916, but was arrested immediately upon landing from a German submarine. He was tried, convicted, and hanged for treason.

Erskine Childers (1905–74)
Statesman. Childers was born in London and came to

Dublin in 1931 to become advertisement manager of the *Irish Press* newspaper. He was secretary of the Federation of Irish Manufacturers (1936–44) before becoming a TD (1938). After serving as a junior minister (1944–48) he held successive ministerial appointments in a number of government departments until 1973. Childers served as *Tánaiste* (deputy prime minister) from 1969 to 1973 before becoming President in 1974.

Michael Collins (1890–1922)
Revolutionary leader. Collins joined the Fenian movement while living in England (1907–16). He took part in the Easter Rising (1916) and was imprisoned for the rest of the year. One of the *Sinn Féin* members who set up *Dáil Éireann* in 1919, he led the Irish Republican Army in the guerrilla campaign against British rule. Although a convinced republican, Collins, with Arthur Griffith, negotiated and signed the treaty (1921) that set up the Irish Free State. They felt it the best settlement with Britain possible at that time. He was briefly finance minister in Griffith's government before being killed by republicans.

James Connolly (1868–1916)
Nationalist and Marxist leader who founded the Irish Socialist Republican Party. Connolly was born in Scotland and came to Ireland while serving in the army. After

BELOW: *Collins Barracks, Dublin, was named in honor of revolutionary leader Michael Collins. It is now part of the National Museum.*

becoming a political activist, he went to the United States (1902–10). He returned in 1910 to work as a labor leader, then became a commander in the Irish Citizen Army, and was executed for his role in the 1916 Rising.

Tom Crean (1877–1938)
Explorer. He joined the Royal Navy at 15 and became involved in notable expeditions to the Antarctic. He participated in Robert Scott's 1901–04 expedition and his doomed 1910 expedition when the party reached the Pole (1912) but perished on the return trek. Crean was in the relief party that found Scott's frozen body. He also worked with Ernest Shackelton's remarkable voyage on *Endurance*.

Michael Davitt (1846–1906)
Revolutionary and land reformer. He joined the Fenian movement (1865) and was imprisoned three times for revolutionary activity. Davitt and Parnell were the leading figures in establishing the National Land League (1879). He broke with Parnell over the question of land nationalization but remained an important Irish leader and was instrumental in bringing the Parnell and anti-Parnell factions together in the United Irish League.

Éamon de Valera (1882–1975)
Statesmen and revolutionary who served as a commandant

during the 1916 Rising. De Valera was born in New York and went to Ireland as a child. He was sentenced to life imprisonment for his involvement in the 1916 Rising but was released (1917). He became president of *Sinn Féin* and an MP. In 1918 he was arrested but escaped from prison and fled to the United States where he raised funds for Irish independence. Although elected president by *Dáil Éireann,* he resigned as the Irish Free State did not include Northern Ireland (1922). *Fianna Fáil* re-entered the Dáil in 1927. De Valera served as *Taoiseach* on three occasions between 1932 and 1959. He then served as President from 1959 until 1973.

Richard Dunwoody (1964–)
Jump jockey. He rode his 1,000th winner on January 30, 1994 and went on to achieve a record 1,699 career victories. He won the Aintree Grand National twice (1986 on West Tip and 1994 on Minnehoma) and the King George three times. He won the Champion Hurdle in 1990 on Kribensis and won 18 times at Cheltenham.

Pat Eddery (1952–)
Jockey. He won his first race in 1969 and was champion apprentice in 1971. Eddery has won the Epsom Derby

RIGHT: *Éamon de Valera, the statesman and revolutionary.*

three times (1975, 1982, 1990). His Irish Classic wins include four Derbies. He has also won the Prix de L'Arc de Triomphe four times.

Edward the Bruce (?–1318)
Scottish King of Ireland and brother of Robert I of Scotland. Edward aided his brother in the war for independence from England and in 1315 was declared heir to Robert's throne. With Robert's approval he then invaded Ulster. He was crowned King of Ireland in 1316 and found many Irish allies against the Anglo-Irish rulers. He failed to consolidate his gains, however, and was killed in battle.

Sir Samuel Ferguson (1810–86)
Irish poet and Celtic scholar. As president of the Royal Irish Academy he gave powerful impetus to the study of early Irish art.

James Fitzmaurice (1898–1965)
Aviator, co-pilot on first east-to-west flight in 1928 from Baldonnel, County Dublin, to Greenly Island, off Labrador. The crew carried two copies of *The Irish Times*, the first European newspaper to cross the Atlantic.

Niall Glundubh (?–919)
High King of Ireland from 915–919. The name O'Neill

meant "grandson of Niall", probably referring originally to *Niall Glundubh*.

Maud Gonne (1865–1953)
Irish nationalist, actress, and daughter of an English colonel. She edited *L'Irlande libre*, a nationalist newspaper published in Paris. She was one of the founders of Sinn Féin.

Arthur Griffith (1872–1922)
Statesman and founder of *Sinn Féin*. Griffith founded the United Irishman newspaper (1899), in which he advocated that Irish MPs withdraw from Westminster and organize their own assembly. In 1905 his supporters formed Sinn Féin. Griffith took no part in the 1916 Rising, but he was imprisoned several times (1916–18) by the British. He was elected to parliament in 1918, then joined the other Sinn Féiners in forming *Dáil Éireann* and was elected its vice-president. He led the Irish delegation that negotiated the treaty establishing the Irish Free State (1921). When de Valera, president of the *Dáil*, rejected the treaty, Griffith succeeded to his office. He died suddenly at the beginning of the Civil War.

Arthur Guinness (1725–1803)
Founder of the famous Guinness brewery. In 1759 he set up a brewery at St. James's Gate, Dublin; 19 years later he

began making his famous porter. It has since become a hugely successful international business empire.

Alfred Harmsworth, Viscount Northcliffe (1865–1922)
Journalist who became one of the most spectacular newspaper publishers in the history of the British press. The publications he launched and acquired formed the basis for what became the world's largest periodical combine, the Amalgamated Press. Northcliffe bought the *London Evening News* (1894), launching his career in newspaper publishing. He founded the *Daily Mail* (1896), the *Daily Mirror* (1903), and gained control of the *Times* in 1908.

Charles J. Haughey (1925–)
Statesman. An accountant and real estate investor, he entered parliament as a *Fianna Fáil* member in 1957. After holding a succession of ministerial positions in the 1960s, he was dismissed as Minister for Finance (1970) for alleged gunrunning to the IRA. He regained his party's favor and held the Ministry of Health and Social Welfare (1977–79) before becoming *Taoiseach* (1979–81, 1982, and 1987–92). A wiretapping scandal forced his resignation in 1992.

Chaim Herzog (1918–97)
Israeli leader who emigrated to Palestine in 1935. Herzog served with the Jewish Haganah fighters, the British Army,

Above: *Charles J. Haughey, the* Fianna Fáil *politician who became* Taoiseach *in 1979, has had his reputation tarnished by scandals.*

and Israeli forces. After serving in various diplomatic and political posts he became Israel's president (1983–93).

Alexander (Alex) Higgins (1949–)
Snooker player. He turned professional in 1971 and became the youngest world champion in 1972. He won the world title again in 1982 and his other major wins included the Benson & Hedges Masters in Britain (1978, 1981), and the UK Championship in 1983. His speed of play earned him the sobriquet "Hurricane".

Patrick Hillery (1923–)
Statesman. Hillery was elected to *Dáil Éireann* in 1951, became Minister for Education in 1959, and then served in various ministerial posts. He became vice-president of the then Commission of the European Communities in 1973. He was inaugurated as president in 1976.

James Hoban (1762–1831)
Architect of the White House. By 1789, Hoban had emigrated to the United States. He won the competition for the design of a mansion for the President which he built from 1792 to 1799. After the White House was burned by the British (1814), President James Madison ordered an immediate rebuilding of the destroyed mansion. Hoban was called back to supervise the reconstruction.

John Philip Holland (1840–1914)

Inventor. He started life as a school teacher in Ireland. He emigrated to the United States (1873) where he offered a submarine design to the US Navy. This was rejected in 1875 as impractical, but he continued his experiments with a submarine, the Fenian Ram, which was launched in 1881. Holland VI, launched in 1898 had almost all the features of a modern, non-nuclear submarine. This convinced the world that his submarines had to be taken seriously as a weapon of war.

John Hume (1937–)

Northern Ireland politician. In the late 1960s he became active in the Northern Ireland Civil Rights Association and the Derry Citizens' Action Committee. He became an MP in 1969 and co-founded the Social Democratic and Labour Party (SDLP). He was MP for Londonderry to the Northern Ireland Assembly (1973–4), and served as Minister of Commerce in the power-sharing Executive (1974). He became SDLP leader and an MEP in 1979. In 1998 Hume was awarded the Nobel prize for Peace (together with David Trimble) for his crucial work in the Northern Ireland peace process.

Douglas Hyde (1860–1949)

Statesman and scholar. Hyde was co-founder and first

president of the Gaelic League (1893–1915), the national movement for the revival of the Irish language. He was a member of *Seanad Éireann* (1925–38), and served as first President of Ireland from 1938–45.

Eddie Irvine (1965–)

Motor-racing driver who made his Formula 1 début with Jordan (1993). In 1999 he won four Grands Prix and finished second in the World Championship. In 2000 he joined the Jaguar racing team.

Eddie Jordan (1948–)

Motor-racing team owner. As a driver he achieved success at every level of racing bar Formula 1. In 1987 he founded Jordan Racing and retired from racing himself the following year to concentrate on running the team. Jordan Grand Prix was founded in 1990 and in 1991 the team entered the Formula 1 championship. His success in Formula 1 has been remarkable with the team progressing steadily from season to season.

Robbie Keane (1980–)

Footballer. His career in England began with Wolverhampton Wanderers before signing for Coventry City (August 1999). A year later he moved to Italian giants Inter Milan, then joined Leeds United in December 2000

and Tottenham Hotspur in August 2002. Keane made his international début in 1998 against the Czech Republic and has been a fixture in the Ireland line-up ever since. He was an integral part of Ireland's success in the 2002 World Cup and is one of the most promising players to come out of Ireland in recent memory.

Roy Keane (1971–)
Footballer. He joined Nottingham Forest in 1990 and transferred to Manchester United in 1994. He became the captain in 1998 and went on to lead them to a historic treble in 1999 winning the FA Premiership, the FA Cup, and the European Champions League. He made his full senior début for Ireland against Chile in 1991.

Herbert Kitchener, 1st Earl (1850–1916)
Field marshal and statesman. He was governor-general of Eastern Sudan (1886–88) and commander-in-chief of the Egyptian Army (1892). In 1896 he began the reconquest of Sudan and was made governor. Kitchener served as chief-of-staff to Lord Roberts in the Boer War (1899–1902), and commander of British forces in India until 1909. After being made field marshal, Kitchener served as consul-general in Egypt (1911–14). During World War I he served as Secretary of State for war but was drowned after a ship carrying him to Russia was sunk by a German mine.

Right: *Posters of Lord Kitchener urging men to enlist became one of the most famous propaganda images of World War I.*

Countess Constance Markievicz (1868–1927)

Revolutionary and leading Anglo-Irish socialite who married Count Casimir Dunin-Markievicz from Ukraine (1900). In 1908 she entered politics, joining *Sinn Féin* and *Inghínidhe na hÉireann*. She participated in the 1916 Rising and was condemned to death. Her sentence was commuted to penal servitude for life, but she was freed in the general amnesty of 1917. Markievicz became the first woman to be elected to the British Parliament (1918), but in accordance with Sinn Féin policy she refused to take her seat. She was a member of the first *Dáil Éireann* in 1919, and Minister for Labor. Although defeated in the 1922 general election, she won Dublin Borough South in 1923 when the Civil War had ended. Markievicz joined the newly formed *Fianna Fáil* Party (1926) and was re-elected in 1927.

William Massey (1856–1925)

Born in County Derry but emigrated to New Zealand, where he served as Prime Minister (1912–25).

Mary McAleese (1951–)

Barrister and professor who became the first president to come from Northern Ireland. In 1994, she became the first

DON'T IMAGINE YOU ARE NOT WANTED

EVERY MAN between 19 and 38 years of age is WANTED!
Ex-Soldiers up to 45 years of age

"YOUR COUNTRY NEEDS
YOU"

MEN CAN ENLIST IN THE NEW ARMY FOR THE DURATION OF THE WAR

RATE OF PAY: Lowest Scale 7s. per week with Food, Clothing &c., in addition

1. Separation Allowance for Wives and Children of Married Men when separated from their Families (Inclusive of the allotment required from the Soldier's pay of a maximum of 6d. a day in the case of a private)

For a Wife **without** Children	12s. 6d. per week
For Wife with One Child	15s. 0d. per week
For Wife with Two Children	17s. 6d. per week
For Wife with Three Children	20s. 0d. per week
For Wife with Four Children	22s. 0d per week

and so on, with an addition of 2s. for each additional child.
Motherless children 3s. a week each, exclusive of allotment from Soldier's pay

2. Separation Allowance for Dependants of Unmarried Men

Provided the Soldier does his share, the Government will assist liberally in keeping up, within the limits of Separation Allowance for Families, any regular contribution made before enlistment by unmarried Soldiers or Widowers to other dependants such as mothers, fathers, sisters, etc.

YOUR COUNTRY IS STILL CALLING.
FIGHTING MEN! FALL IN!!

Full Particulars can be obtained at any Recruiting Office or Post Office.

ABOVE: *Countess Constance Markievicz was a revolutionary and leading Anglo-Irish socialite who married a Ukrainian aristocrat.*

female Pro-Vice Chancellor of Queen's University of Belfast. She is also an experienced journalist and broadcaster. She was inaugurated as the President in November 1997. She has a longstanding interest in many issues concerned with justice, equality, social inclusion, anti-sectarianism, and reconciliation.

Thomas Meagher (1823–67)

Revolutionary and Union general in the American Civil War. A leader of the Young Ireland movement, he was deported to present-day Tasmania for his part in the abortive 1848 rebellion. In 1852 Meagher escaped to the United States where he edited the *Irish News*. In the American Civil War, Meagher fought with the famous 69th Regiment and organized New York's Irish Brigade (1861–62). He resigned as brigadier-general of volunteers (1863), but this was soon canceled. At the end of the war he was serving under General Sherman. He was appointed secretary of Montana Territory in 1865 and also served as temporary governor.

John Mitchel (1815–75)

Patriot, attorney, and editor of *The Nation*, a nationalist publication. Mitchel started the *United Irishman* (1848) and was tried for articles on a charge of "treason-felony". Although he was transported to present-day Tasmania, he

escaped to the United States (1853). He returned home and was elected to parliament (1874), but was declared ineligible. Although re-elected, he died the same month.

Thomas Moore (1779–1852)
Poet. He became one of the first Catholics to be admitted to Trinity College in 1794. He is remembered today for *Irish Melodies*, a group of lyrics published between 1808 and 1834 and set to music by Sir John Stevenson and others. The songs include several of lasting fame, such as "Oft in the Stilly Night", and "The Harp That Once through Tara's Halls".

Liam Neeson (1952–)
Northern Irish actor who made his stage début in *The Risen* (1976). Neeson made his film début in *Excalibur* (1981), and has starred in over 40 films. These include *Schindler's List* (1993) and *Star Wars: Episode I The Phantom Menace* (1999).

Aidan O'Brien (1969–)
Trainer. After a brief career as a jockey he became a trainer at the relatively young age of 23. In 1994 O'Brien took over Ballydoyle stables, and that year he produced a combined total of 176 winners in both flat and National Hunt racing. He went on to break this Irish record the following year and remains a dominant force in Ireland and Britain.

Vincent O'Brien (1917–)
Racehorse trainer. Ballydoyle stables, County Tipperary, which he moved into in 1951, is one of the world's greatest training centers. With jumpers he has won all the major British National Hunt races, including three Grand Nationals (1953, 1954 and 1955). In flat racing, he trained winners of 16 English Classic races, including the Epsom Derby, as well as 27 Irish Classics.

Seán T. Ó Ceallaigh (1882–1966)
Statesman and nationlist. Ó Ceallaigh was one of the founders of *Sinn Féin* and and was an alderman of Dublin Corporation (1906–24). He was jailed for his participation in the 1916 Rising, then served as a TD (1918–45), Speaker of the first *Dáil Éireann* (1919–21), and vice-president of the Executive Council (the Government) of the Irish Free State (1932–38). Other political appointments included Minister for Local Government and Public Health (1932-1939), *Tánaiste* (Deputy Head of Government) (1938–1945), and Minister for Finance (1939–1945). He became the president in 1945.

Daniel O'Connell (1775–1847)
Statesmen and Irish leader in the British House of Commons. He established the Catholic Association (1823) to fight for Catholic rights. He was elected MP in 1828, but

did not take his seat until the Catholic Emancipation bill (1829) was passed. He was imprisoned and fined for conspiracy to raise sedition (1844).

Cearbhall Ó Dálaigh (1911–78)
Statesman and barrister. *Ó Dálaigh* was Attorney General of Ireland 1946–48 and 1951–1953. In 1953 he was appointed a judge of the Supreme Court. He served as Chief Justice and president of the Supreme Court (1961–73) before being appointed a judge of the Court of Justice of the European Communities in 1973. He then became President (1974–1976).

Hugh O'Neill, Earl of Tyrone (c. 1540–1616)
Irish chieftain, son of Matthew O'Neill, the illegitimate son of the 1st Earl. He was made Earl of Tyrone after helping the English fight rebel Gerald Fitzgerald. From 1593 he became the O'Neill chieftain and quickly became Ulster's most powerful nobleman. Hugh O'Neill was angered by the English policy of playing the chiefs against each other and their refusal to restore the lands granted to his grandfather. O'Neill formed an alliance with the other Irish chiefs against England and received Spanish military support. He was forced to make peace with the English in 1603 but never recovered his power. In 1607 Hugh O'Neill joined the "Flight of the Earls".

Charles Stewart Parnell (1846–91)
Nationalist leader who brought the Irish question to the forefront of British politics after being elected an MP in 1875. Parnell became president of the National Land League in 1879, giving him great influence during the "Land War" of 1879–82. He was arrested in 1881, but released in 1882 at the instigation of Gladstone, whom he eventually persuaded of the justice of home rule. However, Parnell's Home Rule bill was defeated in 1886. He was accused and completely acquitted of supporting Irish terrorism (1887–89). Although called the "uncrowned King of Ireland", his influence collapsed when he was cited as co-respondent in the divorce case of Kitty O'Shea. Charles Stewart Parnell never recovered his grip on the Home Rule movement which was soon riven by dissension.

Patrick Pearse (1879–1916)
Nationalist, poet, and educator, who became the first president of the Provisional Government of the Irish Republic. Patrick Pearse was Commander-in-Chief of the Irish forces in the 1916 Rising. He surrendered to the British and was executed at Kilmainham Jail in Dublin on May 3, 1916.

William Petty, Earl of Shelburne (1737–1805)
Statesman and Prime Minister (1782–83). Shelburne studied

ABOVE: *The Dublin monument to the 19th-Century nationalist Charles Stewart Parnell who was called the "uncrowned King of Ireland".*

at Oxford, entered parliament, succeeded to his earldom in 1761, and became president of the Board of Trade (1763) and secretary of state (1766). He became premier on the death of Rockingham, but resigned when outvoted by the coalition between Fox and North. In 1784 he was made Marquess of Lansdowne.

John Redmond (1856–1918)

Nationalist leader elected to parliament as a Home Rule member (1881). When the Irish Nationalist group split as a result of Parnell's involvement in the O'Shea divorce case, Redmond became chief of the pro-Parnell group. On reunion with the majority (1900), he was chosen as chairman and then leader of the combined Irish Party. When the Liberals came to power in 1905, Redmond had no choice but to

RIGHT: *Patrick Pearse, the Nationalist leader, poet, and educator was executed by the British for his role as military commander of the 1916 Rising in Dublin.*

support them, though the policy they advocated was one of "devolution" or merely administrative Home Rule for Ireland. Redmond had declared Ireland's loyalty to the Allies in World War I, and the 1916 Easter Rising was a great blow to him. He supported the plan to begin Home Rule with the temporary exclusion of Ulster, but his influence declined at the end of his life.

Mary Robinson (1944–)

Stateswoman, barrister, and professor. Robinson was a member of *Seanad Éireann* (Upper House of Parliament) from 1969 to 1989. She served on various parliamentary committees before becoming the 7th President (1990–97). She was the first woman president of Ireland. She has been one of the most active presidents in the history of the state, one of her priorities being visits to deprived or disaster-stricken areas of the world. She was also assiduous in visiting places like Warrington and Manchester to show solidarity with the victims of paramilitary violence. She then served as UN High Commissioner for Human Rights (1997–2002).

Sir Ernest Shackleton (1874–1922)

Explorer who made the first of his voyages to Antarctica with Robert F. Scott's 1901–04 expedition. Ernest Shackleton then led a south polar expedition (1907–09).

During this expedition Mount Erebus was ascended, the south magnetic pole was located, and the polar plateau was crossed to a point less than 160km (100 miles) from the South Pole. The scientific results of the expedition were of vast importance. During Shackleton's 1914–16 transantarctic expedition, his ship *Endurance* was crushed in the ice. He led his party some 290 km (180 miles) to safety at Elephant Island. From there he sailed with five companions in a lifeboat through wild seas and crossed South Georgia Island to raise a rescue party. He died on a subsequent expedition.

Hans Sloane (1660–1753)

Physician and naturalist whose collection of books, manuscripts, and treasures formed the basis of the British Museum, London. He succeeded Isaac Newton as the president of the prestigious Royal Society and became first physician to King George II.

Theobald Wolfe Tone (1763–98)

Protestant lawyer and revolutionary who called for Irish independence and a *rapprochement* between Protestants and Catholics. Tone helped found the Society of United Irishmen (1791), but fled to the United States after being implicated in plans for a French invasion (1794). He then went to Paris to secure French aid for an Irish rebellion. He

committed suicide after he was captured during the failed 1798 Rebellion in Ireland.

Arthur Wellesley, Duke of Wellington (1769–1852)
Military commander and statesman. Wellesley entered the British Army in 1787, but also became an MP (1806) and Irish secretary (1807). He gained distinction during the Peninsular campaigns during the French Wars. He was created Duke of Wellington after Napoleon fell from power in 1814. After Napoleon returned from Melba and resumed the war with Britain, Wellington decisively beat his forces at Waterloo (1815). He then resumed his political career and became Prime Minister (1828–30). He refused to form a government in 1834, but served under Sir Robert Peel as Foreign Secretary (1834–35), and as minister without portfolio (1841–46). In 1842 he was made commander-in-chief for life.

ABOVE: *The Wellington Memorial, Phoenix Park, Dublin, was erected in memory of the Duke of Wellington. He was born in Dublin and achieved fame by defeating Napoleon at Waterloo in 1815.*

THE IRISH DIASPORA

The great paradox of Irish history is that because of it there are many more millions of Irish people—Irish born, and of Irish descent—living abroad, than there are living in Ireland today.

Waves of Irish migrants have left home for various reasons to settle in far flung parts of the world. These include Canada, Australia, New Zealand, parts of South America, Great Britain, the United States of America, and the Caribbean. Many of these people have made a valuable contribution to the political, cultural, and economic lives of these lands.

The Irish in the United States

The Irish Catholic millions who fled the Famine of the mid-19th Century certainly changed the story of immigrant America. They were the first group to come in a large, sudden wave that was very different in social makeup from the establishment already here. They were not, however, the

LEFT: *A monument to President John F. Kennedy, the most famous Irish-American in the history of the United States.*

first Irish to come to America. In the early years, the Irish in America were but a scattered few. As early as 1586, Edward Nugent served in North Carolina with Captain Ralph Lane.

An attempt in the 1650s to found a colony in Maryland called "New Ireland" failed, but by the end of the century the Irish were established in Pennsylvania, Maryland, Delaware, and New York.

The rate of emigration to America was at first just a trickle. From North Carolina to upstate New York there had been a few organized Irish settlements before the American Revolution but most were relatively small. The first United States Census in 1790 counted only 44,000 people who had been born in Ireland and 150,000 more of Irish ancestry out of a total population of 3 million. Catholics constituted only a small fraction of the Irish immigrants. No one can say the Irish were not a visible and vital part of the colonies and the young republic, however.

St. Patrick's Day was celebrated in Boston as early as 1737. The Irish even accounted for eight signatories of the Declaration of Independence—four of them born in Ireland. Later Irishman Thomas Fitzsimons was the only Catholic to sign the Constitution of the United States of America. During the revolution some 38 per cent of the American forces were Irish. The Irish were enthusiastic about America and they did anything to get there. Many

who could not afford the passage came to be sold upon arrival as indentured servants along with the merchandize that the ship brought. By the 1770s there were not enough ships to carry all those wishing to leave.

In 1844, a year before the potato blight began, 75,000 Irish emigrated, two-thirds of whom went to the United States. In all, more than a million Irish went to America during the Famine years.

The Irish who fled the Famine and those who followed were different from those who had previously migrated to America. Most of the "Famine Irish" were Catholic. While the earlier immigrants and those who came during the Famine years often traveled as families, those who followed were mostly single people.

There always had been organized Irish settlements and individuals who brought groups of Irish to America. Settlement patterns changed when the "Famine Irish" arrived. Instead of moving to farms, most settled in cities or followed work on the railroads through rural areas until they reached a city. When they did live on the frontier, most settled in frontier towns. Irish settlements, however, were spread thinly outside the cities.

The Irish who arrived after the Famine took mostly unskilled jobs. Some of their success in finding and keeping such work was due to the efforts of labor unions which had many Irish workers in their leadership. They went on to

have strong representation in the police and fire departments. Despite their hard work there was serious anti-Irish violence. By the 1870s, however, the Irish were moving up from laboring positions and were gaining political power. Most notably, in the decade following the Civil War the Irish captured control of Tammany Hall, the New York city political machine.

Political dynasties also emerged, not least the family of President John Fitzgerald Kennedy that became as near in public perception to a royal family as America has known.

Until the 1920s, the Irish in America had suffered from their history. Poverty and oppression at home had been a real handicap, and involvement in Irish nationalist causes had been a distraction from improving their lives in America. By the 20th Century, however, the Famine was ancient history. With the creation of the Irish Free State, nationalism all but disappeared. At the same time, Irish-American accomplishments opened the way for success and assimilation. Today, some 6–7 per cent of the total population are of Irish extraction.

The Irish and Canada

It is not generally known that Irish fishermen were putting down their nets off Newfoundland as early as 1595! Many Irish fishermen settled in Newfoundland in the 1700s, and one-third of the population of Nova Scotia is of Irish

descent. The failure of the 1798 Rising, and the subsequent excesses of the troops in Ireland, sent thousands to Canada, and the famine of 1822 brought more settlers. Today there are millions of Canadians who can claim to be of Irish descent. To escape the Famine in Ireland great numbers came in 1846. The tragedy was that the majority of them, already suffering from the effects of starvation, came from the crowded hulks of the "coffin" ships, bearing with them the last stages of cholera, and burial in mass graves on the shore became the fate of many. Grosse Isle, on the St. Lawrence River at the entrance to the city of Quebec, became the quarantine island in 1834.

Those who survived made good in many places. From 1823–25 emigrants, mostly from Munster, made their homes in Upper Canada. In 1826 some 20,000 settled in the Lake Erie district alone. The Orangemen from Ulster headed mainly for Toronto.

The Irish and Australia

In 1791, Irish prisoners started to arrive, thus forging the first Irish-Australian links. Ireland was then a nation in desperate political turmoil, and the first prison ships contained many country folk, driven in desperation to political "crimes". For many it became, under a fearfully oppressive military goading, a choice of transportation for life or execution. Not all Irish convicts were poor folk.

After the 1798 Rebellion, Presbyterian ministers and professional men were among the more educated revolutionaries to be transported. Regular shiploads of convicts were sent from Cork to Australia.

Fremantle in Western Australia, over 17,700km (11,000 miles) from home, was to be the last port in Australia to receive Irish political prisoners in January 1868. In Australia it is generally reckoned that about half of the population has some link with Ireland.

The Irish and New Zealand

Most of the Irish emigrants to New Zealand were Presbyterians from Ulster, who set up their homes all around the coastline of the north and south islands. Among the very first settlers in the north island, in Wellington, were hundreds of Irish origin. Similarly, many hundreds of Irish who had come via Australia were among the first citizens of Auckland. With the discovery of gold in the 1860s, Irish miners worked their claims, and then settled in Lake Wakatipu, Kingston, and Queenstown. From the 1840s to the 1870s, Irish immigrants were few and far between. Under later settlement schemes, about 20,000 Irish immigrants, mainly from the north of Ireland, and mostly

RIGHT: *Irish migrants have traveled across the globe in search of economic prosperity, political freedom, and also adventure.*

laborers, settled in places such as Katikati which was a successful settlement of Orangemen.

The Irish and South America

Various leaders of Irish stock helped put the South American countries of their adoption on the map, including Bernardo O'Higgins, a founding father of modern Chile. His father was Don Ambrosio, Viceroy of Peru. Don Ambrosio was born near Daingean in County Offaly in 1720. Admiral William Brown, born in County Mayo, founded the

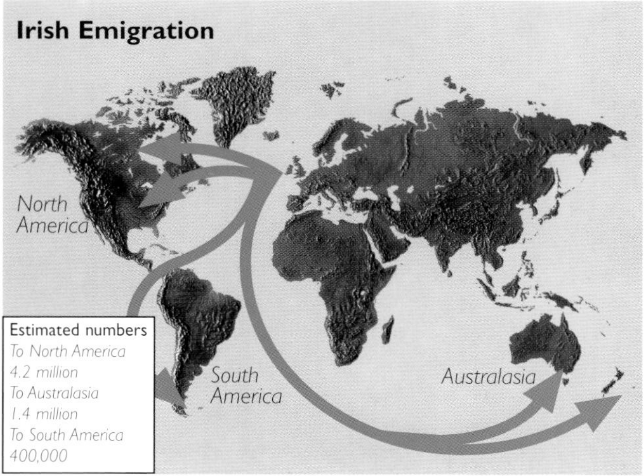

Irish Emigration

Argentinian Navy. The links between Ireland and South America have frequently been forged through soldiers or sailors of fortune offering their services to the emergent republics, and yet there have been many links in peacetime. In our time there are many individual Irish missionaries working on the continent.

Ireland and the Continent

From the 5th Century Irish monks worked as missionaries across Europe. They were followed by young men who trained for the priesthood in France, when persecution forbade such schools of learning in their native Ireland. For centuries, half of the priests of Ireland were trained in the Irish College in Paris. France has been a friend to insurgent Ireland since the days of Henry III of France, who tried to assist a rebellion in Munster against the English in 1572. In 1688 France provided military advisers, troops, and officers to James II in his fight against William of Orange. The French Revolution had a profound effect on the movement known as the United Irishmen.

The Irish struggle for freedom continued, largely with the aid of the French. It was the French who helped inspire the 1848 insurrection. The Fenians—the Irish Republican Brotherhood—were heavily influenced by French revolutionary philosophy.

Austria has had a special fascination for the wandering

Irish since the monks of the 9th Century. When Frederick the Great of Prussia declared war on Maria Theresa of Austria, Irishmen flocked to join her army. At one time there were no less than 30 Irish generals in the Imperial Army. Even in 1915 a Viscount Taaffe was field marshal, minister of state, and chamberlain to the Emperor Franz Joseph. Many other Irishmen achieved eminence and many Austrians today who bear Irish names are unaware of their ancestry.

During the "Flight of the Earls" the O'Donnells and the O'Neills sailed for Spain. After the Battle of the Boyne in 1690, and at Limerick in 1691, 10,000 officers and men sailed into exile and formed Irish brigades in the armies of the continent, known as the "Wild Geese". It is probable that, between the 1600s and the 1800s, up to three-quarters of a million Irishmen fought and died in European wars, starting with the first 30,000 members of the Irish brigades who served under Louis XIV. Some reached the greatest heights. Marshal Patrick McMahon became President of France in the 1870s. During the 20th Century, Irishmen went to fight in Europe during the two world wars, and also on both sides during the Spanish Civil War. Today Irish workers can be found across Europe.

Above: *Farmers gathering hay in County Mayo. This rural county is ideal for those wishing to escape the popular tourist trails.*

A COUNTY GUIDE

◆ ◆ ◆

It is difficult to capture the elusive essence of Ireland by treating it as a single unit as the island's counties are astonishingly varied.

◆ ◆ ◆

The charm of Ireland's regional "subcultures" is part of its unique tradition and the county boundary retains great significance. Irish people identify themselves more with their counties than with any other place, apart from Ireland itself. The county is the core of local identity. Indeed, when the Government of Ireland Act (1920) imposed partition on the island, the two new jurisdictions came to be widely known as "The Twenty-Six Counties" for what is now the Irish Republic, and "The Six Counties" for Northern Ireland. Although the size of each county varies considerably, they are nevertheless a relatively convenient size for identification purposes. The four provinces (Munster, Leinster, Connacht, and Ulster) are too large for people to relate intimately to them at local level. They retain certain uses, however, in such matters as sport where inter-provincial competitions occur in Gaelic games and rugby. Each county offers the visitor spectacular countryside, water features, and recreational opportunities.

Clare

This splendid county has an abundance of visual riches from the famous River Shannon and Lough Derg, which forms its eastern boundary, to its rugged Atlantic coastline with its towering cliffs and golden beaches in the west. Ennis, Kilrush, Ennistymon, Kilkee, Lahinch, Lisdoonvarna, Ballyvaughan, and Doolin are some of the town names associated with fun and enjoyment in the area.

The wondrous Burren National Park consists of scoops in the limestone plains that support dense thickets of hazel and scrub. In spring the Burren stone is colonized by an array of wonderful flora. Blue Spring gentians, cinquefoil, orchids, and plants that are rare in other parts of Ireland may be found here in abundance.

The Cliffs of Moher, a popular destination for visitors, stand against the might of the Atlantic Ocean. O'Brien's Tower, located on the highest cliff, is an exceptional viewing point.

Bunratty Castle, built in 1425 and restored in 1954, is one of Ireland's most complete medieval castles. It is a cross between the earlier Norman castles and later Gaelic tower houses. It has been furnished with the finest collection of medieval furniture in the country, thus preserving a vital part of the Celtic heritage. The 10.5 hectare (26-acre) folk park adjoining the castle re-creates 19th-Century Ireland and includes a village street.

Cork

The county of Cork shares with Kerry the southwestern corner of Ireland. Washed by the warm Gulf Stream and the mild moist south winds, palm trees and bamboo flourish.

Cork is the largest county, and in many ways the most varied. Rich farmlands and river valleys contrast with the wild sandstone hills of the west. Above all there is the magnificent coastline with its great bays and secret coves, strewn with rocky headlands.

What is known as Blarney Castle today, is in fact the keep of a much larger fortress that was built in 1446. All visitors to the castle should kiss the famous Blarney Stone, upon whom it is said to bestow the gift of eloquence. The Rock close, part of the castle grounds is a curiously interesting place of old trees. By legend, the gardens are of Druid origin and were a center of worship.

The town of Kinsale, south of Cork city on the R.600 route, has many popular attractions. These include a heritage center, gourmet restaurants, sailing, and fishing.

Bantry House, built around 1740, contains a wealth of tapestries, furniture, and art treasures. The beautiful gardens are being restored and are home to sub-tropical plants and shrubs. There is also a 1796 French Armada exhibition describing Wolfe Tone's heroic but failed attempt to end British rule in Ireland.

Kerry

No matter from which direction the county of Kerry is approached, the great central spine of mountains draws the eye of the traveler. The relatively high mountains and narrow peninsulas conjure weather patterns which change the face of the mountains, the surface of the water, and the texture of the landscape by the minute.

The south shore of the Shannon Estuary forms the northern boundary of the county. Kerry is one of Ireland's fastest-growing tourism centers. Ballybunion and Ballyheigue have extensive beaches and spectacular scenery. Ballybunion has one of the world's finest golf courses, consistently rated in the world's top ten.

Tralee, known for its annual Rose of Tralee festival, has recently developed the finest range of all-weather visitor attractions in Ireland. These include Kerry the Kingdom (a journey by time-car through medieval Tralee), the Tralee-Blennerville steam train and the Aqua Dome, one of Europe's most exciting water-world centers. The fishing port of Fenit has an excellent sealife visitor center.

Listowel is famous for its writers' week and racing festival while Castleisland boasts a superb natural attraction in Crag Caves subterranean magic!

Muckross House, Killarney, is a mansion set amidst the beautiful Killarney National Park. Visitors can explore the folklife museum, farm, and the superb gardens.

Limerick

County Limerick is a place of quiet beauty and rural charm. Its gentle undulating landscape is pleasing to the eye from the mountains of Ballyhoura, the beautiful Golden Vale in the east of the county through to the tidal estuary of the River Shannon. Birds fly incredible distances, from Canada and Iceland, to winter in the Shannon Estuary.

A particular feature of the county is its range of attractive towns. These include Castleconnell by the Shannon and Adare–which is possibly Ireland's prettiest village–with its thatched cottages and medieval churches.

The county has a whole range of visitor attractions that are well worth exploring. These include the Adare Heritage Center on Adare's main street, and Croom Mills Waterwheel and Heritage Center.

For some years there was a transatlantic seaplane base at Foynes, and its history can be discovered at the Flying Boat Museum. There is also the Celtic Park and Gardens, and Curraghchase Forest Park.

Lough Gur is one of the most important Stone Age sites in the whole of the country. The visitor center, on its lakeside site, explains the incredible story of the area that dates back some 5,000 years. The archaeology of the area provides evidence of the activities of the first farmers in the region, their dwellings, rituals, and burial sites, as well as their tools and implements.

Waterford

"The Crystal County", famed for its glassware, offers a dazzling coastline, beautiful river valleys, and a glorious range of very accessible mountains. The peninsulas each side of the county are both beautiful but quite different in character. West of Dungarvan is a wild and beautiful peninsula containing the historic seaside resort of Ardmore and the *Gaeltacht*, a unique Irish-speaking area. Southeast of Waterford city is the east Waterford Gaultier Coast.

The Celtic Sea, that part of the Atlantic which touches and shapes the Waterford coast, has created a coastline of rugged beauty and contains one of the leading seaside resorts in the country at Tramore.

The Comeragh/Monavullagh Mountains are the spine of the county. The mountain resort of Ballymacarbry has a range of superb leisure facilities.

Dungarvan, the administrative capital for the county, is set in a broad, magnificent bay. In between are a series of seaside resorts, the spectacular Copper Coast, and lovely towns and villages. The town of Lismore was originally a monastic settlement founded in the 7th Century by St. Carthage. It was the centre of ecclesiastical and temporal power for centuries, and is now a popular tourist destination.

RIGHT: *A waterfall in the Comeragh Mountains of County Waterford. The Comeragh Mountains form the spine of the county.*

Tipperary

County Tipperary is the largest inland county and a rich farming area. The Golden Vale, a large, flat plain that stretches through the county and on into Limerick, has some of the best beef and dairy land in the country. Tipperary's great plain has many impressive raised bogs, one of the best being the Littleton Bog that is 12,000 years old. The River Suir flows through Tipperary, with the county's main towns nestling on its banks along the way.

One of the most extensive systems of caves in Ireland can be found in the Galtee Mountains. Mitchelstown Caves extend for 2km (1.2 miles) and are open to the public.

Cahir Castle by the River Suir was built in 1142 by Conor O'Brien, a local chief. The Butler family took possession in 1375. The castle was besieged in 1599 by the Earl of Essex, by Lord Inchiquin (1647), and by Oliver Cromwell (1650). The castel was restored in the 1800s.

The market town of Thurles is the founding place of the Gaelic Athletic Association in 1884, and visitors can find out more about the history and practice of Gaelic Games at the Lár na Páirce center. Holy Cross Abbey in Thurles was one of Europe's most significant early monastic sites.

Lough Derg is the largest of the Shannon's lakes, and is almost an inland sea. It is renowned for game and coarse angling, and sailing. There are many pretty villages along its shores.

Antrim

County Antrim forms the northeast corner of Ireland, where a channel only 20.9km (13 miles) wide separates Torr Head from the Scottish coast. Lough Neagh (the largest lake in Ireland) and the fertile valley of the River Bann occupy the western part of Antrim.

The shallow waters of Lough Neagh and Lough Beg constitute one of the major bird sites in northwest Europe. They are home to thousands of resident and migrant birds, including 10,000 waterfowl.

The Glens of Antrim are the coastal valleys between Lough Larne and the Bush. The nine glens contain examples of nearly every rock formation. The Antrim Mountains rise from the Glens, and at the top there is a great moorland plateau that slopes towards the River Bann valley.

Carrickfergus Castle was built in 1180 to guard the approach to Belfast Lough. This was the first real Irish castle. In the early 1600s, Carrickfergus was the only place in the north where English and not Irish was spoken.

Dunluce Castle, east of Portrush, stands on a rocky headland. During a violent storm in 1639, a portion of the castle's kitchen, along with its cooks, fell into the sea.

The biggest annual event is Ballycastle's Oul' Lammas Fair in August. The event has stalls, music, horse trading, and attracts thousands of people. It used to last a week but today the fun is now packed into two days.

Armagh

The county derives its name from *Árd Macha* (*Macha's* Height), the forest hill where the Celtic goddess *Macha* died. In one of her many guises she married Nemhedh, a mercenary from Scythia in the Black Sea. Árd Macha is now the city of Armagh and was the site on which St. Patrick chose to build his principal church.

Navan, the ancient capital of Ulster, is situated 3.2km (2 miles) from Armagh city. The remains of a 17.2-hectare (18-acre) hill fort are the only visible reminder of the stronghold used by the kings of Ulster from 700 B.C.

To the northeast of Armagh city is the rich fruit growing area called the "Orchard of Ireland". Many of the settlers who came here in the 1600s were from the English county of Worcestershire and laid out the orchards on the same pattern as those of the Vale of Evesham.

The Blackwater River is one of the best fishing rivers in Ireland, and is famous for its big bream. A River Park extends for 4.8km (3 miles) opposite the village of Benburb. There is canoeing over the weirs and a deep pool for subaqua training. The Argory, a neoclassical house with 80 hectares (200 acres) of land overlooking the Blackwater River, is a National Trust property open to the public.

The Armagh Planetarium and Astropark offer fascinating insights into the solar system while Eartharium is a unique earth science center located on the same site.

Cavan

County Cavan, located in the north midlands, is called the "Lake County" as it has 365 lakes. Ireland's two largest rivers—the Shannon and Erne—also rise in the county.

The River Shannon has its source in the western slopes of the Cuilcagh Mountains. The Shannon takes its name from *Sionna*, grand-daughter of Lir, the god of the seas. The River Erne flows from Lough Gowna. A large part of the Shannon-Erne waterway also cuts through Cavan. This is the canal that links the navigable part of the River Shannon to that of the River Erne; for this reason Cavan is a popular destination for boating.

Cavan's water features also make the county a great haven for fishermen who come here from all over the world. Coarse angling remains one of Cavan's most popular attractions, but there is also game fishing for brown trout in Lough Sheelin to the south.

In addition to Cavan's water features, there are also the distinctive drumlins which cover most of the county. These small rounded hills crop up in their thousands. They are also found as islands that rise up out of the lakes. These teardrop-shaped mounds can be up to 0.8km (0.5 miles) long and 304m (100ft) high. The drumlins were formed during the Ice Age and became exposed when the ice melted 10,000 years ago. They are composed of clay and rocky rubble.

Derry

The name Derry (or *Doire* in Gaelic) means "oak grove". The sessile oak, *Quercus petraea*, is one of the great mythical trees from the island. It lends to the early Irish runic ogham script its sign for "D", from *dair* for "oak". The prefix "London" was added in the 17th Century after King James I gave control of Derry city to the livery companies of the City of London. South of the city are the rolling Sperrin Mountains with their forests and river glens. To the east and northeast are Lough Foyle, Magilligan Strand (Ireland's longest beach), and Roe Valley Country Park.

West and north lies rugged County Donegal. Just 4.8km (3 miles) north of Derry is the Earhart Center at Ballyarnet. This tells the story of Amelia Earhart, the first woman to fly the Atlantic solo, who brought her plane down nearby after her epic crossing in 1932.

Limavady is one of Ulster's most characteristically Georgian towns. It was here that Jane Ross noted down the famous "Derry Air" ("Oh Danny Boy") from a passing fiddler in 1851. One of the county's finest attractions is the Roe Valley Country Park. The Roe river winds through gorges where the rapids turned the waterwheels of several mills. The mills and a 19th-Century hydroelectric plant have been restored, and the weaving shed houses a museum.

RIGHT: *Downhill Strand is popular with surfers and gliders.*

Fermanagh

According to legend, Fermanagh was once a vast plain with a fairy well in the middle. It was always kept covered from sunlight in case it bubbled over. One day two lovers met by the well. They eloped, drank a toast from the well and ran off leaving it uncovered. That well has bubbled ceaselessly for centuries and created the Lakelands.

This area is a paradise for fishing, cruising, and other water-based holidays. The largest lake, Lough Erne, is 80km (50 miles) long and has the greatest area of water per boat of any cruising water in Europe. The lakeside is high and rocky in parts and, in addition to the 154 islands, there are coves and inlets to explore. When the wind blows, navigation on Lower Lough Erne can be something of a challenge, with waves of open-sea dimensions.

Shallow Upper Lough Erne is a maze of islands and you need a chart to find your way. With the opening of the Shannon-Erne Waterway there are now 804km (500 miles) of navigable water from Belleek right down to Limerick.

The town of Enniskillen goes back to prehistory when this short nexus was the main route between Ulster and Connacht. Enniskillen Castle was the medieval seat of the Maguires, chiefs of Fermanagh, who policed the lough with a private navy. Coole Castle, at the edge of Enniskillen, is a superb 18th-Century house created by some of the period's leading craftsmen, and is set in fine grounds.

Donegal

The name Donegal comes from the Irish *Dún na nGall* meaning "fort of the foreigner". Ireland's most northerly county is criss-crossed with mountains and inland waters. Blanket bogs, now rare areas, cover much of the county. Donegal's striking coastline has many sandy beaches. The waters around Donegal produce a wealth of fish and seafood, including mussels, crab, and brill.

Donegal has been occupied for over 9,000 years. The Carrowmore tomb site is one of Europe's largest and most important Megalithic sites. The tombs are spread out over 3.8 sq km (1.5 sq miles) in the shadow of the Knocknarea Mountains to the east, over various fields and townlands.

Christianity has had a profound influence in Donegal. Sligo Abbey, built in 1252 but burnt down in 1414, contains many fine carvings, and the only sculptured 15th-Century high altar to survive in any Irish monastic church. The ruins of Colmcille Monastery can be found on Tory Island.

Glebe House is a Regency building set in woodland gardens by Lake Gartan. It has William Morris wallpapers and textiles, and a permanent collection of works by great 20th-Century artists, including Picasso.

Donegal is famed for its tweed and fishing. It has also produced many famous musicians (Enya, Clannad, Daniel O'Donnell and Altan), whose unique and original sounds have no doubt been influenced by the county's character.

Down

This county combines the best characteristics of Ireland. It has clean beaches, shoals of sea and river fish, championship standard golf courses, two cathedrals, castles, gardens, forest parks, mountains, boating, and bird-watching.

Strangford Lough is a great bird sanctuary and an ideal place for yachting. It is said that St. Patrick sailed into the lough in 432 and later died at present-day Downpatrick town from where the county takes its name. The Ards Peninsula with its rolling drumlins and protected coves forms a shelter for the waters of Strangford Lough.

Percy French's song "The Mountains O'Mourne" has made the Mournes the best-known mountains in Ireland. Distinctive and self-contained, they are tucked away in the southeast corner of Northern Ireland. Twelve shapely summits rise above 609m (2,000ft) on the eastern side.

The countryside between Banbridge and Rathfriland was the homeland of the father and numerous relatives of the world-famous Brontë novelists. The ruins of the cottage where Patrick Brontë was born are at Emdale. The hilltop parish church and school at Drumballyroney, where Patrick taught before going to England, is on the "Brontë Homeland" route and is the nucleus of the Brontë Interpretive Center.

LEFT: *Silent Valley in the Mountains of Mourne, County Down.*

Monaghan

The county's name comes from the Irish word *Muineachán* (the place of the little thicketed hills). Bones of the woolly mammoth, arctic fox, and giant Irish deer have been discovered in Monaghan. It may therefore have had a continental climate at one stage. During the 17th Century the Planters, mostly from Scotland, cleared the best land to grow flax and raise sheep.

County Monaghan's undulating countryside is a relaxing haven of gentle hills, woodland, and gorse bushes. Its abundant reserves of water drain over boggy ground into little lakes. The county is also dotted with farmhouses and market towns. The celebrated Irish poet Patrick Kavanagh, who drew much of his inspiration from the Monaghan countryside, was a native of the village of Inniskeen.

There are several Bronze Age sites in the county. Prehistoric remains, such as the Tullyrain Ring Fort near Shantonagh in the south of the county, can be seen.

Carrickmacross is renowned for its traditional crafts, especially lace-making. The Lough Muckno Leisure Park in Castleblayney offers attractive lakeside and woodland trails as well as tennis, canoeing, sailing, and horse-riding.

Monaghan town lies to the northwest of the county, and is a thriving agricultural center with an impressive cathedral and courthouse. The Patrick Kavanagh Literary Resource Center is nearby.

Tyrone

This is the largest county in Northern Ireland. For centuries County Tyrone was the territory of the mighty O'Neill family. In March 1603 Hugh O'Neill, Earl of Tyrone, was finally forced to submit to the English occupiers at Mellifont. This event marked the end of Gaelic Ireland and the dawn of a new era. The Protestant English and Scottish Planters took control of the land and established a major linen trade during the 18th Century.

The Sperrin Mountains, located in northeast Tyrone, run along the border with County Derry. The highest point is Mount Sawel which rises up 678m (2,224ft). There is an abundance of wildlife, and trout fishing is a popular activity.

Many inhabitants of this county migrated to North America. The family of President Woodrow Wilson came from County Tyrone, and several other American presidents can trace their ancestry back to the province of Ulster. The Ulster America Folk Park, 8km (4.9 miles) from the town of Omagh, traces the history of the Ulster people who crossed the Atlantic Ocean during the 18th and 19th Centuries. The outdoor part of the museum re-creates many aspects of 19th-Century Ulster life.

Gortin Glen Forest Park is ideally suited for cars or motorbikes as a tarmac drive runs through the forest that mainly consists of conifers. A herd of Japanese sika deer wander through the park.

Carlow

County Carlow, the smallest inland county in Ireland, has a wealth of scenery—from rich pastureland and colorful mountains to the deep and historical Barrow River Valley. It is here that the coastal mountain ranges of the east meet the rich central plain.

The county of Carlow is considered to be the "Celtic Center of Ireland". It contains some 807 field monuments marking the centuries back to Megalithic times. The county's most prominent feature is the 5,000-year old granite formation known as Browne's Hill Dolmen. It is believed to have the largest capstone in Europe, weighing a colossal 100 tonnes (98 tons).

Located on the banks of the River Barrow, Carlow town is a bustling market center serving a large rural area. The courthouse on Dublin Street, one of the most impressive pieces of architecture in the town, was modeled on the Parthenon in Athens. The courthouse was originally meant for Cork, but the plans for the two buildings got mixed up!

After the arrival of the Normans in neighboring Wexford in the 1100s, they consolidated their conquest by building their first castles in the county. Many of these fortifications have survived, including Carlow Castle. Today only the two towers and an adjoining wall remain of what was once one of the finest Norman castles in Leinster.

Dublin

This is the third smallest county in Ireland but home to a third of the population. The terrain of the county of Dublin is generally flat, except in the extreme southern area, where it rises to join the Wicklow Mountains. Numerous small farms are dotted around the county. County Dublin's magnificent coastline stretches for some 113km (70 miles). It is indented by a series of creeks and bays, most notably Dublin Bay, formed by Howth Head on the north. Dublin Bay receives the waters of the River Liffey. Picturesque coastal villages like Howth and Killiney offer a refreshing break from Dublin city. Popular attractions include Ardgillan Victorian Garden and the popular resort of Dun Laoghaire. Here you will find both a busy harbor but also the prestigious Royal St. George Yacht Club, and the "Dublin Bay Sea Thrill" excursion. Malahide has a pretty marina and castle. Industrial production is mainly confined to Dublin city, the capital and chief seaport. The fishing industry is also important.

Phoenix Park, just 3km (2 miles) from central Dublin, is the largest enclosed city park in Europe. It was founded as a deer park in 1662 by the Duke of Ormond, and some 300 fallow deer can still be seen. The park was opened to the public in 1745. The residence of the Irish president is located within the park. It was built in 1751 but enlarged in 1782 and 1816.

Kilkenny

This county lies inland and has an area of 2,061sq km (796 square miles) with direct access to the sea via Belview Port on the Suir Estuary, and via New Ross on the Barrow River. The county of Kilkenny consists of a highly fertile central plain with uplands in the northeast, the northwest, and the south.

County Kilkenny has a number of important historical sites. These include the famous 13th-Century Kells Priory in its spectacular riverside setting, and the splendid Woodstock Gardens.

The city of Kilkenny is an extraordinary meeting point for ancient history and contemporary culture. Kilkenny was named after St. Canice, a 6th-Century monk. His memory lives on in the beautifully restored St. Canice's Cathedral, built overlooking the city in the 13th Century. Kilkenny Castle, one of the most magnificent in Ireland, was established by the Normans who arrived in the city during the 12th Century. Under the Confederation of Kilkenny (1642–46), the city proclaimed itself Ireland's capital.

Kilkenny holds an international arts festival each year. It plays host to some of the world's leading artists and performers in a range of art forms. These include music, visual arts, theater, and literature. The festival culminates in a spectacular street performance. The creative influence is also seen in the fine craft shops and studios of the area.

Laois

This inland county is located on the central plain of Ireland, although the Slieve Bloom Mountains are a prominent feature in the northwest of the county. The highest peak, Arderin, rises up 528m (1,734ft).

The Bog of Allen stretches across most of the county and has been a valuable source of peat for Bord na Móna (Turf Board). For the past 50 years they have harvested the bog, stripping the wet turf into thin layers, drying it, and using the turf for the production of briquettes, a modern-day version of sods of turf. Today, environmental safeguards are being introduced to protect this precious habitat.

Portarlington, near the border with County Offaly, was home to French Protestant refugees during the 18th Century. A few of their houses still survive today.

One of the finest fortifications in Ireland is situated at the Rock of Dunamase. The site, located about 6km (4 miles) from Portlaoise, is situated on a large limestone mound. Dunamase, first fortified by the Celts, was sacked by the Vikings in 845. When Aoife MacMurrough, daughter of the king of Leinster, married Strongbow in the 12th Century, the fortification was given as part of her dowry. It went through various changes of ownership before Oliver Cromwell sacked the castle in the 17th Century. The site today provides superb views of the surrounding countryside. The castle ruins also remain.

Longford

The Irish name for the county is *Longfort* (stronghold or fortress). The county was named after the ancient castle of the princes of Annaly, the O'Farrells. Longford is located on the central plain of Ireland.

This mainly flat county has fertile agricultural land and peatlands. The Irish peat industry harvests much of its peat here to supply electricity-generating stations.

Longford lies in the Shannon basin and the upper catchment area of the river Erne. The extensive waterways of the county make it a great location for angling and water sports, especially around Lough Ree.

The county's main urban center is Longford. The town is situated on the banks of the River Camlin. A Dominican friary was founded there in 1400.

Ardagh is a very attractive Estate Village rebuilt during the 1860s. The houses of Ardagh are unique in Ireland for their Swiss design. St. Mel's Cathedral, near the town's center, is an imposing 19th-Century Renaissance-style limestone building.

The Corlea Trackway Visitor Center describes an Iron Age bog road built in 148 B.C. across the boglands close to the River Shannon. The oak road is the largest known of its kind to be discovered in Europe. Visitors can view an 18-m (59-ft) stretch of preserved road in a specially designed hall with humidifiers to prevent the wood from cracking.

Louth

County Louth stretches from the River Boyne to Carlingford Lough. It mainly consists of fertile land alongside a coastline of wide sandy bays and occasional rocky headlands. It is Ireland's smallest county. The county figures prominently in legends and folktales, especially the story of *Cuchulain*.

The Cooley Peninsula, in the northeastern part of County Louth, is a mountainous stretch of land. Only one road runs around the peninsula, but there is a 25-mile (40.2-km) walking route called the *Táin* Trail. It is the setting for the legend of Queen Maeve of Connacht's capture of the highly prized Brown Bull of Cooley.

Monasterboice, near Drogheda, was founded by St. Buite, a disciple of St. Patrick, in the 5th Century. It is one of Ireland's most famous religious sites, which includes the ruins of the medieval monastery and two fine high crosses. These are richly carved with images from the Bible that were used to explain the Gospels to the people.

Mellifont Abbey, also near Drogheda, was the first Cistercian monastery in Ireland. The monastery, which was built by St. Buite in the 12th Century, took 15 years to build. At the abbey's peak it housed some 400 monks and presided over 38 other monasteries. The site today contains the remains of a 13th-Century church, a chapter house, and a lavabo (an ancient type of launderette).

Kildare

County Kildare borders Dublin to the west and is situated on the edge of the island's central plain. This is a county of open grasslands, green pastures, and ancient peatlands. The landscape of the county is crossed by canals, and the Rivers Barrow and Liffey.

This county is a sporting, racing and hunting center. The home of the horse offers year-round racing at the Curragh, Punchestown, and Naas. Some of the biggest meetings in the racing calendar take place here, including the Irish Derby in June.

The Irish National Stud, near Kildare town, covers 387 hectares (958 acres), and was established in 1900 by Colonel William Hall-Walker of Johnnie Walker whisky. His eccentric approach to breeding included the belief that the stars dictate the destiny of all living creatures. Skylights were consequently built into the roofs to ensure the moon and stars could exercise their maximum influence on his precious horses.

Hall-Walker's Japanese Gardens, created between 1906 and 1910, were planned to symbolize the "Life of Man". The garden traces the journey of a soul from Oblivion to Eternity. The gardens are now of international renown and are open to the public.

RIGHT: *Conolly's Folly in the grounds of Castletown House, Maynooth.*

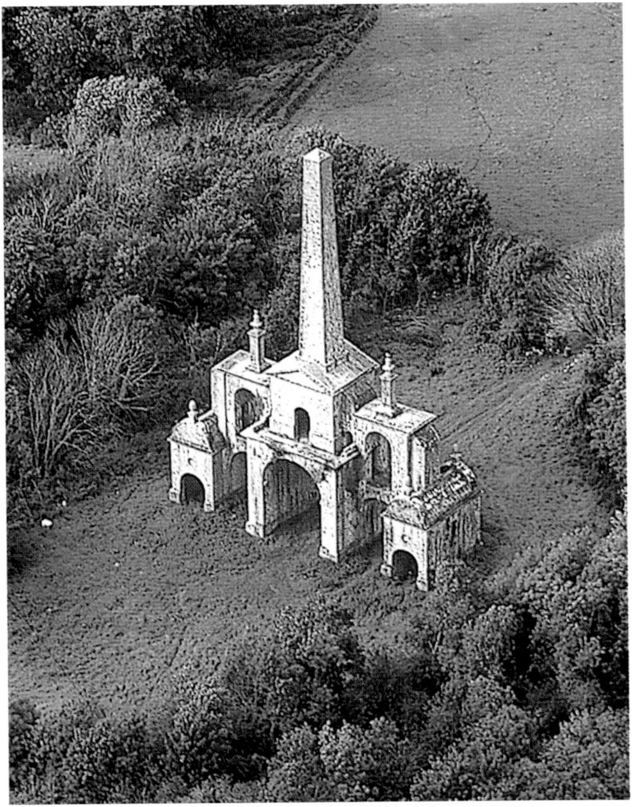

Meath

County Meath is largely flat, with some small hills, providing rich agricultural land. Meath is known as the Royal County because of its connections with the High Kings of Ireland.

The Hill of Tara is a place where myth and history are one. It has been associated with gods, druids, warriors, and nobility. The hillside is marked by ancient earthworks, mound formations, and the ruins of royal enclosures.

Brú na Bóinne (Palace of Boyne) is a United Nation's World Heritage site. It comprises the Neolithic-Age burial chambers of Newgrange, Knowth, and Dowth. They are situated on the banks of the River Boyne.

The Irish heritage town of Kells situated on the River Blackwater is surrounded by historical sites. The Kells Heritage Center gives visitors an insight into important places of interest. This includes the nearby monastery founded by St. Columba in 559. The monastery is most famously associated with the famous *Book of Kells* depicting stories from the four Gospels.

Butterstream Gardens, near Trim, were established in the 1970s and comprise a series of integrated compartments. It is considered to be one of the most imaginative gardens in Ireland.

LEFT: *Slane Castle by the River Boyne. Rock concerts, featuring bands such as U2, have been held here regularly since the 1980s.*

Wexford

County Wexford is bordered on the north and west by the mountains of south Wicklow, Carlow, and Kilkenny. To the south and east it is bordered by the Irish Sea. The county consists mainly of rich, relatively flat agricultural land. A third of the land is under cultivation.

Wexford is known as the "Maritime Center of Ireland". The county has wonderful seashores and attractive coastal villages. It also has a number of Ireland's newest attractions, including the Dunbrody Famine Ship and the Hook Lighthouse Visitor Center.

The Kennedy Homestead at Dunganstown, New Ross, is the birthplace of President John F. Kennedy's great-grandfather Patrick Kennedy. The center celebrates the story of five generations of the Kennedy dynasty and the land is still today farmed by his descendants.

Wexford, the county's largest town, was founded by the Vikings who turned it into a major trading center. The Normans then developed the town further. It was seized by Cromwell in 1649 and was the center of the 1798 Rebellion. Today it is a lively market and tourist town. The Opera Festival, the last of the area's annual festivals, is held in October and November.

RIGHT: *The J. F. Kennedy Arboretum, New Ross, dedicated to the famous US president, has 4,500 types of trees and shrubs.*

Wicklow

County Wicklow is known as the "Garden of Ireland". Its scenery is graduated; the great massif slopes gently to the sea on the east and to the central plain on the west. The county is dominated by the domed granite mountains that run through most of its center. Eastern Wicklow is low and sandy. Farmland can be found in western parts. Northern Wicklow is developing rapidly as the population of Dublin city moves southwards.

The Wicklow Mountains contain the ruins of many tombs and forts which indicate humans have inhabited the region since ancient times. Despite being close to the capital, the mountain terrain has always made it difficult to control and its inhabitants participated in various uprisings.

The county town of Wicklow was founded by the Vikings. Wicklow takes its name from the original settlement of Vikingalo. It is now a small port and popular seaside town.

The Glendalough monastic settlement is one of the country's most important Early Christian sites. It was founded by St. Kevin in the 5th Century and is set in a glaciated valley with two lakes. The monastery did not decline until an attack by the English from Dublin in 1389. The monastic remains include a fine round tower, stone churches, and decorated crosses. The visitor center has an interesting exhibition and an audio-visual show.

Offaly

The inland county of Offaly, bordered by the River Shannon to the west and the Slieve Bloom Mountains to the south, consists mainly of bogland. Clara Bog is one of Western Europe's largest remaining inland boglands.

Offaly, along with neighboring Laois, was one of the first counties to be "planted" by the English. It was known as King's County from 1556 until the Irish Free State was established in 1922.

Tullamore, the largest town, was designed by the Earls of Charleville in the mid-1700s. Today, Tullamore is a prosperous market and manufacturing center.

There are several important sites from the Early Christian period. These include Durrow, Gallen, Kinnity, and Rahan.

The monastery at Clonmacnoise is the most important site and its foundation stone was laid by St. Kieran in 544. This major ecclesiastical site contains churches, high crosses, and one of the finest collections of grave slabs in Ireland. Clonmacnoise has also been the burial place for some of Ireland's High Kings, including Turlough O'Conor, and his son, Roderick.

Birr town is home to Birr Castle Demesne, built in the 17th Century by Sir Laurence Parsons. It is famous for its gardens and home to the Great Telescope. It is also renowned as a center of astronomy.

Westmeath

County Westmeath is situated on Ireland's central plain. It stretches from the River Shannon's Lough Ree in the west to the shores of Lough Sheelin in the northeast, and to Kinnegad and the Royal Canal in the south. Other large lakes in Offaly include Loughs Owell, Ennell, Derravaragh, and Lene.

Athlone or *Áth Luain* (the Ford of Luan), the county's largest town, is regarded as the center of Ireland. The town has played an important part in Ireland's history because of its strategic location on the River Shannon. In 1129 King Turlough O'Conor recognized its strategic importance and built a wooden castle here. In 1210 King John of England ordered the building of a stone castle and bridge. The castle was built by John de Gray, Bishop of Norwich. It is now a focal point for tourism.

Tullynally Castle, located in Castlepollard, dates from the 17th Century. It was remodeled in the Gothic revival style in the early 1800s. The house is one of the largest in Ireland to survive as a family home. It has magnificent grounds, including a Chinese garden, and a Tibetan garden with waterfalls.

Belvedere House, near Mullingar, is a superbly restored 18th-Century hunting lodge. It has a large park with a fine rare plants collection in the spectacular walled garden, and also the Jealous Wall (Ireland's largest folly).

Galway

This is Ireland's second-largest county and is situated on the Atlantic coast. A series of harbors and island clusters, including the islands of Inishbofin and Aran, are situated on its coastline. The county is divided by Lough Corrib with fertile farmland to the east and the Connemara Mountains to the west.

The county of Galway was first inhabited some 5,000 years ago and many ancient sites can be explored. The spectacular stone fort of *Dún Aonghusa* on *Inis Mór* is perched on a cliff overlooking the Atlantic Ocean. This is the largest of the prehistoric stone forts of the Aran Islands. It is enclosed by three massive dry-stone walls and a *chevaux-de-frise* consisting of tall blocks of limestone set vertically into the ground to deter attackers. Its legendary owner, *Aonghusa*, was a chief of the *Fir Bolg* who are said to have been the earliest inhabitants of the island.

Athenry is one of the most important medieval, walled towns surviving in Ireland, owing its foundation to Meiler de Bermingham who built his castle there around 1250. The great three-storey tower is surrounded by defensive walls, and is entered at first-floor level.

Galway hosts a variety of popular events throughout the year. These include festivals for oyster lovers, sea anglers, blues enthusiasts, traditional music fans, and racing events in the summer and early fall.

Leitrim

This is a boggy county bordered by the River Erne and its lakes, Lough MacNean, and Lough Melvin, on its northern border. The county is bisected by the River Shannon and Lough Allen.

The Shannon-Erne Waterway, formerly the Ballyconnell-Ballinamore Canal, was reopened in 1994. This is Europe's longest navigable inland waterway.

Leitrim originally formed part of the old Gaelic kingdom of Breffni, which was ruled by the O'Rourkes. The Normans invaded the county in the 13th Century. They seized the south of the county but failed to conquer the northern portion, which remained under the control of the O'Rourkes until the 1500s.

Carrick-on-Shannon became the chief town of the county, which had one other borough, Jamestown, built for settlers in the 17th Century. There are three other market towns, Manorhamilton, Ballinamore, and Mohill. The poor agricultural productivity of Leitrim has led to a high rate of emigration since the 19th Century.

Leitrim has a variety of tourist attractions. These include the superbly restored Parks Castle dating from the 1600s, scenic Lough Gill, and the old narrow-gauge Cavan and Leitrim Railway. The Organic Center, in north Leitrim, is Ireland's leading center for education and information on organic farming and gardening.

Mayo

The landscape of County Mayo varies from the relatively flat land in the south and east, through large island-studded lakes, such as Lough Conn and Lough Mask, to the quartzite peaks along the indented Atlantic coast. Inland bog is prevalent, and the Nephin Beg mountain range dominates the center of the county.

The *Céide* Fields, situated 8km (4.9 miles) west of Ballycastle, contain a 1,500-hectare (3,760-acre) archaeological site of stone walls, field systems, enclosures, and tombs, around 5,000 years old. These have been preserved beneath the bog. It is one of the most extensive Stone Age sites in the world.

The National Folklife Collection, in Turlough Park, Castlebar, portrays Ireland's rural communities and traditions established for several hundred years and lasting into the 20th Century. Admission is free. Visitors can also admire the spectacular scenery of Turlough Park.

Knock Shrine is Ireland's national Marian shrine and pilgrimage center. Knock Folk Museum tells the story of the Knock apparitions of 1879 and places them in the context of life in Ireland at that time. From this miraculous occurrence Knock has grown to the status of an internationally recognized Marian Shrine. Pope John Paul II visited the shrine in 1979; Mother Teresa of Calcutta visited in 1993. One and a half million pilgrims visit annually.

Roscommon

This is a county of fertile farmland, undulating hillsides, quiet country lanes, and silver lakes. The area has strong musical connections, being the birthplace of the song writer Percy French who wrote "The Mountains O'Mourne". The 18th-Century harpist-composer Turlough O'Carolan often played there. O'Carolan was so popular with both Protestants and Catholics in the county that thousands from both traditions attended his funeral in 1738.

Lough Key Forest Park, close to the town of Boyle, is home to one of Ireland's principal lakeside attractions. Herds of deer wander through this stunning park. Its amenities include a well-landscaped caravan and camping park, nature walks, a bog garden, observation tower, ice house, and underground tunnels. The lake is navigable from the River Shannon via the River Boyle.

Strokestown Park House is an impressively restored 18th-Century edifice that retains its original furnishings. The 4-acre walled garden includes the longest herbaceous border in Britain and Ireland. The Famine Museum housed on the estate explains the circumstances surrounding the Great Irish Famine of the 1840s. The collection includes an extensive archive of papers and images.

King House, Boyle, is a magnificently restored 18th-Century Georgian mansion. Visitors can explore the estate's history through fascinating interactive exhibitions.

Sligo

The celebrated poet William Butler Yeats, a native of Sligo, described his birthplace as the "land of heart's desire". It is a county of great beauty with the Ox Mountains in the west of the county forming a background to the coastal plain, while north of Sligo town the landscape is dominated by steep-sided and flat-topped limestone hills. The loaf-shaped Benbulben is Sligo's most famous mountain. There are some excellent beaches at Strandhill, Mullaghmore, Rosses Point, and Enniscrone.

Sligo was first populated 6,000 years ago by Mesolithic hunter-gatherers, and the county is rich in archaeological remains. There are important prehistoric cemeteries, such as Carrowmore. This is the largest cemetery of Megalithic tombs in Ireland and is also among the country's oldest. Over 60 tombs have been located by archaeologists, the oldest pre-date Newgrange by some 700 years. A restored cottage houses a small exhibition relating to the site. Important Early Christian monastic sites can be found on the island of Inishmurray just off the coast and at Drumcliff. William Butler Yeats is buried at Drumcliff.

The town of Sligo was sacked by the Vikings in 807, and was granted to Maurice FitzGerald after the Norman invasion of Connacht in 1235. It was a major point of emigration in the 1800s. Today Sligo is a busy town with a thriving commercial and cultural life.

IRELAND'S CITIES

No two cities in Ireland are the same. They have contrasting appearances and locations, but all have fascinating histories and attractions for the visitor.

Ireland's cities perform service, cultural, industrial, administrative, and commercial functions. The main concentration of cities is in the east and south of the country and all of the larger centers grew up as ports.

Dublin

The city and county of Dublin has a population of 1,056,000. The city is located on the edge of the Irish Sea, straddling both sides of the River Liffey, and rimmed by a semicircle of inland mountains. It is the chief commercial, industrial, administrative, educational, and cultural center of the Republic of Ireland.

Dublin has an international airport and seaport. The city is the seat of the Irish government, and the headquarters of various banks and financial institutions. It is also the center of Ireland's cultural life with its great theaters, museums, art spaces, and the National Concert Hall.

The capital celebrated its official millennium in 1988, but

Below: *The Four Courts, by the River Liffey, has housed Dublin's Courts of Law since 1796.*

there were settlements there long before 988. Dublin's Irish name *Baile Átha Cliath* (Town of the Hurdle Ford) comes from the ancient river crossing that was there in early Celtic times.

Viking raiders then came in the 9th Century. They

eventually settled, inter-married with the Irish and set up a prosperous trading port where the River Poddle meets the River Liffey in a black pool, in Irish *dubh linn*. Today the River Poddle flows mainly underground.

The Anglo-Normans then invaded and took the city. Dublin Castle, built on the orders of King John in 1204, became the center of British power in Ireland.

ABOVE: *A view of Dublin's sprawling suburbs from the Dublin Mountains. This expanding city is one of Europe's most vibrant capitals.*

BELOW: *Trinity College, one of Dublin's most beautiful sights, was founded by Queen Elizabeth I in 1592.*

Dublin enjoyed great prosperity and prominence during the 18th Century. At one point London was the only city in the British Empire larger than Dublin. During this period the wealthy middle classes left the medieval city to the south of the River Liffey for the northern Georgian squares surrounded by imposing townhouses. As Dublin's poorer districts spread northwards, the city's wealthy families

moved south of the river again to areas such as Merrion Square, Fitzwilliam Square, and St. Stephen's Green.

The union of Britain with Ireland in 1801 led to the end of the Irish Parliament in Dublin. Control was returned to London. This period saw unrest and a decline in the fortunes of the "Fair city".

Parts of central Dublin were badly damaged during the 1916 Rising. Subsequent violence caused further damage, including the burning of the Custom House in 1921. The Four Courts was also burned during the Civil War the following year.

The city remained depressed until Ireland joined the European Economic Community (now the European Union) in 1972. This led to an injection of funding into the country and an economic upturn. During the 1980s and 1990s the miracle of the Celtic Tiger economy led to a further rise in the fortunes of the city. Greater Dublin has expanded considerably as people continue to leave rural areas for the employment opportunities of the city. Culture and tourism also flourish and Dublin is now regarded as a thriving European capital.

Belfast

The city of Belfast has a population of some 400,000 and is the second-largest city on the island. To the west of the city are the Belfast Hills, to the north looms Cave Hill, and

Belfast Lough lies to the northeast.

Belfast is an administrative and engineering center and has a fine harbor. The city's name in Irish is *Béal Feirste* (Mouth of the Sandy Ford). This is a reference to the River Farset that once flowed through Belfast and is now confined to an underground pipe. A Norman castle was built on the River Lagan in 1177, and a settlement was established around this until it burned down some 20 years later. After another castle was constructed in 1611 the city of Belfast began to emerge. Protestant Scottish and English Planters settled there in the early 1600s, and they were followed by French Protestants (Huguenots) fleeing religious persecution in France. Industries such as rope-making, engineering, tobacco, and ship-building helped the city develop.

Belfast flourished during the Industrial Revolution and was given city status by Queen Victoria in 1888. Following the partition of Ireland, the city became the capital of Northern Ireland. Following the end of World War II, the city's economic fortunes declined rapidly. This economic depression was exacerbated by "The Troubles" that saw the city separated by sectarianism.

Since the Good Friday Agreement the city has enjoyed a revival in its fortunes. There have been huge injections of money into Belfast, unemployment has fallen and the security situation is stabilizing.

The visitor can admire some fine architecture, such as City Hall and the Linen Hall Library. Belfast boasts a vibrant night life and is proud of its cultural amenities. Lagan Weir, completed in 1994, is the first stage in an ambitious scheme to regenerate the city's docklands and Cathedral quarter. New parks, public spaces, sculptures, and restaurants are springing up. Historic buildings in the city center are also being restored.

Belfast has entered the 21st Century with high hopes. Inevitably divisions and sectarian passions remain, but there is also optimism and a determination to transform this great city.

Cork

The city of Cork is the third-largest city on the island with a population of some 127,000. It has traditionally been associated with the processing and marketing of agricultural products, but it benefits also from the presence of large-scale industrial development around its outer harbor and the use of natural gas from the offshore Kinsale field.

Cork, the center of Ireland's southwest coast, is actually built on an island. The city is closely identified with the River Lee and sits between the two channels of the river, with a "midtown" area that spills over on to the north and south river banks.

The city dates back to the 7th Century and it became a

ABOVE: *The English Market in Cork city has a great selection of local and imported produce. It is open from Monday to Saturday.*

major commercial center, especially for the butter market, during the 18th Century. The Famine years led to depression and mass migration. The nearby port of Cobh remained a major point of emigration until 1970. Cork was heavily embroiled in the fight for Irish independence in the early part of the 20th Century. The infamous Black and Tans set the city ablaze. Today, Cork is a an attractive city popular with tourists. There is some fine Georgian architecture, the imposing St. Finbarr's Cathedral completed in 1879, a range of retail outlets, and many pubs.

Derry

Derry is the island's fourth-largest city and has a population of 190,000. *Derry* is situated on the River Foyle and there has been a settlement here since the 6th Century when St. Columba founded a monastery. During the 1100s and 1200s the city prospered and remained an Irish powerbase while other towns fell to Norman conquerors. It withstood a series of conflicts until 1566 when English forces briefly seized the city. Control of the city was eventually given to London's livery companies. Twice during the 1640s the city walls held out against Irish attacks, and twice Parliamentarians repulsed the Royalist besiegers.

Today the city is being redeveloped. Major operations include the Foyleside, Quayside, and Richmond Shopping Centers. Visitors can walk along Derry's famous city walls,

RIGHT: *The historic city of Derry is situated on the River Foyle. There has been a settlement here since the 6th Century.*

built in the 1600s, which were the last complete set of city walls to be built in Europe.

Galway

The city of Galway is the island's fifth-largest city and has a population of 57,000. Galway became an important walled town when the Anglo-Normans captured the territory in 1232. Richard II granted a charter to the city in 1396. Today it is one of Europe's fastest-growing cities. The beautiful Collegiate Church of St. Nicholas of Myra is the largest medieval parish church in Ireland still in use. It is said that Christopher Columbus prayed at the church. He supposedly made this trip because one of his crew came from Galway. The city's other great religious building is Galway Cathedral. The modern architecture of the cathedral is not to everyone's taste!

Placenames

◆ ◆ ◆

Investigating the name of a place can give you a fascinating insight into the history of a town or district.

◆ ◆ ◆

It is often possible to work out the origins of an Irish placename. Many of them are made up of descriptions of the neighborhood. For example, if there are two features, say lakes, close together, the larger one will often have -more in its name, and the smaller one -beg.

Human structures also find their way into names: *droichead* is a bridge, and *dún* is a fortress. Many others are named after people, usually the lords who owned the lands on which they were built. Castledawson and Manorhamilton are examples.

When investigating the origins of a placename, it is always important to remember that a large number of Irish words sound similar, and in many cases the Anglicization of Irish placenames has confused the spelling. This makes the word look as if a placename means one thing when it actually means something completely different. Too many people fall into the trap of taking the English spelling, looking it up in an Irish dictionary and assuming they have the right meaning.

This is a list of some of the more common placename components in Ireland:

Ard

Signifies a high place in Irish. This ususally means a physically high place, but it can also mean a place of importance, for example, the Ards Peninsula in County Down, Ardstraw (a high, or important rath) in County Tyrone, and Ardfert in County Kerry.

A few places seem to be an Ard, but are actually not. For example, Ardee in County Louth is actually an abbreviation of the older name Atherdee, where Dee is the name of the river on which it stands.

Bally, Ballyna, Ballina

Bally is an extremely common prefix to town names in Ireland. This prefix is derived from the Irish phrase *Baile na*, (place of). It is not quite right to translate it as "town of", as there were few, if any, towns in Ireland at the time these names were formed, for example, Ballyjamesduff (Place of James Duff) in County Cavan, and Ballymoney in County Derry.

The Irish name for the site of present-day Dublin was *Baile Átha Cliath* which, if Anglicized, would be spelt something like Ballycleeagh. Note that "Dublin" is actually a Viking word.

...beg

This means "small" in Irish. Usually used at the end of a name, this often means that this feature is the smaller of a pair of adjacent features. A similar name ending in "more" is often found nearby, for example, Killybegs in County Donegal, and Lambeg in County Antrim. North of Lough Neagh is a much smaller lake called Lough Beg.

...bridge

When found at the end of a name, this means that the town developed beside a bridge, or became famous as a bridging point. These town names are usually of English language origin, for example, Banbridge in County Down, which grew up around a bridge over the River Bann. Newbridge in County Kildare grew up when a bridge over the Liffey was built at that point. Newbridge is increasingly being called *Droichead Nua*, which is an Irish version of the original English name. This illustrates the importance of bridges to trade.

Carrick, Carrig

Carrick means "rock" in Irish, and Carricks are abundant across Ireland, for example, Carrickfergus

RIGHT: *Farmland in County Down. The prefix Down evolved from the Irish word* Dún *(a fortified place).*

(Rock of Fergus) in County Antrim, Carrickmacross (Rock of MacRoss) in County Monaghan, and Carrick-on-Suir in County Tipperary.

Castle

A prefix whose origins are in the English language. Towns with this name once, and in a few cases still do, have a castle, for example, Castlederg in County Tyrone, Castlebar in County Mayo, and Castleisland in County Kerry.

Clon, Cloon

An Irish word meaning a "dry place". This name is much more common in Connacht than elsewhere in Ireland. This is because the province is known for its wetland areas, so a dry and well-drained site was more valuable and well regarded, for example, Clonmel in County Tipperary, and Clonmacnoise in County Offaly.

Derry

This term evolved from the Irish name for "a place of oak trees", or sometimes a grove or clearing of the same. Oak trees are found in many places in Ireland, so there are many examples of the name Derry. The most famous is Derry city. Other examples include Derryaghy in County Antrim (a former village which is now part of Belfast city), and Edenderry in County Offaly.

Down, Dun, Don

These prefixes all evolved from the Irish word *Dún* (a fortified place). As Ireland has always had wars, there are many examples of fortified places—Donegal (Fortress of the foreigners) in County Donegal, Dungannon in County Tyrone, Portadown (Port of the fortress) in County Armagh, Dungarvan in County Waterford.

Droichead

An Irish word meaning "a bridge". The prime example is Drogheda in County Louth, which is an evolved spelling derived from the Irish word. Also the town of Droichead Nua (Newbridge) in County Kildare.

Drum, Drom

An Irish word meaning "a ridge". Examples include Drumquin (Quinn's ridge) in County Tyrone, and Drum (the ridge) in County Monaghan.

...ford

Names containing "ford" could have either an Irish or Viking origin. If the place is by a narrow bay, it is likely to be of Viking origin. The word evolved from the Viking fjord. Alternatively, it could be an Irish/English word meaning "a shallow crossing point in a river", for example, the county town of Longford.

ABOVE: *Drumcliff Church seen looking towards Glencar Lough in County Sligo.*

Gal, Gael

An Irish word meaning strangers or foreigners, for example, Donegal (Fortress of the foreigners). Note that Galway is not an example of this word. It translates to something like "a port at some small islands".

ABOVE: *Galway Bay. The city's name means "a port at some small islands". Today Galway is one of Europe's fastest-growing cities.*

RIGHT: *Glenelly Valley in County Derry. The Irish word* gleann *means "a valley situated between mountains". Other examples of places with the prefix Glen include the village and glen of Glengarriff, County Cork, and the wild valley of Glenmalure in County Wicklow.*

Glen

From the Irish word gleann meaning "a valley between mountains", for example, Glenariff in County Antrim, and Crossmaglen, County Armagh.

...hill

An English word used for any town on or near a hill, for example, Markethill, County Armagh, and Richill in County Armagh.

Kil, Killy

An Irish word meaning "a church". Famous examples include Kildare (*Cill Dara*) meaning "the second church", Kilkenny, and Belfast's Shankill is Irish for "old church".

Knock

An Irish word meaning "a hill". There are many examples of this, including Knock in County Mayo, Knock in County Down, and Knockmore (the great hill) in County Antrim. For a period several centuries ago, Carrickfergus in County Antrim was known as Knockfergus.

Ireland's Landmarks

◆ ◆ ◆

The island of Ireland is rich in stunning landscapes, architectural masterpieces and historic sites.

◆ ◆ ◆

For a small island, Ireland is astonishingly diverse. It is criss-crossed with streams, rivers, lakes, and canals. The central plain of Ireland is surrounded by a ring of hills and bleak mountains. Hues vary from the deep purple of heather to the black of turf bogs. Ireland's vistas range from the gentle slopes of the Slieve Bloom Mountains through to the steep, wooded valleys of County Wicklow and the dramatic Cliffs of Moher.

Ireland has a fantastic array of buildings, monuments, and archaeological sites that date back to Neolithic times. These include ancient burial sites and stone circles. There are imposing medieval castles, walls, and round towers.

Magnificent Norman castles are found across the country. There are grand stately homes from the 18th and 19th Centuries. Sacred sites are to be found in every county. These include cathedrals, monasteries, shrines and graveyards dating back to the time of St. Patrick. All these landmarks give the visitor a wonderful insight into Ireland's culture, history, and geography.

The Giant's Causeway, Country Antrim

This major landmark is a world-famous and truly remarkable natural geological formation on the north Antrim coast, lying 3.2km (2 miles) from the village of Bushmills. It is associated with the mythical Ulster giant Finn MacCool. According to a legend, when he fell in love with a lady giant on Staffa, an island in the Hebrides, he built this wide commodious highway to bring her across to the province of Ulster.

Over 37,000 dark basalt columns, most of them perfect hexagonals, are grouped together like honeycombs from the cliff to the shore for about a 1km (1,100 yards). The tallest column, known as the Giant's Organ, is about 12m (39ft) high. Elsewhere along the Giant's Causeway there are strange terraces and shapes that have given rise to other fanciful names, such as the Giant's Horseshoe, the Giant's Loom, the Fan, and the Giant's Coffin.

Before the famous coast road was built in the 1830s visitors complained about the ruggedness of the trip. But there was one shining compensation on the journey: the town where tourists made their last stop before the final push to the Causeway was Bushmills. Ever since 1608 travellers had been revived with Bushmill's famous whiskey.

FOLLOWING PAGE: *The Giant's Causeway, near Portrush, is one of Ireland's most famous landmarks.*

Newgrange Passage Tomb, County Meath

This great burial mound was constructed nearly 5,000 years ago and overlooks the River Boyne. The powerful Stone Age people, whose cult center it was, dominated the whole northern midlands of Ireland, but we have no clue as to the language they spoke and can only speculate about their customs and beliefs. Not only were they great builders, but they also specialized in abstract art, as is clear from the many spirals, lozenges, triangles, zig-zags, and cup-marks inscribed on the kerbstones which girdle the mound.

A long passageway leads to the center of the mound, which is in cruciform shape, with three recesses and a granite basin in each. Cremated bones in these recesses suggest that the basins contained the remains of chieftains. Most remarkably, a "roof-box" is located over the entrance, and at the winter solstice the sun shines directly through this and lights up the whole passage. The nurturing sun took away the spirits of the dead chieftains and guaranteed the welfare of the people under their new leaders. When the Celts reached Ireland in the final centuries B.C., they echoed this ritual and regarded the place as the residence of their own great father-deity, the sun-like *Daghdha*. They called it *Brú na Bóinne* (Palace of Boyne).

RIGHT: *Tomb interior at Newgrange, County Meath. This is one of the most remarkable prehistoric sites in Europe.*

Jerpoint Abbey, County Kilkenny

This was a Cistercian abbey founded around 1160 by the King of Ossory, *Donncha Mac Giolla Phádraig*. It was under the patronage of the Virgin Mary, and its first abbot was *Felix Ó Dubhshláine*, later to become Bishop of Ossory and whose effigy can be seen carved on a tomb in the chancel. In the 15th Century the lofty square tower was erected, being raised on four arches—three of these are in Gothic style, and the fourth is rounded.

The Norman conquest came within a dozen years of the foundation of Jerpoint, and the abbey soon found itself under pressure to conform with the new control of ecclesiastical affairs. Contrary to Norman policy, Jerpoint continued to admit native Irishmen as monks, and as a result its influence over sister houses was reduced. Its future was, however, guaranteed by the protection of strong Norman families of the locality. The more elaborate stone carvings in the abbey date from the 15th and 16th Centuries and are the work of a special school of masons located some distance away at Callan. These worked under the patronage of the Butlers, Lords of Ormond, but they were inspired by the art forms found in the illuminated manuscripts of early Irish Christianity.

LEFT: *The ruins of Jerpoint Abbey, County Kilkenny. According to local legend, St. Nicholas (or Santa Claus) is buried near the abbey.*

The Townhouses of Dublin City

The 18th Century ushered in a period of great house-building in Dublin. Many of the fine houses were town dwellings for the new gentry who had received vast estates in rural Ireland due to their loyalty to the Hanoverian dynasty. St. Stephen's Green was laid out to provide sites for such houses, and this was followed soon afterwards by the formation of Dawson Street, Grafton Street, and Molesworth Street, after which the building extended to Merrion Square, Fitwilliam Square, and areas north of the River Liffey. The beauty of the houses in all that area remains as a testimony to an age of affluence among the ruling class, and to their fine taste in architecture.

These townhouses have a basement, topped by four storeys, and are built in terraces with long brick facades. They have impressive doorways, the lintel resting on two pillars and an arched fanlight overhead. The vertical rectangular windows are in two shafts and are multi-paned, while internally the ceilings were often decorated in Neo-classical style. As the century wore on, successful merchants and businessmen became more numerous as neighbors of the gentry, but the latter continued to attract most of the attention with their more colorful lifestyles.

RIGHT: *Dublin's Georgian streets were the product of public planning. This provided the public spaces in which architects could flourish.*

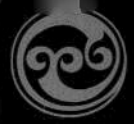

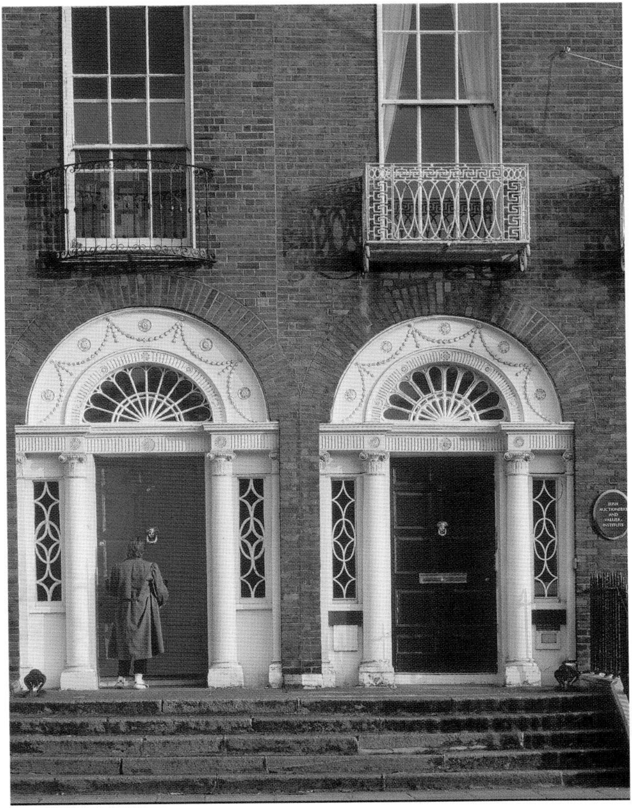
IRISH
AUCTIONEERS
AND
VALUERS
INSTITUTE

Wicklow Mountains, County Wicklow

The Wicklow Mountains are visible from most parts of Dublin. These beautiful peaks lie to the south of the capital and form its dramatic backdrop. Visitors from the city can reach them in less than an hour and are usually surprised at their wild appearance so soon after the cultured refinements of the metropolis. For the most part the Wicklow Mountains are inhabited only by sheep; the eye rests on a panorama of waterfalls, and solitary loughs.

The Wicklow Mountains themselves are comprised of a large mass of granite which, as it solidified many millions of years ago, compressed and baked the adjacent sedimentary rocks forming mica-schist. Much of this has now been washed away, but the geological boundary holds high concentrations of lead, iron, and zinc which were mined in the past. It is Ireland's fourth National Park and is centered on Glendalough.

Nearby can be found the lavish gardens of the Powerscourt mansion. The Powerscourt estate has one of Europe's greatest gardens. The terraces were laid out between 1843 and 1875, and the Japanese garden was added in 1908. The demesne is enormous and offers a magnificent view of the Sugarloaf Mountain.

RIGHT: *The Great Sugar Loaf Mountain, near Enniskerry. At its foot are the beautiful gardens of Powerscourt.*

Kilkenny Castle, County Kilkenny

In the year 1192, one of the leading Norman conquerors, William Marshal, built a large castle on an eminence over the River Nore. Soon after, King John granted control of the wine patent for the whole of Ireland to Theobald, brother of the Archbishop of Canterbury. From this Theobald derived his surname de Bouteillier (bottle-bearer); but the later Butlers turned it into a myth whereby their great ancestor had landed in Arklow, unsheathed his sword there and formally announced that he would not rest until he had control of the whole island. He did not achieve that, but his descendants inter-married with those of Marshal, and in 1391 the great castle of Kilkenny was acquired by James Butler, 3rd Earl of Ormond.

From that time on, Kilkenny Castle has been synonymous with the Butler family. The occupants have been varied and dramatic. James, created 1st Duke of Ormond (1607–88), remodeled the castle and immense grounds on French patterns in the 17th Century, by removing the defenses, erecting the classical entrance, and placing lofty roofs on the towers. The whole structure was again remodeled in the 19th Century, this time in the castellated style, and a great picture gallery was built.

LEFT: *Kilkenny Castle was home to the mighty Butler family from the end of the 14th Century until 1935.*

Kilmainham Jail, Dublin

This place takes its name, *Cill Mhaighneann*, from St. Maighniu who founded his church there in the late 6th Century. This grew into a monastery, which gave rise to the village of Old Kilmainham. Of the monastery only a small graveyard now remains. After the Norman invasion, a fortified priory of the Knights Hospitallers was established nearby. A County Jail was built by the English on the site in the 17th Century, and in 1796 this was replaced by a larger prison on Kilmainham Commons, a little to the west. There was plenty of demand for prison spaces, especially after the crushing of the 1798 Rising, and until it closed in 1924 Kilmainham Jail included among its inmates some of the most famous personalities in Irish history, such as William Smith O'Brien and the great parliamentary leader Charles Stewart Parnell. He was an unwilling guest there for a while in 1881 until released by Prime Minister Gladstone. In 1883 the group known as the Invincibles were hanged there for the assassination of Lord Cavendish and his secretary in Phoenix Park. The leaders of the 1916 Rising, including Pádraic Pearse and James Connolly, were executed by firing squad at Kilmainham, the place of execution now marked by a simple cross.

RIGHT: *Kilmainham Jail was used to imprison many of Ireland's nationalists, including Charles Stewart Parnell.*

The Rock of Cashel, County Tipperary

This great eminence, rising commandingly over the Golden Vale of Munster, was the royal seat of the sept called *Eoghanacht* (people of the yew), which from the 4th Century onwards dominated the southern half of Ireland. The original myth of the *Eoghanacht* recalled how their ancestor, *Conall Corc*, came from Britain with his wife and three sons. They went astray in a snowstorm, through which only this massive rock could be discerned. Finding their way to it, they lit a fire at a yew-tree there. On the same night, a druid dreamt that whoever lit such a fire on the rock would be king of all Munster. The local people rushed to the place and, finding Conall there with his fire, they gave homage to the surprised stranger.

Christianity came early to the Rock of Cashel, and it was even claimed that St. Patrick himself visited the place. The surviving ecclesiastical buildings include the round tower, and a richly decorated Romanesque chapel which was completed in 1134. A cathedral was constructed on the site in 1169, but it was replaced about a century later by the present cathedral with its massive tower. Finally, a castle was constructed at the western part of this cathedral in the early 15th Century.

LEFT: *The Rock of Cashel is one of the country's most impressive historical sights and is built on a huge limestone rock.*

Christchurch Cathedral, Dublin

When the raiding Norsemen sailed up the mouth of the River Liffey in 837, there was a pre-existing small Irish settlement on the northern bank. Within 15 years the newcomers had founded their own settlement. This new fortified town grew into the strong Norse kingdom of Dublin. These Norsemen in time became Christianized, and the original Christchurch was founded by their king, Sigtrygg Silkbeard, in or about 1038; but their power was overthrown when the Normans captured Dublin in 1171. The Norman leader known as Strongbow determined to replace the church with a new cathedral, and the building of this began almost immediately. Strongbow himself was buried there on his death in 1176, and the work was completed by 1234, with an Augustinian priory on the southern side. The priory was dissolved in 1539, and the Roman liturgy was replaced by the Anglican in 1551. The building was badly dilapidated before it was restored, in Gothic style and with drastic alterations, in the 1870s by George Edmund Street. He rebuilt the tower, and added the present Chapter House. He also incorporated the old bell-tower into a new Synod Hall, linking it to the cathedral by the covered footbridge which spans the adjacent roadway.

RIGHT: *The magnificent Christchurch Cathedral was founded by Norse converts during the 11th Century.*

FAMILY NAMES

◆ ◆ ◆

The history of Ireland is a drama of war, invasion, plantation, and migration. Like all history it is composed of individual family histories. Surnames are the point where history and family history intersect.

◆ ◆ ◆

Aherne

Aherne is an Anglicization of *Ó hEachthianna*, from *Eachthiarna* (lord of horses) and is also found in the variants Hearn and Hearne. *Eachthiarna* was a relatively common personal name in Gaelic society, borne by, for instance, a brother of Brian Boru. The surname originated, in fact, in the sept or tribe of Brian, the *Dál gCais*, and has always been strongly associated with their homeland in County Clare. The family territory was in the southeast of Clare, around Sixmilebridge, up to the end of the Middle Ages, when they migrated south and east, to Counties Cork, Limerick, and Waterford. To this day, Ahernes are most numerous in Cork and Waterford.

Allen

The name has two quite distinct origins, one Scots Gaelic, the other French. *Ailín* (little rock) is the root of the

Scottish name, originally MacAllan. The first recorded arrivals bearing the Scottish name came in the 15th Century, as hired soldiers (gallowglasses) imported to Donegal by the O'Donnells, and the migrations of the following two centuries brought many more. In other cases, the surname derives from the old Breton personal name *Alan*, which in turn came from the Germanic tribal name *Alemannus* (all men). The same root provided the modern French name for Germany, *Allemagne*. Followers of the invading Normans were the first to carry the Breton version of the name to Ireland. Irish families bearing the name may be of either origin, though the fact that two-thirds of the Allens are to be found in the province of Ulster—they are especially numerous in Counties Antrim and Armagh—suggests that the majority are of Scottish extraction.

Barrett

The name Barrett is now concentrated in two widely separated parts of Ireland, in County Cork and in the Mayo-Galway region. The Irish version of the name is *Baróid* in the south and *Bairéid* in the west, and this may reflect two separate origins. At any rate, families of the surname first appeared in these areas in the 13th Century, after the Anglo-Norman invasion. Its Norman origin derives from the old Germanic personal name, *Bernard* or *Beraud*. A

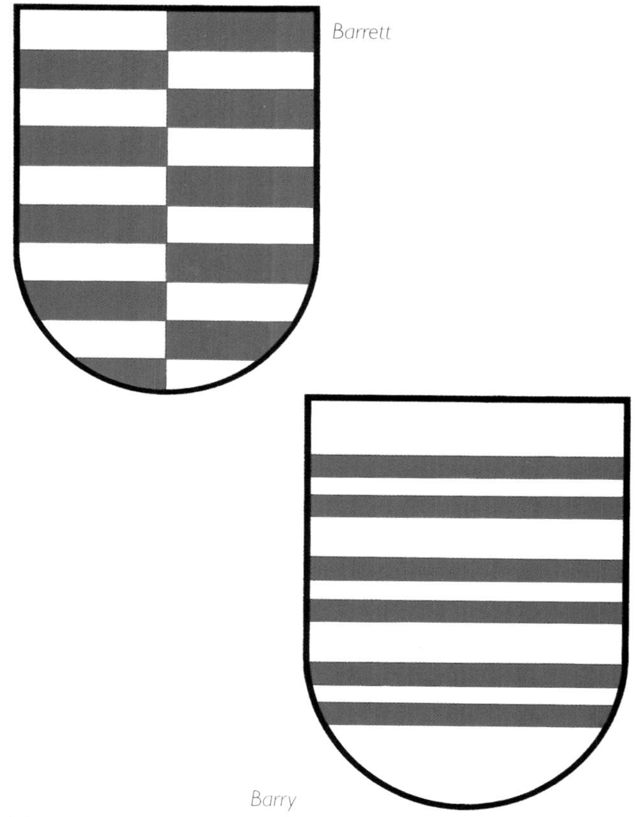
Barrett
Barry

separate derivation gives its origin as the Middle English *Barat*, a nickname for a quarrelsome or deceitful person. The western family, originally based around Killala in County Mayo, were thoroughly absorbed into Gaelic society very quickly, and in the Middle Ages began to split into various sub-clans, among them McAndrew, Timmons, and Roberts. The Cork settlers were not so Gaelicized, giving their name to the large barony of Barretts in the middle of the county. The arms of the family are based on word play, a pictorial version of the French *barrettes* (short bars).

Barry

The first bearer of the surname to arrive in Ireland was Robert de Barri, one of the original band of Norman knights who landed at Bannow Bay in County Wexford in May 1169, and a brother of Giraldus Cambrensis, historian of the invasion. The name comes from the earlier association of the family with the island of Barry, southwest of Cardiff in Wales. From the start the family were prominent in the settlement of east Cork, and were soon absorbed into the native culture, forming sub-septs on Gaelic lines, the most important being Barry Mór, Barry Óg and Barry Roe. The names of two of these are perpetuated in the names of the Cork baronies of Barrymore and Barryroe, and many others. The surname is now very

numerous in Ireland. As well as the Norman origin, two relatively uncommon Gaelic surnames, *Ó Béargha* and *Ó Báire*, have also been Anglicized as Barry.

Boyd

This surname originated in Scotland, and is now most common in Ulster, particularly in Counties Antrim and Down. Two separate derivations are claimed for the name. The most commonly accepted links it with the Scottish island of Bute in the Firth of Clyde, in Gaelic *Bód, Bóid* (of Bute). Another derivation connects the family with the Stewarts, claiming that the descent is from Robert, son of Simon, one of the Norman founders of the Scottish Stewarts. Robert was known as *Búidhe*, meaning yellow, from the color of his hair, and this is taken as the origin of the surname. Whatever the truth, the earliest recorded bearers of the name certainly used the Norman prefix "de".

Boyle

Boyle, or O'Boyle, is now one of the 50 most common surnames in Ireland. In Irish the name is *Ó Baoghill*, the derivation of which is uncertain, but thought to be connected to the Irish *geall* (pledge). In the Middle Ages the family was powerful and respected, sharing control of the entire northwest of the island with the O'Donnells and the O'Dohertys, and the strongest association of the family is

Boyd

Boyle

Brady

Breen

still with County Donegal, where (O)Boyle is the third most numerous name in the county. The majority of those bearing the name are of Gaelic origin, but many Irish Boyles have separate, Norman origins. In Ulster, a significant number are descended from the Scottish Norman family of *de Boyville,* whose name comes from the town now known as *Beauville* in Normandy. The most famous Irish family of the surname were the Boyles, earls of Cork and Shannon, descended from Richard Boyle, who arrived in Ireland from Kent in 1588 and quickly amassed enormous wealth.

Brady

The surname derives from the Irish *Mac Brádaigh*, coming, possibly, from *brádach* (thieving or dishonest). The name is among the 60 most frequently found in Ireland, and remains very numerous in County Cavan, their original homeland, with large numbers also to be found in the adjoining county of Monaghan. Their power was centered on an area a few miles east of Cavan town, from where they held jurisdiction over a large territory within the old Gaelic kingdom of *Breifne*.

Breen

There are several distinct Gaelic origins of the surname, both *Mac Braoin* and *Ó Braoin*, from *braon* (moisture or drop). The Mac Braoin were originally located near the

town of Knocktopher in County Kilkenny, but migrated to Wexford after the Anglo-Norman invasions in the 12th and 13th Centuries. County Wexford is still the area of the country in which the surname is most common, though a separate Wexford sept, the *Ó Briain*, also had their surname Anglicized as Breen. These were descended from *Bran Finn*, son of *Lachta*, King of Munster, and uncle of Brian Boru. However, the O'Breens, rulers of Brawney, a territory near Athlone in Counties Offaly and Westmeath, were the most powerful of the name in the Middle Ages; as they lost power the name mutated, and many in the area are now to be found as O'Briens. The surname is now also quite common in north Connacht, County Fermanagh, and in County Kerry.

Brennan

This is one of the most frequent surnames in Ireland and is to be found throughout the country, though noticeably less common in Ulster. It derives from the two Irish originals *Ó Braonáin* and *Mac Branáin*. The Mac Branáin were chiefs of a large territory in the east of the present County Roscommon, and a large majority of the Brennans of north Connacht, Counties Mayo, Sligo, and Roscommon, descend from them. Ó Braonáin originated in at least four distinct areas: Kilkenny, east Galway, Westmeath and Kerry. Of these the most powerful were the Ó Braonáin of Kilkenny, chiefs

Brennan

Browne

of Idough in the north of the county. After they lost their land and status to the English, many of them became notorious as leaders of bands of outlaws. A separate family, the *Ó Branáin*, are the ancestors of many of the Brennans of Counties Fermanagh and Monaghan, where the name was also Anglicized as Brannan and Branny.

Browne

This is one of the most common surnames in the British Isles, and is among the 40 commonest in Ireland. It can derive, as a nickname, from the Old English *Brun*, referring to hair, complexion or clothes, or from the Norman name *Le Brun* (the Brown). In the three southern provinces of Munster, Leinster, and Connacht, where the name is usually spelt with the final "e" it is almost invariably of Norman or English origin, and was borne by some of the most important Norman-Irish and Anglo-Irish families, notably the earls of Kenmare in Kerry and Lord Oranmore and Browne and the earls of Altamont in Connacht. The assimilation of the Connacht family into Gaelic life is seen in their inclusion as one of the "Tribes" of Galway. In Ulster, where it is more often plain Brown, the surname can be an Anglicization of the Scots Gaelic *Mac a' Bhruithin* (son of the judge) or *Mac Gille Dhuinn* (son of the brown boy). The largest concentrations of the name in this province are in Counties Derry, Down, and Antrim.

Burke

Burke, along with its variants Bourke and de Burgh, is now by far the most common Irish name of Norman origin; there are over 20,000 Burkes in Ireland, a fraction of the world-wide total. The first person of the name to arrive in Ireland was William Fitzadelm de Burgo, a Norman knight from Burgh in Suffolk, in the invasion of 1171. He succeeded Strongbow as chief governor. He received the earldom of Ulster, and was granted vast tracts of Connacht. His descendants adopted Gaelic customs almost wholesale, and very quickly became one of the most important families. In Connacht, which remained the center of the family's power, new septs were formed on native Irish lines. William Liath de Burgh, a great-grandson of the original William, was the ancestor of the two most influential clans, the MacWilliam *Uachtar* of County Galway, and the MacWilliam *Íochtar* of County Mayo. Other descendants founded families with distinct surnames; Philbin derives from *Mac Philbín*, son of Philip (de Burgh); Jennings is an Anglicization of *Mac Sheóinín*, son of John (de Burgh); Gibbons, found in Mayo, was originally *Mac Giobúin*, son of Gilbert (de Burgh).

Butler

The surname Butler, found in both England and Ireland, is Norman in origin, and originally meant "wine steward" from

Byrne

Carroll

the same root as modern French *bouteille* (bottle). The name was then extended to denote the chief servant of a household and, in the households of royalty and the most powerful nobility, a high-ranking officer concerned only nominally with the supply of wine. In Ireland the most prominent Butler family is descended from Theobald de Bouteillier, who was created Chief Butler of Ireland by Henry II in 1177. His descendants became the earls of Ormond in 1328 and dukes of Ormond after the restoration of Charles II in 1660. Up to the end of the 17th Century, the Butlers were one of the most powerful Anglo-Norman dynasties, sharing effective control of Ireland with their great rivals the Fitzgeralds, earls of Desmond and earls of Kildare. From the Middle Ages right up to the 20th Century their seat was Kilkenny Castle.

Byrne

Byrne or O'Byrne, together with its variants Be(i)rne and Byrnes, is one of the ten most frequent surnames in Ireland today. In the original Irish the name is *Ó Broin*, from the personal name *Bran* (raven). It is traced back to king *Bran* of Leinster, who ruled in the 11th Century. As a result of the Norman invasion, the O'Byrnes were driven from their original homeland in County Kildare into south County Wicklow in the early 13th Century. There they grew in importance over the years, retaining control of

the territory until the early 17th Century, despite repeated attempts by the English authorities to dislodge them. Even today, the vast majority of the Irish who bear the name originate in Wicklow or the surrounding counties.

Carroll

One of the 25 most common Irish surnames, Carroll comes, in the vast majority of cases, from the Irish *Ó Cearbhaill*, from *Cearbhall*, a very popular personal name thought to mean "fierce in battle". It is widespread today throughout the three southern provinces of Connacht, Leinster and Munster, reflecting the fact that it arose almost simultaneously as a separate surname in at least six different parts of Ireland.

The most famous of these were the Ely O'Carrolls of *Uíbh Fhailí*, including modern County Offaly as well as parts of Tipperary, who derived their name from *Cearball*, king of Ely, one of the leaders of the victorious native Irish army at the Battle of Clontarf in 1014. Although their power was much reduced over the centuries in the continuing conflict with the Norman Butlers, they held on to their distinctive Gaelic customs until the start of the 17th Century.

Connolly

Again, a number of original Irish names have been Anglicized as Connolly. The *Ó Conghalaigh*, from *conghal* (as

Connolly

Cullen

fierce as a wolf), were based in Connacht, where the English version is now often spelt Connelly. The name arose as *Ó Coingheallaigh* in West Cork, while Ulster Connollys derive from both the *Ó Conghalaigh* of Fermanagh, who gave their name to Derrygonnelly (Connolly's oakwood), and the Monaghan Connollys, for whom a number of separate origins are suggested, as a branch of the southern *Uí Néill*, or as a branch of the MacMahons. Whatever their origin, the Monaghan family have been the most prominent of the Connollys, recorded as having "Chiefs of the Name" up to the 17th Century, and producing, among others, Speaker William Conolly (sic), reputedly the richest man in 18th-Century Ireland.

Cullen

The surname Cullen may be of Norman or Gaelic origin. The Norman name has been derived both from the city of Cologne in Germany, and from Colwyn in Wales. In Ireland this Norman family was prominent principally in County Wexford, where their seat was at Cullenstown Castle in Bannow parish. Much more numerous in modern times, however, are descendants of the *Ó Cuilinn*, a name taken from *cuileann* (holly tree). The name originated in southeast Leinster, and this area has remained their stronghold, with the majority to be found even today in Counties Wicklow and Wexford.

Delaney

In its form, Delaney is a Norman name, from *De l'aunaie* (from the alder grove), and doubtless some of those bearing the name in Ireland are descended from the Normans who came in the 11th and 12th Centuries. However, in the vast majority of cases the name was adopted as the Anglicized form of the original Irish *Ó Dúbhshláine*, from *dubh* (black) and *slán* (defiance). The original territory of the *Ó Dúbhshláine* was at the foot of the Slieve Bloom Mountains in County Laois. From there the family spread into neighboring County Kilkenny, and the surname Delaney is still strongly associated with these counties.

Doyle

This name, one of the most common in Ireland, derives from the Irish *Ó Dubhghaill*, from *dubh* (dark) and *gall* (foreigner), a descriptive formula first used to describe the invading Vikings, and in particular to distinguish the darker-haired Danes from fair-haired Norwegians. The common Scottish names Dougall and MacDougall come from the same source, and reflect the original pronunciation more accurately. In Ulster and Roscommon, these names now exist as McDowell and Dowell carried by the descendants of immigrant Scottish gallowglasses, or mercenaries. The strongest association of Doyle, however, is with southeast

Doyle

Farrell

Leinster, Counties Wexford, Wicklow, and Carlow in particular, though the name is now found everywhere in Ireland. The stag portrayed in the arms is regarded as a symbol of permanence and endurance, a theme reflected also in one of the family mottoes *Bhí mé beidh mé* (I was and will be).

Farrell

As both (O')Farrell and (O')Ferrall, this name in Irish is *Fearghaíl*, from the personal name *Fearghal*, made up of *fear* (man) and *gal* (valor). The original Fearghal or Fergal, from whom the family claim descent, was killed at Clontarf in 1014. His great-grandfather *Angall* gave his name to the territory they possessed, Annally in County Longford. The present name of both the county and the town derives from the family, the full name in Irish being *Longphuirt Uí Fhearghaíll* (O'Farrell's Fortress). The family ruled this area for almost seven centuries, down to the final catastrophes of the 17th Century, after which many members of the family fought with distinction as mercenaries in the armies of continental Europe. Today the surname is one of the most common in Ireland, with a wide distribution throughout the country, though the largest concentration remains in the historical homeland of Longford and the surrounding areas.

Fitzgerald

Fitzgerald is a Norman name, made up of *Fi(t)z*, Norman French for "son of" and Gerald, a personal name of Germanic origin from *geri* (spear) and wald (rule). The family traces its origin to Walter FitzOther, keeper of Windsor forest in the late 11th Century, whose son Gerald was constable of Pembroke Castle in Wales. Gerald's son Walter accompanied Strongbow in the invasion of Ireland, and adopted the surname Fitzgerald. Over the following eight centuries the family became one of the most powerful and numerous in Ireland. The head of the main branch, the Duke of Leinster, known historically as the Earl of Kildare, is the foremost peer of Ireland.

Flaherty

In Irish Flaherty and O'Flaherty are *Ó Flaithbheartach*, from *flaitheamh* (prince or ruler) and *beartach* (acting or behaving). Although the literal translation is "one who behaves like a prince", a more accurate rendition would be "hospitable" or "generous". The family's original territory included the whole of the west of the modern County Galway, including Connemara and the Aran Islands, whence the title of their chief, lord of Iar-Chonnacht and of Moycullen. They occupied and controlled this area from the 13th Century on, and survived as a power in the area down to the 18th Century. Although the name is now common

Flaherty

Kearney

and widespread, the largest numbers are still to be found in County Galway.

Kearney

Kearney is common and widespread in Ireland, and has a number of different origins. In the west it originated in County Mayo, near Moynulla and Balla, the territory of the *Ó Cearnaigh* from *cearnach* (victorious), where it has sometimes also been anglicized as Carney. A separate family of the same name, but anglicized as (O)Kearney, arose in Clare, and migrated in early times to the area around Cashel in County Tipperary. In Ulster the name derives from *Mac Cearnaigh*, also from *cearnach*; they were part of the *Cinéal Eoghain*, the large group of families descended from King Eoghan, son of Niall of the Nine Hostages, who founded the *Uí Néill* dynasty and was supposedly responsible for the kidnapping of St. Patrick to Ireland. The most historically important family, however, were the *Ó Catharnaigh*, from *catharnach*, meaning warlike. These were chiefs of a large territory in the midlands, in the modern Counties of Meath and Offaly. The composer of the Irish national anthem was Peadar Kearney.

Kelly

Kelly comes from the Irish *Ó Ceallaigh*, based on the popular personal name *Ceallach*, which may mean either

"bright-haired" or "troublesome". The most prominent families are the O'Kellys of *Uí Máine*, or Hy Many, an ancient territory taking in east Galway and south Roscommon, also known simply as "O'Kelly's Country". Their pedigree takes them back to *Máine Mór*, first chief of the area bearing this name, who lived in the 5th Century. His descendant *Ceallach* I (died *c.* 874) was the 12th chief, and the surname derives from him. Despite the loss of most of their possessions in the catastrophic wars of the 17th Century, the succession to the position of head of the sept has continued unbroken down to the present incumbent, Walter Lionel O'Kelly of Gallagh and Tycooly, count of the Holy Roman Empire, known as "the O'Kelly", and recognized as such by the chief herald of Ireland. Today, Kelly and O'Kelly are almost as numerous in Ireland as Murphy, and are to be found throughout the island.

Kennedy

Kennedy in Irish is *Ó Cinnéide*, from a compound word meaning "ugly-headed" or "rough-headed". The original bearer of the name, from whom the family claim descent, was a nephew of Brian Boru. His descendants were one of the most powerful families in the famous *Dál gCais* tribal grouping, who migrated from their homeland near Killaloe in County Clare into adjoining north Tipperary, to become lords of Ormond for over four hundred years up to the

Kelly

Kennedy

16th Century. From there the surname spread further afield, becoming one of the most numerous and widespread in Ireland. In Ulster, many Kennedys are originally of Scottish stock, the MacKennedys being a branch of the Clan Cameron. The surname is now also common in Galloway and Ayrshire. The most famous modern bearer of the name was John F. Kennedy, 35th President of the United States, descended from a Wexford branch of the Dalcassian family.

Lynch

Lynch, which is today one of the most common surnames throughout Ireland, is unusual in that it has two completely distinct origins. The first is Norman, from *de Lench*, possibly derived from a placename now forgotten. The family settled initially in County Meath, and a branch then established itself in Galway, where they rapidly became one of the strongest of the "Tribes of Galway"; one of their number, James Lynch, mayor in 1493, is reputed to have hanged his own son for murder when no one else could be found to carry out the sentence. The second origin for the name is Gaelic, from the Irish *Ó Loingsigh*, from *loingseach* (seaman). This arose quite separately in a number of areas, including Clare/Limerick, Sligo, west Cork, Cavan, Donegal, and the north Antrim/Derry region, where they were chiefs of the old kingdom of *Dál Riada* in medieval times. As the variety

of geographical sources implies, the Gaelic origin is responsible for the wide frequency of the surname today.

Lyons

Lyons is one of the commonest surnames in Ireland, particularly in the three southern provinces. In Ulster especially it may be a variant of the English and Scottish surname Lyon which can derive, as a nickname, from "lion" from the first name Leo or Leon, or from the placename *Lyon-la-Forêt* in Normandy. Elsewhere, however, Lyons is virtually always the Anglicized version of one of two Irish names, *Ó Laighin*, from *laighean* (spear) or *Ó Liatháin*, possibly from *liath* (grey). *Ó Laighin* originated in two areas, in County Kerry and in east County Galway, where the family's territory was centered on Kilconnell. In Kerry, however, the name was almost invariably Anglicized as Lyne. The *Ó Liatháin* family are reputed to have originated in County Limerick, but are now to be found much more frequently in County Cork, particularly in the north of the county, where the village of Castlelyons records their presence.

Moore

Moore is today one of the most common surnames in Ireland, among the top 20. It may be of English, Irish, Welsh, or Scottish origin. In England the name may derive either

from someone who lived near a moor or from a nickname for someone of dark complexion, from "moor" meaning Negro. This is frequently also the ultimate origin of the name in Scotland and Wales, where it is often rendered Muir, although in places it is thought to come from *mór* (big). The Irish origin of Moore is *Ó Mórdha*, also Anglicized O'More, from *mórdha* (stately or noble). The principal family of definite native Irish origin were of County Laois, where they were the leading sept of the famous "Seven Septs of Laois" whose resistance to the English led to the forced resettlement of the most prominent individuals in County Kerry. At this point, it is virtually impossible to say in any single case which of the various origins of the surname is the most accurate.

Murphy

Murphy is the Anglicized version of two Irish surnames, *Ó Murchadha* and *Mac Murchadha*. Both of these names are derived from the popular early Irish personal name *Murchadh* (sea-warrior). *Mac Murchadha* (son of Murchadh) is exclusive to Ulster, where the family were part of the *Cinéal Eoghain*, the tribal grouping claiming descent from Eoghan, himself a son of the 5th-Century founder of the *Uí Néill* dynasty, Niall of the Nine Hostages. In Ulster today, the name Murphy remains most numerous in County Armagh. Elsewhere in Ireland, *Ó Murchadha* (descendant of

Murchadh) is the original Irish. This arose separately in Cork, Roscommon, and Wexford. The most prominent were the Wexford *Uí Murchadha*, who took their surname from Murchadh or Murrough, grandfather of Dermot MacMurrough. Their chief seats were at Morriscastle (O Murchu's Castle), Toberlamina, Oulart, and Oularteigh. In the late 16th Century, *Dónal Mór* O'Morchoe (as the name was then Anglicized) was overthrown, and virtually all his territory confiscated. The branch of the family based at Oularteigh managed to retain their lands.

Murray

Murray is a common surname throughout Ireland, among the 20 most numerous. It can be of Scottish or Irish origin. The Scottish surname, Murray or MacMurray, derives from Moray in the northeast, a name that originally meant "settlement by the sea". The earliest recorded ancestor of this family was one Hugh Freskin, a Flemish settler who obtained large grants of land in Morayshire in 1130; his descendants took their name from his property. Many in Ireland, in Ulster particularly, are of this connection.

In Ireland the surname came from *Ó Muireachaidh* (descendant of the seaman). The most prominent family was based in the south Roscommon/east Galway region, and were part of the *Uí Máine* tribal grouping. As well as these, however, a separate family is recorded in Cork, in the

Murphy

Nolan

barony of Carbery, and *Mac Muireachaidh*, Anglicized as Murray and MacMorrow, is found in County Leitrim and north County Down. In addition *Mac Giolla Mhuire* (son of the servant of Mary), another County Down name, has sometimes been Anglicized as Murray, as well as the more obvious MacIlmurray and Gilmore.

Nolan

Nolan is now among the most common surnames in Ireland. It is the Anglicized form of *Ó Nualláin*, from a diminutive of *nuall* (famous or noble). The family is strongly linked with the area of the modern County Carlow, wherein in pre-Norman times they held power in the barony of Forth, whence their ancient title of Princes of Foharta. Their power was greatly diminished after the arrival of the Normans, but the surname is still strongly linked with the area.

The prevalence of the surname in the modern counties of Mayo and Galway is explained by the migration of a branch of the family to that area in the 16th Century; they obtained large tracts of land, and their descendants are many. The most famous modern bearer of the surname was Brian O'Nolan (1911–66), better known under his two pen-names, Flann O'Brien and Myles gCopaleen, whose genius for comic invention has only been fully appreciated since his death.

Quinn

Quinn is now one of the most numerous of Irish surnames, among the 20 most common, and is to be found throughout the country. The name arose separately in four distinct areas. In three of these, near the modern town of Corofin in County Clare, in the glens of north Antrim, and in County Longford, the Irish original from which the surname derives is *Ó Coinn*, from *Conn*, a popular personal name meaning "chief" or "leader". The most notable of these families is that based in Clare, where the barony of Inchiquin bears their name; in early times they were chiefs of the Clan Heffernan, and their descendants are today earls of Dunraven and Mountearl. The fourth area is Tyrone, where the surname is today the most common in the county. Here the individual from whom descent is claimed was *Coinne*, a great-great-grandson of Niall of the Nine Hostages, the 5th-Century monarch who founded the dynasty of the *Uí Néill*. In the fighting forces of the O'Neills, the *Ó Coinne* were traditionally quartermasters.

Reid

Reid, with its variants Reed and Read(e), is now one of the 100 most common surnames in Ireland. In form it is English, and can derive from a nickname for someone who is red-haired or ruddy (from the Old English *read*), from a name for someone who lived in a clearing in a wood (Old English

Quinn

Reilly

ried), or from the various places in England called Read or similar. No doubt many bearing the name in Ireland are of English stock. In addition, a number of Scots Gaelic surnames—MacRory, *Ruaidh* (red), and MacInroy—were frequently Anglicized Reid, and many Reids in Ulster especially are descended from Scottish settlers. However, there were also two Gaelic families, the *Ó Maoildeirg* (*Mulderrig* meaning "red chieftain") of Mayo and Antrim, and the *Ó Maoilbhríghde* (Mulreedy—"devotee of St. Brigid") of County Roscommon, whose surnames have often been Anglicized to Reid, by semi-translation and abbreviation respectively.

Reilly

Reilly, with its variants Riley and (O')R(e)ily, comes from the Irish *Ó Raghallaigh*, and is extremely common and widespread throughout Ireland. It originated in the old kingdom of *Breifne*, which included areas now in Counties Cavan and Longford, where the O'Reillys were long the dominant family. Their prosperity may be gauged by the fact that "reilly" was at one point a colloquial term for money in Ireland. After the collapse of Gaelic power in the 17th Century, large numbers emigrated to serve in the armies of France, many in Colonel Edmund O'Reilly's regiment of foot. The connection with the original homeland is still strong, however; even today (O')Reilly is the single most

numerous surname in Cavan and Longford.

Rogers

Rogers is one of the most common surnames in Britain and Ireland. Its English origin is simple: it means "son of Roger", a very common personal name made up of two Germanic elements: *hrod* (renown) and *geri* (spear). It is also common in Scotland, where it is frequently spelt Rodgers. Many bearing the name in Ireland are of English and Scottish descent. However, the Gaelic Irish surname *Mac Ruaidhrí*, from the personal name *Ruaidhri* (red king) was also Anglicized as Rogers. Two Mac Ruaidhrí families are notable in early times: one based in County Tyrone, a branch of whom migrated north to County Derry; the other in County Fermanagh, possibly an offshoot of the Maguires. In these areas the surname was also Anglicized MacRory and MacCrory. In addition, many individuals in the 16th and 17th Centuries were identified by the fathers' names. A son of *Ruaidhrí Ó Briain* might, for example, be known as *Mac Ruaidhrí Ó Briain*. In a significant number of cases *Mac Ruaidhri* became an hereditary surname in its own right, instead of *Ó Briain*, and was then Anglicized to Rogers.

Ryan

Ryan is today one of the commonest surnames in Ireland. Unlike many other common surnames, however, it has one

major origin, in the family of *Ó Maoilriaghain* (descendant of a devotee of St. Riaghan). The Anglicization Mulryan began to fade as early as the 17th Century, and is today virtually unknown apart from a few pockets in Counties Galway and Leitrim, possibly derived from a different family. The surname first appears in the 14th Century in the barony of Owney, on the borders of Counties Limerick and Tipperary, where the *Ó Maoilriaghain* displaced the O'Heffernans. Even today the surname is highly concentrated in this area.

Walsh

Walsh is among the five most numerous surnames found all over Ireland with particular concentrations in the province of Connacht. The name is especially common in Counties Mayo and Galway. It is also common in the Munster counties of Cork and Waterford, and in the Leinster counties of Kilkenny and Wexford. The name Walsh is a semi-translation of the Irish surname Breathnach (British or Welsh). It is also sometimes Anglicized as Brannagh. The surname thus has the same origin as Wallace, but arrived at its present form by a more circuitous route. Unlike most Hiberno-Norman families, such as the Burkes and the Fitzgeralds, who can trace their ancestry to a small number of known individuals, the Walshes have many different origins, since the name arose independently in many different places, for obvious reasons. Two exceptions should

Ryan

Walsh

perhaps be mentioned: the descendants of Haylen Brenach, one of those who arrived in 1172, became well known and prosperous in the south and east of the country, while Walynus who arrived in 1169 is said to have been the progenitor of the Walshes of Tirawley in County Mayo, and the brother of Barrett, the ancestor of the Barretts of the same county.

Ward

Ward is common and widespread throughout Ireland, England, and Wales. In Britain it is generally an occupational surname, derived from the Old English *weard* (guard). Some in Ireland may be of English stock as, for example, in the case of the family who now hold the title of Viscount Bangor in County Down. In the vast majority of cases, however, Ward in Ireland is the Anglicization of *Mac an Bháird* (son of the poet or bard). Two families are historically prominent, one based near the modern town of Ballinasloe in County Galway, and the other near Glenties in County Donegal. Both families were professional hereditary poets, as their surname implies, to the O'Kellys and the O'Donnells respectively. A branch of the northern family also became poets to the O'Neills in County Tyrone. Today the largest single concentrations of the surname are to be found in the original homelands, Galway and Donegal.

Whelan

Whelan, along with its common variant Phelan, comes from the Irish *Ó Faoláin*, from a diminutive of *faol* (wolf). Taken together, the two names come among the 50 most numerous in Ireland. The family originated in the ancient kingdom of Decies, part of the modern county of Waterford, where they were rulers up to the Norman invasion. From this center the surname has now spread to the adjoining counties of Kilkenny, Cork, Wexford and, further north to Carlow. But it is also to be found throughout the country.

White

White is one of the most common surnames in England, Wales, Scotland, and Ireland. In England its most common origin is as a descriptive nickname for someone who was fair-haired or pale, and a sizable proportion of those bearing the name in Ireland will be of English extraction; such families were prominent in Counties Clare, Waterford, and Kilkenny. In some cases, as families were absorbed by Gaelic culture, White was phonetically Hibernicized *Mac Faoite*. After the final collapse of the Gaelic order in the 17th Century this was re-Anglicized as MacWhitty and MacQuitty, as well as the original White. In the north of Ireland, many Whites are of Scottish extraction. The surname was a semi-translation of the Highland Gaelic *Mac*

Gille Bháin (son of the fair-haired servant or youth), and was also adopted by many of the MacGregors and Lamonts when they were outlawed and their own names proscribed. Elsewhere in Ireland White was sometimes used locally for many Irish originals containing, or thought to contain, the elements *bán* (white) or *fionn* (fair).

ABOVE: *A view of Skellig Michael from Little Skellig off the coast of County Kerry. The name Michael or Mícheál is one of the top 100 boys' names today. One famous Irish Michael is the celebrated football manager Mick McCarthy.*

IRISH FIRST NAMES

◆ ◆ ◆

First names in Ireland have a variety of origins. Here you will find some of these names, how to pronounce them, alternative spellings, and the English equivalent. The meaning behind many of these names is explained, and also the places or historical figures connected with them.

◆ ◆ ◆

Aengus (m)

(AYN-gus). An alternative spelling is *Aonghus*. The name means "one choice". The English spelling is Angus.

Aidan (m)

(AY-dan). Alternative spellings include *Aodán, Aodh, Aodhán*, and *Aodhagán*. The name means "fire". The English spelling is Hugh.

Aideen (f)

(AY-deen). Alternative spellings include *Eadaoin*, and *Aedín*. *Eadaoin* was the goddess of beauty.

Áine (f)

(AWN-ya). The name means "joy" or "praise". Áine was said

to be the queen of the South Munster fairies, living at Knockany.

Brendan (m)
(BREN-dan). An alternative spelling is *Breandán*.

Brian (m)
(BRY-an). An alternative spelling is *Briain*. The name means "noble" or "strong". Brian Boru, King of Ireland, was slain after his victory at the Battle of Clontarf in 1014.

Briana (f)
(BREE-ana). Alternative spellings include *Brianagh*, *Breena*, and *Brianne*. This name is the female form of Brian. The English spelling is Briony.

Bríd (f)
(BREED). An alternative spelling is *Bríghid*. The name means "strength". St. Bríd/Brighid is one of Ireland's patron saints. The English spelling is Brigid.

Bridie (f)
(BRY-dee). The name means "strength". It comes from *Bríd*.

Bronagh (f)
(BRO-na). An alternative spelling is *Brona*. The name

means "sorrow".

Caelan (f)
(KEE-lin). Alternative spellings include *Caoilfhionn*, Keelin, and *Caoilin*. The name means "slender and fair".

Cáit (f)
(Coyt). The name means "pure" in Greek. The English spelling is Kate.

Cáitlín (f)
(Coyt-leen). The name means "pure" in Greek. The English spelling is Kathleen.

Caitríona (f)
(Cat-REE-ona). Alternative spellings include Catríona, and Caitrín. The name means "pure" in Greek. The English spelling is Catherine.

Cara (f)
(CAR-a). An alternative spelling is Caragh. The name means "friend".

Cathal (m)
(CA-hal). An alternative spelling is Cahal. The name means "battle-mighty". The English spelling is Charles. St. Cathal

was born in Munster and was noted for his great learning. He became Bishop of Taranto, Italy.

Ciara (f)
(KEAR-a). An alternative spelling is Kyra. St. Ciara, who was born in County Tipperary, was the founder and abbess of the monasteries at Kilkeary, and Tehelly.

Clíona (f)
(CLEE-ona). An alternative spelling is Clíodhna. According to the legend *Tonn Cliona* (Cliona's Wave), a girl called Clíona drowned off the coast of Cork while attempting to escape from her father's wrath with her beloved.

Clodagh (f)
(Clo-da). This name is likely to have originated from the River Clóideach in County Tipperary. In recent years it has been used as a first name.

Coileán (m)
(Col-AUN). An alternative spelling is *Cuileán*. This is an old Irish name meaning "youth" or "young hound". The English spelling is Colin.

Conor (m)
(CON-or). Alternative spellings include *Conchobhar* and

Connor. The name means "high will" or "desire". The English spelling is Cornelius.

Cormac (m)
(COR-mac). The name means "charioteer" or alternatively "son of the raven". St. Cormac was a king of Munster. He was probably also the first Bishop of Cashel. He was killed in battle in A.D. 908.

Críosa (f)
(KREE-osa). An alternative spelling is Christian. The English spelling is Christina.

Críostóir (m)
(CREE-store). The name means "Christ-bearing" in Greek. The English spelling is Christopher.

Dara (f) (m)
(DA-RA). The name means "oak tree".

Dearbhla (f)
(DERV-la). Alternative spellings include Derval, *Deirbhle*, and Dervla. The name means "true desire".

Deirdre (f)
(Deir-drey). A name of uncertain meaning, perhaps signifying

"fear", or perhaps "broken-hearted one".

Dermot (m)
(DER-mot). Alternative spellings include *Diarmuid*, and *Dermod*. The name means "freeman". The English spelling is Jeremiah.

Desmond (m)
(DES-mund). Alternative spellings include *Deasmhumhan*, *Deasún*, and Des. The name means a "native of south Munster".

Dónal (m)
(DOUGH-nal). An alternative spelling is *Domhnall*. The name means "mighty in the deep". The English spelling is Daniel.

Eamon (m)
(EY-mon). An alternative spelling of Éamonn. The English spelling is Edmund.

Eibhlín (f)
(Ev-LEEN). The name means 'fair'. The English spelling is Evelyn.

Eileen (f)
(EYE-leen). Alternative spellings include *Eibhlín* and *Eilín*. The

name means "sunlight" in Greek. The English spellings are Helen or Elene.

Eilís (f)
(EYE-leesh, AY-lish). Alternative spellings include Ailish, and Eilish. The name means "God has sworn" in Greek. The English spelling is Elizabeth.

Eimear (f)
(Eem-er). An alternative spelling is Emer and *Eimear*. Emer, the wife of legendary super-warrior Cuchulainn, possessed all six gifts of womanhood. These are beauty, chastity, a soft voice, clear speech, skill with a needle, and wisdom.

Enda (f) (m)
(EN-ya). An alternative spelling of Eanna.

Eoghan (m)
(OWE-an). An alternative spelling is Owen. The name means "well born". The English spelling is Eugene.

Felim (m)
(FEE-lim). Alternative spellings include Phelim and *Feidhlim*. The name means "ever good". The English spelling is Philip.

Fergal (m)
(FUR-gal). An alternative name is *Fearghal*. The name means "bright man" or "manly".

Fergus (m)
(FER-gus). An alternative spelling is *Fearghus*. The name means "strong".

Fiachra (m)
(FEE-a-cra). This is the name of eight Irish saints.

Finbar (m)
(FIN-bar). An alternative spelling is *Fionnbar*. The name means "fair head". The English spelling is Barry.

Finian (m)
(FIN-ee-an). An alternative spelling is *Finghín*, Finan, Finn, Finnian, and Fintan. The name means "fair birth". The English spelling is Finlay.

Fionnabhair (f)
(FIN-a-vair). The name means "fair". The English spelling is Jennifer.

Fionnuala (f)
(Fin-NOO-la). An alternative spelling is Finola. The name

means "fair shoulder".

Flann (m)
(Flan). An alternative spelling is *Floinn*. The name means "Ruddy". This was the name of a 9th-Century king of Tara.

Gearóid (m)
(GA-road). An alternative spelling is Garrett. The name means "spear-mighty". The English spelling is Gareth or alternatively Gerard.

Gráinne (f)
(GRAW-nya). The name means "love". The English spelling is Grace.

Hugh (m)
(Hyoo). An alternative spelling is *Aodh*. The name means "fire".

Iarla (m)
(EAR-la). An alternative spelling is *Iarfhlaith*. St. Iarla is the patron saint of Tuam. The English spelling is Jarlath.

Kevin (m)
(Kev-in). An alternative spelling is *Caoimhín*. The name means "comely birth".

Kieran (m)
(KEAR-an). An alternative spelling is *Ciarán*. The name means "black".

Killian (m)
(KIL-ee-an). Alternative spellings include *Cillín*, *Cillian*, and *Ceallach*. The name means "war" or "strife".

Laoise (f)
(LEE-sha). An alternative spellings is *Labhaoise*. The English spelling is Louise.

Liam (m)
(LEE-am). The name means "protection". The English spelling is William.

Lorcan (m)
(LOR-can). An alternative spelling is *Lorcán*. The name means "fierce". The English spelling is Laurence.

Maeve (f)
(MAYV). Alternative spellings include *Meadhbh*, and *Medbh*. Queen Maeve of Connacht is featured in several Irish legends.

Máire (f)
(MAW-ra). Alternative spellings include Moira or Maura. The

name means "bitter" in Hebrew. The English spelling is Mary.

Mairéad (f)
(Ma-RAYD). An alternative spelling is *Maighréad.* The name means "pearl" in Greek. The English spelling is Margaret.

Malachy (m)
(MAL-a-key). An alternative spelling is *Maolseachlann.* St. Malachy was a disciple of St. Patrick. The English spelling is Malachi.

Manus (m)
(MAN-us). An alternative spelling is *Maghnus.* The name means "great" in Latin. Manus is a Roman name introduced to Ireland by the Vikings.

Mícheál (m)
(MEE-haul). The name means "who is like God" from the Hebrew. The English spelling is Michael. St. Michael is the guardian of the Christian at the hour of death.

Milo (m)
(MILE-oh). Alternative spellings include *Maolmórdha*, Miles, and Myles. The name means "majestic chief".

Molly (f)

Alternative spellings include *Máille* and *Mallaidh*. This is the pet form of *Máire*. The English spelling is Mary.

Muiris (m)

(MAN-ee). The name is short for Maurice or Morris. The name is of Moorish descent. The English spelling is Maurice.

Niall (m)

(NEE-al, NY-al). Alternative spellings include Neill and Neil. It is an ancient Ulster name. Niall Noigíallach was a High King of Ireland in the 5th Century.

Niamh (f)

(NEE-uv, NEEV). The name means "bright" or "lustrous". According to legend Niamh was the daughter of the lord of Tír na nÓg (Land of youth).

Noreen (f)

(KNOWR-een). Alternative spelling is *Noirín*. The name means "honorable" in Latin. The English spelling is Nora.

Nuala (f)

(NOO-la). The name means "fair shoulder". It is a

diminutive spelling of the name is Fionnuala.

Orla (f)
Alternative spellings include *Orlaith* and *Orfhlaith*. The name means "golden lady".

Owen (m)
(OWE-in). Alternative names include *Eoin* and *Eoghan*. The name means "gracious gift of God" (Hebrew). The English spellings are John, and Eugene.

Pádraig (m)
(PAW-drig). An alternative spelling is Pádraic. The name means "noble" in Latin. The English spelling is Patrick.

Pádraigín (f)
(PAWD-rig-een). The name means "noble" in Latin. It is the female version of Pádraig.

Peadar (m)
(PAD-er). The English spelling is Peter.

Pearse (m)
(PEERS). Alternative spellings include *Piarais* and Pierce. The name means "rock" in Latin. The English spelling is Peter.

Róisín (f)
(RO-sheen). An alternative spelling is Rosaleen. The English spelling is Rose.

Ronan (m)
(ROW-nan). An alternative spelling is *Rónán*. The name means "seal" in Irish. There is a St. Ronan or Rumon who lived in the 6th Century.

Rory (m)
(ROAR-ee). Alternative spellings include *Ruairí* and *Ruaidhrigh*. The name means "red" in Irish. The English spellings are Roger, or Roderick.

Saibh (f)
(SIVE). Alternative spellings include *Saidhbh* and Sive. The name means "goodness". The English spelling is Sonya.

Saoirse (f) (m)
(Sear-sh). The name means "freedom" in Irish. This has been a popular name since Irish independence in the 20th Century.

Séamus (m)
(SHAY-mus). The English spelling is James.

Seán (m)
(SHAWN). The English spelling is John.

Seosaimhín (f)
(SHOW-siv-een). The name means "God shall add" in Hebrew. The English spelling is Josephine.

Shauna (f)
(Shawna). The female form of *Seán*, meaning "Gracious gift of God" in Hebrew.

Síle (f)
(SHEE-la). Alternative spellings include Sheila and Sheelagh. The name means "blind" in Latin. The English spellings are Cecilia, and Julia.

Sinéad (f)
(Shin-AYD). It is an alternative version of the name Shauna. The English spelling is Jane.

Siobhán (f)
(Shi-VAWN). The English spelling is Joan.

Siún (f)
(SHOON). The English spelling is Joan.

LEFT: *This ancient document, known as the Rawlinson B502 manuscript, is the oldest Irish resource containing genealogical material, in this case about the Kings of Leinster. Such documents reveal that many Irish first names have been passed down through the generations and are still in use in the 21st Century.*

Sorcha (f)
(SOR-a-cha). The name means "clear" or "bright". The English spelling is Sarah.

Tadgh (m)
(TY-g). Alternative spellings include *Taidgh*, Teige, and Tad. The name means "poet" or "philosopher" in Irish. Blessed Tadhg MacCarthy was made Bishop of Ross in 1482 and was then appointed by Rome to the diocese of Cork and Cloyne, but was prevented from taking up his appointment by powerful local families.

Treasa (f)
(TRA-sa). The name means "strength". The English spelling is Theresa.

Una (f)
(OO-na). Alternative spellings include Oona, Oonagh, and Unagh. The English spelling is Winifred.

THE IRISH LANGUAGE

Irish is the first official language of Ireland. Today Irish is enjoying a revival and there is a growing movement to promote this ancient language.

There are two official languages in Ireland. Irish is the national language, and English which is the language of the majority of the population. Irish is a Celtic language and, as such, is a member of the Indo-European family of languages.

The Irish language has evolved from a form of Celtic which was introduced into the country at some period during the great Celtic migrations of antiquity between the end of the second millennium and the 4th century B.C. Old Irish, the country's vernacular when the historical period begins in the 6th Century A.D., is the earliest variant of the Celtic languages.

Written literature in Old Irish dates from the 6th Century A.D. Heroic sagas depicting the deeds of mythical warriors, along with lyrical and conventional poetry, survive from that time.

LEFT: *Killary Harbor and the Mweelrea Mountains in County Galway. This is part of the Irish-speaking or Gaeltacht area of the west.*

New forms of language developed with the Viking and Norman arrivals during the 12th Century. Irish, however, remained dominant. The main towns prescribed English for the formal conduct of administrative and legal business. The early modern period (1250–1650) produced bardic verse and prose, but the literary language was then displaced by the vernacular form, which gave rise to an extensive, popular, poetic literature.

The events of the later 16th and 17th Centuries for the first time undermined the status of Irish as a major language. They had the cumulative effect of eliminating the Irish-speaking ruling classes and destroying their cultural institutions. They were replaced by a new ruling class, or Ascendancy, whose language was English. Irish continued as the language of the greater part of the rural population.

From the mid-1700s the more prosperous of the Irish-speaking community began to conform to the prevailing middle-class ethos by adopting English. Irish thus began to be associated with poverty and economic deprivation.

Revival

Towards the end of the 1700s the Anglo-Irish Ascendancy began to develop an academic interest in the Irish language and its literature. Academic interest later merged with a concern for the survival of spoken Irish as its decline became increasingly evident.

Language-related activity grew throughout the 1800s and, following the establishment of the Gaelic League, there was a move to maintain and extend the use of Irish as a vernacular. This fused with the renewed separatist movement which culminated in the establishment of the Irish Free State.

Numbers of Irish Speakers

The rapid growth of the rural population meant that the actual number of Irish speakers increased substantially. In 1835 their number was estimated at four million. This impoverished rural population was decimated by the Famine (1845–48) and by the resultant mass emigration. By 1891, the number of Irish speakers had been reduced to 680,000. When the position began to stabilize early in the 20th Century, Irish remained as a community language only in small peripheral regions.

The Gaeltacht

Irish is the principal language in areas known as the *Gaeltacht*, situated mainly along the western seaboard. These Irish-speaking pockets are found in various localities within several counties. About 86,000 people live in the *Gaeltacht* and around 70 per cent are *Gaeilgeóirí* (speakers of Irish). It is considered the last bastion where Irish is spoken as a community language.

The Galway (or Connemara) *Gaeltacht* extends from the west of the city of Galway to the Aran Islands. This is the largest *Gaeltacht*. The Donegal *Gaeltacht* is found in the northwest of the country. The Kerry *Gaeltacht* is situated at the western extremity of the Dingle Peninsula and the Cork *Gaeltacht* is situated inland in the Muskerry area. The smallest *Gaeltachtaí* are in Counties Mayo, Waterford, and Meath. The latter was purposely created in the mid-1930s from poor people from the depressed coastal *Gaeltachtaí*.

Today Irish speakers across the island are drawn to the *Gaeltacht*. Visitors will find these often remote areas have stunning scenery as well as a unique cultural heritage.

Údarás na Gaeltachta, a state body, promotes industrial development in these areas. *Bord na Gaeilige* (the Irish Language Board), also a state agency, promotes the use of Irish throughout the country and as a core school subject. *Radio na Gaeltachta* and the television service *Telifís na Gaeilige* broadcast nationally in Irish.

The number of Irish speakers, however, is a decreasing proportion of the total because, for a variety of complex reasons, some of the population of the *Gaeltacht* continue to shift to English, and because new English-speaking households are settling there.

There has, however, been an increasing interest in the Irish language throughout the rest of the country, particularly in Dublin. The latest figures available (1996

Census) show that 43 per cent of adults claim to be able to speak some Irish.

Literature

Over 100 new titles in the Irish language are published each year. Writers in Irish from the modern period include Patrick Pearse (1879–1916) and *Pádraic O'Conaire* (1883–1928), who helped open Irish literature to European influences after centuries of isolation. They were followed by a number of talented authors and poets such as *Seán Ó Ríordáin* (1916–77), *Máirtín Ó Díreáin* (1910–88), *Máire Mhac an tSaoi* (1922–), *Liam Ó Flaitheartaigh* (1897–1984), *Seosamh Mac Grianna* (1901–90), *Máirtín Ó Cadhain*, and Brendan Behan (1923–64). Today there are figures such as *Nuala Ní Dhómhnaill* (1952–), *Micheál Ó Siadhail* (1947–), and *Liam Ó Muirthile* (1950–). A number of these writers have also produced acclaimed works in English.

ABOVE: *It is still common to hear Irish being spoken in the rural areas around the town of Letterkenny in County Donegal.*

Simple Irish Phrases

Irish is not only spoken in the Gaeltacht region but across the island. There are even Irish-speaking restaurants, bars, and social events where the language is used.

Irish has three main dialects. These are from Connacht (Galway and north Mayo), Munster (Cork, Kerry, and Waterford) and Ulster (Derry). The following pronunciation guidelines are in an Anglicized form of modern Irish.

Irish divides vowels into long (which have an accent) and short (without an accent). More importantly they are either broad or slender. This can affect the way preceding consonants are pronounced.

a – as in bat
á – as in claw
e – as in yet
i – as in hit
í – as the ee in three
o – as in son
ó – as in bow
u – as in the oo in look
ú – as in mule

Consonants are normally less difficult than vowels for beginners in the language. Most of them are pronounced as they would be in English.

bh –	as the v in voice
bhf –	as the w in well
c –	always hard, as in cat
ch –	as the ch in loch
d –	as in do when followed by a broad vowel, as the ju in jug when followed by a slender vowel.
dh –	as in the g in gap when followed by a broad vowel, as the y in year when followed by a slender vowel
mh –	as the w in well
s –	as in said when before a broad vowel, as the sh in shift when before a slender vowel, and at the end of a word
t –	as the t in toast when before a broad vowel, as the ch in church before a slender vowel
th –	as the h in house, as the t in sat or silent at the end of a word

The following is a list of basic words and phrases that are ideal for those beginning to learn the Irish language. They are presented in a system to help memorize the words in question.

Greetings, Introductions, and Civilities

English	*Irish*	*Pronunciation*
Hello	Dia Dhuit	dee a gwit
Good morning	Maidin mhaith	maw jin wah
Goodbye	Slán	slawn
Good night	Oíche mhaith	eeha wah
Please	Le do thoil	le du hull
Thank you	Go raibh maith agat	goh rev meeleh maw agut
You're welcome	Tá fáilte romhat	taw fawl-ta rowit
Excuse me	Gabh mo leithscéal	gawvh mu lash kayl
Yes/It is	Tá/Sea	taw/sheh
No/It is not	Níl/Ní	neel/nee heh
How are you?	Conas tá tú?	kunas taw too?
(I'm) fine	(Tá mé) go maith	(taw may) go maith
Irish (language)	Gaelige	gwayle guh
Irish (person etc.)	Éireannach	ayrah nuk
English	Béarla	bare lah
Ireland	Éire	ayrah

Questions and Responses

English	*Irish*	*Pronunciation*
Do you speak Irish?	An bhfuil Gaelige agat?	on will gwayle-guh a gut?

Speak in Irish to me!	Labhair as Gaelige dom!	lawur oss gwayle-guh dum!
I don't understand	Ní thuigim	nee higgin
Why?	Cén fáth?	kane faw?
How much/many?	Cé mhéad?	kay vade?
What's your name?	Cad is ainm duit?	kod is anim dwitt?
My name is (Sam)	(Sam) is ainm dohm	(Sam) is anim dom
Where is...?	Cá bhfuil ...?	kaw will...?

Out and About

English	*Irish*	*Pronunciation*
town center	an lár	an lawr
city	cathair	kawher
street	sráid	shrawd
shop	siopa	shoppa
bank	banc	bonk
post office	oifig an phoist	iffig on fwisht
toilet	leithreas	lehrass
men	fir	fear
women	mná	m'naw
telephone	telefón/teileafón	taylayfon
hotel	óstán	oh stahn
bed and breakfast	lóistín oíche	leestin eek heh

Numbers

English	*Irish*	*Pronunciation*
1	haon	hayin
2	dó	doe
3	trí	tree
4	ceathaír	kahirr
5	cúig	koo ig
6	sé	shay
7	seacht	shocked
8	hocht	hukt
9	naoi	nay
10	deich	jeh
11	haon déag	hayin jague
12	dó dhéag	doe yague
20	fiche	fiha
21	fiche a haon	fiha un hayin
30	tríocha	tree okha
40	daichead	day khayd
50	caoga	kowga
60	seasca	shaska
70	seachtó	shocked-ow
80	ochtó	ukth-ow
90	nócha	nokha
100	céad	kade
1,000	míle	meeleh

Time

English	*Irish*	*Pronunciation*
What time is it?	Cén tam é?	kane tawm ay?
5 o'clock	cúig a chlog	koo ig ah klug
today	inniu	in you
tomorrow	amárach	amawrok
hour	uair	oor
minute	nóiméid	nomade
week	seachtain	shocktin
month	mí	mee

Days of the Week

English	*Irish*	*Pronunciation*
Sunday	Dé Domhnaigh	day downick
Monday	Dé Luaín	day loon
Tuesday	Dé Máirt	day mawrt
Wednesday	Dé Ceádaoin	day kaydeen
Thursday	Déardaoin	daredeen
Friday	Dé hAoine	day heeneh
Saturday	Dé Sathairn	day sahern

Months of the Year

English	*Irish*	*Pronunciation*
January	Eanáir	anir
February	Feabhra	fiow ra

March	Márta	mawrta
April	Aibreán	ebb rawn
May	Bealtaine	bywoltana
June	Meitheamh	me hiv
July	Iúil	lool
August	Lúnasa	loonassa
September	Meán Fómhair	mian fore
October	Deireadh Fómhair	derra fore
November	Samhain	sowin
December	Nollaig	null ig

LITERARY IRELAND

◆ ◆ ◆

Ireland has a rich literary tradition dating back to the oral tradition of pre-Celtic times.

◆ ◆ ◆

Irish literature dates to the pre-Celtic peoples inhabiting the area now known as Ireland. The earliest known written form of Irish is Ogham. This is a stick-like script dating mainly from the 5th to 6th Centuries. Examples of Ogham writing can still be seen on ancient stones throughout the Irish countryside. The predominant format for writing in Irish, however, has been an uncial-style script, although the English alphabet is now used interchangably.

In the pre-Celtic period, the two groups who contributed most to the stability of society were the *breitheamh* (judges) and the filí (poets). Through their oral and written traditions, they formed and preserved a body of knowledge and thought from as early as the 1st Century B.C.

Amongst the earliest literature are two heroic cycles of legend. The Ulster, or Red Branch Cycle centers around Conor Mac Nessa, the king of *Uladh*, and his chief warrior

LEFT: *Marsh's Library, Dublin, is the oldest public library in Ireland.*

Cuchulainn. The central story to this cycle is the *Táin Bó Cuailgne* (*The Cattle Raid of Cooley*).

The earliest surviving Irish poems are anonymous nature poems written in the 8th Century. Between the 9th and 17th Centuries, a patronage system supported classical or bardic poetry, the most prevalent form of literature. The *filí* were not only poets but orators of traditional tales, recorders of genealogies, and composers. The next major group responsible for preserving Ireland's poetry, laws, and stories were the monks. They recorded the earlier oral histories and verse.

The language of the ordinary people, and their poetry and stories, was Irish. English, under the Norman Ascendancy, was spoken in a limited area extending outside Dublin known as the Pale. Gradually the bards and the poets gave way to the Anglo-Irish conquerors.

17th-Century Literature

In the 17th Century advances in writing from Ireland were made both through fictional and political avenues. Jonathan Swift (1667–1745), Dean of St. Patrick's Cathedral in Dublin, addressed issues of political concern to the Protestant Ascendancy in Ireland through a number of satirical pieces. A contemporary of Swift, Sir Richard Steele (1672–1729) was best known for publishing journals including *Tatler* and the *Spectator*. George Farquhar

(1677–1707) used rural realism to replace the more artificial comedy of earlier plays. Other writers of the period include Oliver Goldsmith (1728–74), Edmund Burke (1729–97), and Richard Sheridan (1751–1816). The audience for these writers was limited by the fact that most people in Ireland spoke Irish. With that in mind, these writers targeted their efforts to the Protestant Ascendancy in Ireland, or audiences in England.

Anglo-Irish Writers

In the 19th Century, as a result of various policies and out of economic necessity, English was spreading rapidly in Ireland. By 1840 the majority of the Irish population read and spoke English.

This situation created a wider audience for literature written in English and a new writing style emerged. Written in English by Irish writers, this writing is referred to as Anglo-Irish literature. In its earliest years, fiction emerged as the main strength of its writers. They included Maria Edgeworth (1767–1849), Lady Morgan (1776–1859) and Thomas Moore (1779–1852). William Carleton (1794–1869) was the first Irish-based writer to support himself with his writing for the better part of his life.

Two brothers from Kilkenny, Michael (1796–1874) and John Banim (1798–1842) paired up to write a series of Irish stories, *Tales by the O'Hara Family* (1825). John also wrote

ABOVE: *The imposing Old Library in Trinity College, Dublin, was built in 1712. Its many precious works include the Book of Kells.*

the long poem *The Celt's Paradise* (1821). Portraits and mementoes of the brothers are on display at the Rothe House Museum in Kilkenny.

George Moore's (1852–1933) *The Untilled Field* (1903) remains a popular reflection of Irish life during the period. Standish O'Grady (1846–1928) uncovered a rich body of history and mythology in his research into the country's heroic past at the Royal Irish Academy. He put that information together in two volumes of the *History of Ireland* (1878 and 1880).

The first half of the 19th Century included the famines of 1840 and 1847 which led to mass emigration and subsequent political weakening. This condition continued until the rise of political movements such as Home Rule and the creation of the Land League resulted in the first mass-organization of the Irish people. An interest in restoring Irish as the national language accompanied some of these movements, and the Gaelic League was founded in 1893.

The Irish Literary Revival

One emerging poet of the time, William Butler Yeats (1865–1939), had visions of creating a new image for Ireland which would escape sectarian and political limitations. He was the catalyst behind the Irish Literary Revival (1880–1916). He founded the Irish Literary Society

in 1891, serving as a mentor to potential writers, and helped create one of the strongest periods of Irish writing. For the first time authors were writing mostly on Irish themes using the tradition of the past to inform their styles. The term "Celtic" took on the connotations of the ethereal and mysterious. The area of his childhood home in Sligo has become known as the "Yeats Country" and visitors today can view the places that inspired him.

Lady Gregory (1852–1932) translated and compiled the basic and lesser stories of the heroic cycles in *Cuchulain of Muirthemne* (1902) and *Of Gods of Fighting Men* (1904). Yeats and Lady Gregory were the leading forces behind the establishment of Dublin's Abbey Theater, which would later become the Irish National Theater. It was the first truly Irish forum for dramatic literature.

John Millington Synge (1871–1909) is viewed as the premier Irish playwright of the national theatre. Oscar Wilde (1854–1900) and George Bernard Shaw (1856–1950) are also celebrated Irish-born writers, though both resided and worked in England in their adult years. In his time, Wilde was the most popular playwright in London. James Joyce (1882–1941) wrote one of the most important 20th-Century novels in English.

The End of the Literary Revival

The writers of the next generation shifted their focus in

line with the political climate of the time. Following independence, these writers addressed issues of identity arising from this era. They had real insight into the Irish people and the conditions they faced. They included Daniel Corkery (1878–1964), Seán O'Faolain (1900–91), Frank O'Connor (1903–66), Liam O'Flaherty (1896–1984), and Patrick Kavanagh (1904–67).

Kate O'Brien (1897–1974) considered the struggle of Irish women, while Belfast-born C.S. Lewis (1898–1963) wrote *Chronicles of Narnia* (1950), a series of acclaimed children's books. Samuel Beckett (1906–89), writing in French and English, won international acclaim. Edward O'Brien (1880–1952) won fame for his books on the sea.

In the 1960s, a generation of poets, such as John Montague (1929–) and Thomas Kinsella (1928–), established themselves with their creative responses to Irish questions of identity and individuality. Eavan Boland (1944–) is generally esteemed for her sharp observations on daily life in modern Ireland. Seamus Heaney (1939–) won the Nobel prize for his poetry in 1995.

Other figures in this "literary renaissance" include Edna O'Brien (1932–), Hugo Hamilton (1953–), Dermot Healy (1947–), Roddy Doyle (1958–), Patrick McCabe (1955–), Paul Muldoon (1951–), Brendan Kennelly (1936–), and Maeve Binchy (1940–). Their talents continue to be recognized at home and internationally.

ABOVE: *Dublin's Palace Bar was popular with writers and poets, such as Patrick Kavanagh, in the early 1900's. The many photographs in the bar immortalize an illustrious past.*

AUTHORS AND POETS

The Irish writer holds a special spot in the soul of Ireland, sometimes shaping its character by scripting the course of her actions and sometimes characterizing her features by recording her political and social developments.

John Banim (1798–1842)
Author. With his brother Michael he conceived the idea of a series of national tales and wrote the first, *Crohoore of the Billhook* in1825.

Michael Banim (1796–1874)
Novelist, playwright, and poet. In 1822 he suggested to his brother John that they write a series of novels. The *O'Hara Tales* became their most famous work. Michael wrote about 13 out of their 24 works.

Samuel Beckett (1906–89)
Novelist, poet, playwright, and winner of the Nobel prize for Literature. He is regarded as one of the most influential avant-garde writers. His first novel, *Dream of Fair to Middling*, written in 1932, was not published until 1992. His trilogy *Molloy, Malone Dies*, and *The Unnamable*, completed in 1950,

is now considered a major work. His other acclaimed works include *Waiting for Godot* (1957), *Endgame* (1957), and *Krapp's Last Tape* (1958).

Maeve Binchy (1940–)
Journalist and author. She was appointed women's editor of *The Irish Times* in 1968, and was also a popular columnist. Her first collection of short stories, *Central Line* (1977) was followed by two more. Her novels include *Circle of Friends* (1990), which was made into a film starring Minnie Driver.

Eavan Boland (1944–)
Poet, lecturer, and broadcaster on literary subjects. Her poetry collections include *New Territory* (1967), *In Her Own Image* (1980), and *Object Lessons* (1995). She won a Macaulay fellowship for poetry in 1968.

William Carleton (1794–1869)
Novelist. His works provide a fascinating insight into rural Ireland in the 19th Century. His works include *Traits and Stories of the Irish Peasantry* (1830), *Fardorougha the Miser* (1839) and *The Black Prophet* (1847).

Daniel Corkery (1878–1964)
Writer and teacher. His works revealed the riches of Irish poetry from the 1700s back through to ancient times. His

works include the play *The Labour Leader* (1919), the short story collection *The Hounds of Banba* (1920), and the book *The Hidden Ireland* (1924).

Roddy Doyle (1958–)

Novelist. He originally wrote satirical plays for Dublin's Passion Machine Theater Company. His popular novels include *The Commitments* (1987) and *Paddy Clarke Ha Ha Ha*, for which he won the 1993 Booker prize. He has also written scripts for films based on his works.

Maria Edgeworth (1767–1849)

Novelist. Her first novel, *Castle Rackrent* (1800) broke new ground in reporting the speech and customs of the Irish characters with almost documentary accuracy. Her other works include *The Absentee* (1809) and *Ormond* (1817).

George Farquhar (1678–1707)

Dramatist. He produced a series of highly successful comedies in London. His play *The Recruiting Officer* is based on his experiences as a lieutenant in England.

Oliver Goldsmith (1728–74)

Author, poet, and dramatist. He became known in London literary circles after publishing *The Citizens for the World* (1762). His verse, such as *The Deserted Village* (1770), is

highly acclaimed, and he achieved great success on the stage with *She Stoops to Conquer* (1773).

Lady Augusta Gregory (1852–1932)
Playwright. She devoted herself to the foundation of the Irish Literary Theater and Abbey Theater. She published versions of the old heroic sagas and was a gifted dramatist.

Hugo Hamilton (1953–)
Novelist and short-story writer. Hamilton was born in Germany but grew up in Ireland. He has traveled widely abroad. Many of his works are set in Germany. His novels include *Surrogate City* (1990) and *Headbanger* (1996).

Seamus Heaney (1939–)
Poet, essayist, and translator. He was awarded the Nobel prize for Literature in 1995. He has received most of the British and Irish literary awards, including the Whitbread Book of the Year twice for *Spirit Level* (1996) and his reworking of the Anglo-Saxon tale *Beowulf* (2000). He is regarded as one of the greatest poets from the British Isles during the second half of the 20th Century.

James Joyce (1882–1941)
Poet, novelist, and playwright. James Joyce first published a series of short stories, *Dubliners* (1914), and then achieved

PREVIOUS PAGE: *James Joyce, the 20th-Century literary genius who challenged readers with his experimental literary style.*

success with *Portrait of the Artist as a Young Man* (1916). His masterpiece, *Ulysses* (1922), was written using the "stream of consciousness" technique. It baffled readers and revolutionized 20th-Century fiction. He is one of the most significant Irish writers of the 20th Century.

ABOVE: *A tribute in a Dublin pub to Joyce's Ulysses that recounts the hour-by-hour events of one day in Dublin—June 16, 1904.*

Patrick Kavanagh (1904–67)

Poet. In 1938 he published his first collection, *Ploughman and Other Poems*. His verse was formed to a large extent by his experiences in his native Monaghan and later in his

adopted Dublin. His *Collected Poems* (1964) confirmed his full stature as one of Ireland's leading poets.

Brendan Kennelly (1936–)
Poet, dramatist, and novelist. His poetry includes *My Dark Fathers* (1964), *Good Souls to Survive* (1967), and *Dream of a Black Fox* (1968). He is a popular national figure.

Thomas Kinsella (1928–)
Poet and translator. He is one of Ireland's most stimulating poets to emerge in the 1950s. His acclaimed translations from early Irish include *The Táin* (1969). He has also written *Madonna* and *Open Court* (1993).

Clive Staples (C.S.) Lewis (1898–1963)
Novelist and critic. Lewis was born in Belfast but lived most of his life in England. He won great acclaim for his literary criticism, allegorical fantasy, and religious works. His series of children's books known as *The Chronicles of Narnia*, include *The Lion, the Witch, and the Wardrobe* (1950).

Patrick McCabe (1955–)
Novelist and short-story writer. After receiving the Hennessy award for a short story in 1979, he published his first novel, *Music on Clinton Street* (1986). The acclaimed *Butcher Boy* (1992) was made into a film in 1996.

John Montague (1929–)
Poet. He worked for *The Irish Times* in Paris (1961–64) and has lectured in the United States and Ireland. His work mostly deals with exile. His publications include *Poisoned Lands* (1961 and 1978) and *The Great Cloak* (1978).

George Moore (1852–1933)
Novelist. Moore's novel *Esther Waters* (1894) established his reputation as an author. He published more than a dozen books, including *The Brook Kerith* (1916).

Thomas Moore (1779–1852)
Poet. His *Odes of Anacreon* (1800) received high praise. He then published *Odes, Epistles and Other Poems* (1806) and in 1807 began his *Irish Melodies* (1807–34), with music arranged by Sir John Stevenson from traditional tunes.

Paul Muldoon (1951–)
Poet and translator. His volume of poetry *The Annals of Chile* (1994) won the T. S. Eliot prize and *New Selected Poems 1968–1994* (1997) won *The Irish Times* Poetry prize. He has also published several volumes of translations.

Edna O'Brien (1932–)
Novelist. A dominant theme in her writing is the position of women in society and their lack of fulfilment. Her works

include *The Country Girls* (1960), *Girls in their Married Bliss* (1963) and *A Fanatic Heart* (1985).

Edward O'Brien (1880–1952)
Novelist. His *Across Three Oceans* (1926) described his yacht voyage around the world. This first book was followed by a dozen more works, mostly on sailing.

Kate O'Brien (1897–1974)
Novelist and dramatist. She began her career with the play *Distinguished Villas* (1926). This was followed by the novel *Without My Cloak* (1931). The novel *That Lady* (1946), a historical novel set in Spain, was dramatized in 1949 and played on Broadway.

Frank O'Connor (1903–66) (born Michael O'Donovan)
Author. His first book of short stories, *Guests of the Nation* (1931), was followed by a novel, *The Saint and Mary Kate* (1932). He was a director of the Abbey Theater (1935–39), but became best known for his short stories. He also translated noted works from Irish.

Sean O'Faolain (1900–91)
Novelist. *Midsummer Night Madness* (1932) was the first of 10 volumes of short stories he published. He also wrote

four novels, five biographies, and several prose works, including *The Irish* (1947). This work established him in the forefront of contemporary Irish writing.

Liam O'Flaherty (1896–1984)
Novelist and short-story writer. His first novel, *Thy Neighbour's Wife* (1923), was followed by *The Black Soul* (1924) and *The Informer* (1925), which was made into a successful film (1935). *Skerret* (1932) and *Famine* (1937) are considered his masterpieces. He wrote over 150 short stories, mostly dealing with peasants, fishermen, and nature.

Standish James O'Grady (1846–1928)
Novelist and historian. After publishing *The History of Ireland: Heroic Period* (1878–80), he wrote a series of novels based on Irish history. *Red Hugh's Captivity* (1889) was followed by *Finn and His Companions* (1892).

George Bernard Shaw (1856–1950)
Playwright. George Bernard Shaw's plays, including *Pygmalion* (1913) and *Heartbreak House* (1919), established him as the leading English-language playwright of his time. His plays treated of themes previously aired only in parliament or church but with great wit and eloquence. In addition to being a prolific playwright, he was also a celebrated pamphleteer, music critic, theater critic, and letter writer.

Richard Brinsley Sheridan (1751–1816)
Playwright and orator. Sheridan's first play, *The Rivals* (1775), quickly became popular. His masterpiece is *The School for Scandal* (1777). He was also a gifted political orator.

Sir Richard Steele (1672–1729)
Essayist and playwright. With Joseph Addison he launched the *Tatler*, *Spectator*, and *Guardian* periodicals. He entered parliament in 1713. His works include *The Funeral* (1701), *The Lying Lover* (1703), and *The Tender Husband* (1705).

Jonathan Swift (1667–1745)
Writer. He is recognized as one of the greatest satirists in the English language. His masterpiece, *Gulliver's Travels* (1726), is a ruthless satire of human follies but subsequently became an expurgated children's story.

John Millington Synge (1871–1909)
Playwright. The plays of Irish peasant life on which his fame rests were written in the last six years of his life. His celebrated works include *In the Shadow of the Glen* (1903), a comedy, and *Riders to the Sea* (1904).

Oscar Wilde (1854–1900)
Dramatist. He was the chief proponent of the aesthetic movement, based on the principle of art for art's sake.

LEFT: *Oscar Wilde, the 19th-Century wit and dramatist, who grew up in Dublin. He propounded the philosophy of "art for art's sake".*

Wilde's most distinctive and engaging plays are the four comedies *Lady Windermere's Fan* (1892), *A Woman of No Importance* (1893), *An Ideal Husband* (1895), and *The Importance of Being Earnest* (1895). *The Ballad of Reading Gaol* (1898) is the most powerful of all his poems.

RIGHT: Poems by Osar Wilde, *published in 1892, was a collection of the writer's remarkable verse. Wilde wrote both plays and poetry during his career.*

William Butler Yeats (1865–1939)

Poet. This mystic and romantic was one of the greatest poetical figures of his age. Yeats received the Nobel prize for his dramatic works in 1923, but his significance today rests on his poems. His poetry included *The Wild Swans at Coole* (1919), *Michael Robartes and the Dancer* (1921), *The Tower* (1928), *The Winding Stair and Other Poems* (1933), and *Last Poems and Plays* (1940).

ABOVE: *Samantha Mumba, the Dublin singer-songwriter who achieved her first hit in 2000 and made her Hollywood début in 2002.*

MUSIC

◆ ◆ ◆

The Irish nation is renowned for its musical talent. This ranges from the famous tunes of Percy French to acclaimed pop exports such as Samantha Mumba.

◆ ◆ ◆

The precise origins of traditional Irish music are not known although it played a central part in the cultural life of the island's inhabitants. The music of medieval Ireland was orally transmitted and few records survive. The harp was the dominant and characteristic instrument in early historical times, and was adopted as the arms of Ireland in the 17th Century. One of the few early composers whose work has survived is Turlough Carolan (1670–1738), a poet, harpist, and composer. Some 220 pieces are attributed to him. Following the Belfast Harp Festival of 1792, Edward Bunting transcribed and published the traditional airs of the participants, including the blind harpist Arthur O'Neill (1727–1816), one of the last wandering bards.

Traditional vocal music includes English and Scottish ballads imported centuries ago, and Anglo-Irish songs and ballads dating mostly from the 19th and early 20th Centuries. These were popularized by Thomas Moore and Percy French. The form of singing Irish in the old style or

sean nós is a unique feature of traditional music. *Sean nós* is sung solo, and the music is usually ornamented by melismatic, rhythmic, and intervallic variation.

During the 18th Century, Dublin became an important center of music, attracting such composers as Francesco Geminiani (1687–1762) who played and taught music in the city. In 1742 Georg Friedrich Handel (1685–1759), one of Germany's musical geniuses, held the premiere of *Messiah* in the capital in 1742. John Field (1782–1837), one of the foremost pianists of his day, had considerable influence on Romantic composers from Chopin to Glinka.

Ireland's 19th-Century composers included Michael Balfe (1808–70), and Vincent Wallace (1812–65) who composed *Maritana*. Charles Villiers Stanford (1852–1924) established himself as a leading musical figure by composing many operas, orchestral pieces, and choral music. Compositions such as *Irish Symphony* and *Six Irish Rhapsodies* reflect his origins. Victor Herbert (1859–1924) also composed operas, and Hamilton Harty (1879–1941) composed a celebrated symphony based on traditional songs. More recently, Brian Boydell (1917–2000) wrote for both orchestra and string quartet.

Composers A. J. Potter (1918–80), and Gerard Victory (1921–95), through their links with the RTE Symphony Orchestra from 1967, have been major figures on the music scene in recent times.

Some 60 composers are currently working in Ireland. These include Seóirse Bodley (1933–), James Wilson (1922–), John Kinsella (1932–), Frank Corcoran (1944–), and Jerome de Bromhead (1945–). Gerald Barry (1952–) has established a high profile internationally.

A new generation of composers have fused Irish traditional/world music with jazz. Bill Whelan (1950–) has become famous for combining the classical and the traditional in the internationally successful music and dance show *Riverdance*.

Ireland has a wealth of individual classical musical talent. This includes the well-known pianists John O'Conor, Micheál O'Rourke, Philip Martin, and Hugh Tinney, up and coming pianists Finghín Collins, Peter Tuite, and Maria McGarry, renowned singers Bernadette Greevy, Ann Murray, Suzanne Murphy and, more recently, Linda Lee, Patricia Bardon, and Orla Boylan. Violinists include Fionnuala Hunt and Catherine Leonard who are well established on the international concert circuit, while tenor Finbarr Wright enjoys popular appeal, as did the late Frank Patterson.

Professional music performance in Ireland involves a number of organisations. There are three main opera companies operating in Ireland: DGOS Opera Ireland present two seasons of operas in Dublin annually; the Wexford Festival Opera, a 15-day event at the end of October, has achieved a major international reputation; and

the Opera Theatre Company tour opera to centers around the country. There are three full-time professional orchestras: the National Symphony Orchestra, the RTE Concert Orchestra, maintained by RTE (the national broadcaster), and the Ulster Orchestra, funded by the Arts Council of Northern Ireland.

During the 20th Century there was a renewed interest in North America and domestically in Irish traditional music. The *Fleadh Cheoil* (Music Festival) in the 1950s enabled the older rural-based traditions to find urban enthusiasts in dance halls. New instruments were added to the traditional line-up of drum, elbow pipes, tin whistle, and fiddle. Seán Ó Riada (1931–71) set up a band, *Ceoltóirí Chualann*, that performed music to listen to rather than dance to. Members of the band went on to form The Chieftains in the 1970s, who helped bring traditional music on to the world stage.

Traditional instrumental music, therefore, enjoys great popularity in Ireland at the present time. These include dance tunes such as jigs, reels, hornpipes, slides, and polkas as well as slow airs based on vocal music. The main national collection of materials relating to traditional music is housed in the Irish Traditional Music Archive in Dublin.

Ceol—the Irish Traditional Music Center—was established in the Smithfield Village area of Dublin as an interactive cultural center in 1999. Visitors are guided

through the history and development of Irish traditional music in a most innovative way.

The two main varieties of popular music at the present time are country music and the more cosmopolitan rock/pop music. The growth of maturity in Irish rock bands since the 1970s has seen rock/pop music emerge as a natural expression for a growing number of musicians.

The vibrancy of the music scene is emphasized by the international recognition of acts such as U2 who began their musical careers at school in Dublin back in 1977. Today the band is indisputably one of the most popular rock acts in the world,

The singer Sinead O'Connor, from Dublin, combined her highly distinctive vocal range with striking post-feminist imagery to great commercial effect on both sides of the Atlantic. Another female vocalist, Enya, from County Donegal, is a classically trained pianist who was formerly a member of Clannad before embarking on a solo career that blossomed unexpectedly with her *Orinoco Flow* (1988).

The Cranberries from Limerick boast the honeyed voice of frontperson Dolores O'Riordan. Their début EP *Uncertain* was released in late 1991.

The male pop quintet Boyzone was tailored for mainstream success by Polydor Records. The group's UK breakthrough came with a cover of the Osmonds' "Love Me For A Reason". The single became a Top 10 hit in most

European countries. The band's début album, *Said And Done*, was released in August 1995 and sold over one million copies worldwide. Although the band broke up, Ronan Keating, the lead vocalist, has established himself as a successful television presenter, entrepreneur, and solo artist.

Another Irish boy band, originally known as Westside (now Westlife), emerged in the late 1990s as the highly successful successor to Boyzone. The Corrs were one of Ireland's most successful pop exports of the 1990s. The family group's 1995 début, "Forgiven, Not Forgotten", was a striking work, deftly combining traditional music with a strong pop sensibility.

The talented singer-songwriter Samantha Mumba, from Dublin, burst into the lucrative pop/R & B scene in 2000. Mumba inaugurated her acting career in 2002 with a role in Simon Wells' adaptation of *The Time Machine*.

Finally, Daniel O'Donnell now dominates the musical genre known as "Country'n' Irish". His success can be attributed to the fact that he is a clean-cut and gimmick-free vocalist.

ARTS AND CRAFTS

◆ ◆ ◆

Ireland offers a wide range of goods which reflect the quality and craftsmanship of her traditional industries.

◆ ◆ ◆

Many Irish arts and crafts are known throughout the world. A large number of these products are made using traditional materials and designs. Even the influence of Irish Celtic art can be seen in many goods such as lead crystal, chinaware and jewelry. Traditional materials and skills, however, have also been adapted to contemporary culture and design. Today Irish arts and crafts are also to be found in the forefront of the fashion and design worlds.

Irish handwoven tweed, traditionally crafted, is acclaimed for its quality, individuality, versatility, and color blends. It is used in a wide range of clothing as well as soft furnishings. The weaving of tweed is one of Ireland's oldest crafts. Each bolt of Irish tweed, painstakingly produced in factories or small workshops, is as distinctive as the weavers and looms that produce it. Donegal tweed is a sturdy and complex fabric, characterized by nubby textures and speckles of diverse colors. This robust and waterproof tweed is much in demand for jackets and traditional caps. Equally prized tweeds are woven elsewhere, especially in

LEFT: *A traditional weaver at her loom on Clare Island, a tiny area of land off the coast of County Mayo.*

Connemara and Wicklow.

Knitwear has undergone a revolution in Ireland in recent years and has become a flagship small industry. The intricate stitchwork of the traditional Aran sweater has been incorporated into a wide variety of stylish designs and patterns. The patterns of the original *báinín* sweater (so called because of the undyed wool from the Aran Islands which was used to knit them) was unwritten and handed down from family to family. Often imitated but never equalled, every Aran hand-knitted sweater is unique.

Linen-weaving is one of Ireland's earliest crafts. It is said that the growing of flax for linen can be traced back to the Bronze Age. As well as the more traditional bed linen and tableware, fashion clothing now makes up a large part of the linen range. The damask variety, introduced some 300 years ago, brought international fame to Ireland as a linen producer. Irish damask tableware has distinctive patterns, many of which reflect the swirls and shapes of the country's foliage.

Glass factories existed in many parts of Ireland until the early 19th Century when heavy duties forced most to close. Today's industry is a restoration of the old craft and glass-cutting companies now produce fine crystal and cut-

glass in Waterford, Cork, Cavan, Galway, Kilkenny, Tipperary, Tyrone, Sligo, and Dublin. Handblown glass is produced in Waterford, Jerpoint in County Kilkenny, Kerry, Dublin, and Tipperary. It takes finely honed skills to produce the exquisite handcut glass. Veteran glassblowers begin this process by lifting fiery balls of molten glass on to iron rods from the depths of huge furnaces. They use only their breath, artistic instincts, and wooden blocks to transform these white-hot masses into traditional glassware shapes. Intricate patterns are later cut into the glass.

The ceramic industry is flourishing in Ireland and factories, as well as studio potteries, produce a variety of designs in ovenware, tableware and decorative items throughout the country. Belleek Pottery in Fermanagh, which opened in 1857, is widely acclaimed. Only Belleek of the highest quality is ever put on sale. When the firm began, the founder, John Caldwell Bloomfield, declared that any piece with even the slightest flaw should be destroyed. More than 150 years later, this golden rule is still strictly adhered to. Irish porcelain is produced too in Cork, Clare, Galway, Leitrim, and Kilkenny. Irish Dresden, a line of porcelain figurines, is produced at Drumcolligher in County Limerick. These delicate pieces are fashioned in the tradition of a business originally founded in Volkstedt, Germany, and brought to Ireland some 40 years ago. Many of the designs are inspired by life in rural Ireland. Other

leading names include Royal Tara China in Galway, and Donegal Parian China in Ballyshannon.

The working of precious metals in Ireland dates from about 2000 B.C. and the tradition of Celtic ornamentation inspires many of today's jewelry-makers. Handwrought jewelry is available from studios and workshops throughout the country. The Claddagh ring, first developed in the 1500s by a goldsmith from Galway, is a simple design featuring a pair of hands holding a crowned heart. It was originally worn as a wedding ring in the west of Ireland but is now worn worldwide. The Claddagh ring has come to be accepted as a universal symbol of friendship, love, and loyalty.

Other leading Irish crafts include basketry, patchwork, stained glass, beaten copper art, pewter-casting, leatherwork, enamel painting, bookbinding, candle-making, and instrument-making.

On the practical side, the craft of thatching is still in much demand in remote rural areas. The style of putting a thatched roof over a whitewashed stone cottage goes back hundreds of years in Ireland. Only the richest people could once afford slates, tiles, or other imported materials.

With such creativity it is easy to understand why George Bernard Shaw equated Irish hearts with pure imagination. Inspired by Ireland, its traditions, and resources, the Irish people have added much to the world.

ROUND TOWERS

◆ ◆ ◆

The stone structures known as round towers are a distinctive architectural feature of the Irish landscape.

◆ ◆ ◆

The remains of round towers are scattered across the country. They soar up to 34m (111.5ft) above the ground. Some still have a conical cap and it is thought that all the others would also have had this. Initially the round towers were free-standing structures. Some, however, have been surrounded by other structures, mainly ecclesiastical buildings such as churches or monasteries built between the 7th and 12th Centuries. Battlements have been added to a small number of round towers, but these were later additions to the original towers.

The round towers were built using the same design principles. Two walls of block and mortar construction were built at a short distance from each other, then the cavity was filled with rock rubble. This method of wall construction was used by the Romans and it is assumed that this practice was brought to the country by

LEFT: *The 30m (98.4ft) high round tower at Monasterboice, County Louth, is one of the tallest in Ireland.*

PREVIOUS PAGE: *The round tower and church at Ardmore, County Waterford. The round tower, standing 29m (95ft) high, dominates this sacred site. This monastic center, founded by St. Declan in the 6th Century, was one of the first in Ireland.*

missionaries from mainland Britain or continental Europe.

Dimensions

The basic dimensions of the round towers in Ireland do not vary very much. Lennox Barrow in *Irish Round Towers* records how the circumference at the base of most round towers lies between 14m (46ft) and 17m (55ft) and the thickness of the wall at the lowest point at which it can be measured varies from 0.9m (2.9ft) to 1.4m (4.5ft). Doorways, windows, storey heights and diameters also follow clearly defined patterns. It has therefore been concluded that most of the towers were the work of teams of builders who moved from one monastery to another using standard designs.

Refuge

Most round towers had doorways that were raised above the ground. The common explanation for this is that the towers were places of safety. The monks would take refuge inside the towers with their treasures and relics if their community was attacked by Viking raiders. The round tower

also served as an observation point to spot approaching warriors. It has also been suggested that the doorways were raised to help the stability of the tower. The higher you could build before making an opening in the wall, the stronger the base would be.

Antennas

New theories surrounding the purpose of the round tower, however, have emerged. These include the amazing suggestion that they may have been constructed and utilized as huge resonant systems for collecting and storing meter-long wavelengths of magnetic and electromagnetic energy coming from the earth and sky. The subtle magnetic radiation from the sun was passed on to monks meditating in the tower and plants growing around the base. The towers were able to function in this way because of their form and also because of their materials of construction. There is also the suggestion that the arrangement of the round towers mirrors the positions of the stars in the northern sky during the time of winter solstice.

Today these structures still tower above many of Ireland's most sacred sites. A tower has also been erected at the Island of Ireland Peace Park, Messines, Belgium, in memory of the thousands of Irish troops killed during World War I.

ABOVE: *Church ruins on the Hill of Slane, County Meath. This is the site where St. Patrick lit the first paschal candle in Ireland.*

Sacred Ireland

◆ ◆ ◆

The Irish national psyche has been significantly shaped by the Christian faith which arrived in the 5th Century.

◆ ◆ ◆

Religion has played a major role in the life and culture of Ireland. The religious beliefs of the Neolithic people can be seen in the large monuments, called megalithic tombs, that they built for their dead. The Roman empire never considered the island worth invading, but eventually it was the coming of Christianity, the official religion of the late empire, which opened Celtic Ireland to the wide world.

St. Patrick was not the only Christian missionary in Ireland during the 5th Century. In 431 Palladius was recorded as being "the first bishop to the Irish who believed in Christ". This clearly suggests that Christians were already present on the island even at this early date. By the 7th Century paganism had virtually disappeared.

Irish Christianity soon diverged from continental norms. In the social sphere the effect was limited. Divorce, for example, remained a secular matter, and was still available under the Celt's Brehon Law, while the Irish Church was monastic rather than episcopal. There were no towns to act as foci for diocesan organization, so monasteries assumed

great importance as centers of Christian learning, scholarship, and discipline.

The monastery as Clonmacnoise, County Offaly, was one of Europe's powerhouses of learning. Most of all, the early Irish Church was a missionary Church, reintroducing Christianity to continental Europe after the collapse of the Roman Empire. Irish missionaries founded religious settlements all over Europe. Even France and Italy needed to be re-evangelized, while Germanic and Slav lands were brought within the Christian world for the first time.

In the 12th Century the Church was reformed, which lead to the introduction of the Cistercian and Augustinian orders to Ireland. By the 13th Century Franciscan, Dominican, Augustinian and Carmelite friars were arriving from the continent.

The religious, social, and economic life suffered during the 14th and 15th Centuries. This was exacerbated by the Black Death

RIGHT: *A stained glass window in St. Anne's Church, Dublin.*

BELOW: *A wayside shrine in County Kerry depicting the crucifixion. Similar shrines may be found across Ireland.*

ABOVE: *Christchurch Cathedral, Dublin, has vied for supremacy with nearby St. Patrick's Cathedral through much of its history.*

that had devastated the whole of Europe. When religious life resurfaced it had taken on a much more Gaelic feel. The Protestant Reformation that was initiated in Britain by King Henry VIII then led to the suppression and dissolution of the monasteries that were such a focal point of the Roman Catholic faith.

In the 17th Century new orders began to appear in Ireland, including Jesuits. Communities of Augustinians, Dominicans, and Poor Clare nuns were also established. But the Franciscan and Dominican friars continued to be the largest group among the regular friars. Life for Roman Catholics was often severely restricted by the political and social circumstances of the time. During the 17th and 18th Centuries a number of religious houses closed. The Protestant Church of Ireland, however, enjoyed the protection of the state.

Catholicism enjoyed a revival during the 19th and early 20th Centuries. The formation of the Irish Republic led to the Church assuming a dominant role in national life. The final decades of the 20th Century, however, saw many people increasingly question the Church's dominance over society. Secular and liberal thinking led many to challenge established beliefs. The Church has adapted to the "New Ireland" and is addressing pressing social issues. Today 4,500 Irish missionaries give pastoral care and aid in 85 countries. Present-day Ireland has various religious traditions.

Den schwantz regete si want der qual von dem wasser als gross
vor dem schiff das er den kiell uff hub als ob er

in die lufft wolte tragen und viel den wider hernider
als ob er in abgrund wolte wallen dem selben fisch was
ouch uff dem schwantz gewachssen holtz und gras do waren si alle

IRELAND'S SAINTS

The nation's many holy men and women have carried the Gospel message far beyond their homeland.

St. Aidan of Lindisfarne (d. 651)

Aidan was an Irish monk from the monastery St. Columba founded on the island of Iona. He led a mission of 12 monks to Northumbria in northeast England and they settled on the island of Lindisfarne. Aidan, who became a bishop, led his monks out into the countryside to speak to the people and ensured that a new generation of priests and nuns in England would carry on his work. They trained in his school and worked for the conversion of much of Anglo-Saxon England. His feast day is August 31.

St. Brendan (c. 484–c. 577)

This saint was born in County Kerry and was educated under St. Ita and St. Erc who ordained him around 512. He then helped establish various monastic communities in Ireland. Amazing stories surround this saint who is believed to have built a coracle boat on the Kerry coast and chose

LEFT: *St. Brendan and his monks at sea during their seven-year voyage.*

14 monks to join him on a mission to a mystical land. He may have reached the Canary Islands, although his exact movements cannot be determined. After a voyage lasting seven years he returned to Ireland. Brendan founded a great monastery at Clonfert, County Galway. This contained 3,000 monks and a convent under his sister, St. Briga. He also made missionary journeys in Ireland and to Scotland. His feast day is May 16.

St. Brigid (c. 451–500)
The patron saint of infants, farmers, dairy workers, cattle, and mariners is believed to have been born in County Louth. Her mother was a Christian Pictish slave who had been baptized by St. Patrick. According to legend she prayed that her beauty be taken from her so no one would seek her hand in marriage. Her prayers were granted and she became a nun. Brigid established the famous Convent of Cill-Dara, County Kildare. Many miracles are attributed to this holy woman who is one of the three patron saints of Ireland. Her feast day is February 1.

St. Colman/Columbanus (c. 543–615)
This saint was born in Leinster and trained in a monastery in Bangor, County Down. Around 590 he joined 12 companions on a mission to the Gauls in Burgundy, France. He founded monasteries at Luxeuil and Fontaines. He was banished from

Burgundy around 610 by the King for condemning the immorality of his court. Colmán then travelled through Switzerland and founded a monastery at Bobbio, Italy, where he died. His feast is celebrated on November 21.

St. Columba (c. 521–597)

The patron saint of bookbinders was descended from Irish royalty and was born in County Donegal. His baptismal name was Colum which signifies a dove. Columba was the Latinized form of his name. It also assumes another form, Columcille, the suffix meaning "of the Churches". While training in the monastery at Moville he began performing miracles. By tradition, it is said his prayers turned water into wine. The itinerant preacher, bard priest, and teacher traveled throughout Ireland. He later became abbot of Iona and helped convert the Picts on the British mainland. Columba is one of the three patron saints of Ireland. His feast day is June 9.

St. Fiacre (d. 670)

The patron saint of florists, gardeners, and taxi drivers was raised in a monastery. Fiacre sought isolation but his knowledge and holiness gained him a great number of followers. He therefore fled to France and was given land for a hermitage by St. Faro of Meaux. Fiacre wanted the land to make a garden where he could grow vegetables and

healing herbs. St. Faro, the bishop of the area, offered him all the land he could entrench in a single day. Fiacre walked around the perimeter with a spade. Wherever his spade touched the trees fell, bushes were uprooted, and the soil was entrenched. The garden became a place of pilgrimage for centuries. Fiacre's connection to cab drivers is because the Hotel de Saint Fiacre in Paris, France, rented carriages. The saint healed many conditions, including blindness and fistulas. His relics have been distributed to several churches across Europe. Fiacre's feast day is celebrated on August 30.

St. Gall (c. 550–645)
The patron saint of birds is believed to have been educated at Bangor under St Colman. He then joined him on a mission(*c.* 590) to France and Switzerland. He established a hermitage along with 12 followers at the source of the Steinach River. This later became a famous monastery and a great center of learning. The present-day town and canton of Sankt Gallen is named in his honor. According to legend he twice refused bishoprics offered by King Sigebert, whose betrothed he had freed of demons which fled from her in the form of blackbirds. Gall is known as "The Apostle of Switzerland" and his feast day is celebrated on October 16.

St. Ita/Ida (c. 475–570)
This saint, descended from Irish nobility, was born in

County Waterford. She refused to marry and received her father's blessing to enter the convent at *Cluain Credhail*, now known as Killeedy, in County Limerick. Ita founded a school for boys there and one of her students was St. Brendan. Many extravagant miracles have become associated with her including healing a man who had been decapitated, and living solely off food delivered from heaven. Her feast is celebrated on January 15.

St. Kevin (c. 498–618)

Various miracle stories surround this popular saint who was born in Leinster. Kevin was baptized by St. Cronan of Roscrea, and educated by St. Petroc of Cornwall from the age of 7. From the age of 12 he lived with monks and studied to be a priest. After his ordination he lived as a hermit for seven years in a cave at Glendalough, a Bronze Age tomb now known as St. Kevin's Bed, to which he was reportedly led by an angel. He wore skins and ate the nettles around him. His reputation as a holy man spread and he attracted followers, including St. Moling. Kevin founded the monastery at Glendalough, County Wicklow, which included relics brought back during a pilgrimage to Rome. This monastery, in turn, founded several others, and around it grew a town which became a see city, though now subsumed into the archdiocese of Dublin. He withdrew to live as a hermit once the monastery was

established. Four years later, however, he returned to Glendalough at the entreaty of his monks, and served as abbot until his death at the age of 120. Kevin performed many miracles. On one occasion a young man with severe epilepsy received a vision that he would be cured by eating an apple. There were, however, no apple trees about. Kevin, seeing his need, ordered a willow to produce apples; 20 yellow apples appeared on the tree. His feast day is June 3.

St. Kieran/Ciaran (c. 516–556)

Among the many Irish saints of this name, St. Kieran of Clonmacnoise is the most celebrated. This learned man lived for several years as a hermit with St. Enda before becoming a monk at the abbey of Isel in central Ireland. He was driven out by his fellow monks because his charitable assistance to the local poor threatened to bankrupt the community. He then

RIGHT: *A cross at Clonmacnoise Abbey, the great religious center in County Offaly founded by St. Kieran in the 6th Century.*

lived as a hermit again before founding the Conmacnoise Abbey in County Offaly. He became its first abbot and established an austere rule. It was known for centuries as a center of learning. His feast day is celebrated on September 9.

St. Malachy (c. 1094–1148)
This prophetic saint was born in Armagh and became a priest at the age of 25. Malachy then studied under St. Malchus to perfect his knowledge of theology. This zealous preacher was a clerical reformer who instituted celibacy regulations and other disciplines on the clergy after a period of laxity. Malachy was instrumental in establishing a priory in Downpatrick and the great Mellifont Abbey. He was also a great healer. While in Rome in 1139 he received a vision showing him all the popes from his day to the end of time. His feast day is celebrated on November 3.

St. Oliver Plunkett (1625–1681)
This martyr from County Meath came from Irish nobility who were supporters of King Charles I of England. He was ordained in 1654 and in 1669 became Archbishop of Armagh. During this period harsh penal laws suppressed the Church. In 1679 he was arrested for treason. Oliver was falsely accused of conspiring against the state. He was executed in London. His feast day is celebrated on July 1.

ST. PATRICK

◆ ◆ ◆

Ireland's patron saint was brought to the island as a slave but became one of the land's most revered figures.

◆ ◆ ◆

Ireland's patron saint came from mainland Britain. His missionary work was crucial to the conversion of Ireland to Christianity during the 5th Century. Patrick's Celtic name was *Patricius* and he was the son of a deacon and grandson of a priest. He was seized by an Irish raiding party as a teenager near his home, brought across the Irish Sea and sold into slavery. After several years herding animals he escaped to mainland Europe where he studied for the priesthood. In a dream he was called to return to Ireland and he did so. This story is told in one of the few documents believed to have been written by Patrick himself, his *Confessio*.

Missionary Life

Traditionally the dates 432–461 have been given for his mission in Ireland, and there is little doubt but that his feast day, March 17, was the date of his death. Ireland did have

LEFT: *Statue of St. Patrick at the foot of Croagh Patrick, County Mayo.*

some scattered Christian communities before his arrival. Patrick's misson, however, was the impetus for the conversion to Christianity across the island.

Fact and Fiction

Two biographies were written about St. Patrick around 200 years after he died. The authors were *Muirchú* and *Tíreachán*. They were monks who had some knowledge of Patrick's writings and some traditions concerning the saint. The value of these works, however, is dubious and much of the information was included in order to portray Patrick's prophetic profile. These and later medieval biographies are not highly valued by present-day scholars although they do show how a number of legends have developed around the saint.

Preaching the Gospel

The stories recorded by *Muirchú* and *Tíreachán*, however, do have some connections with Patrick's preaching. In the *Confessio*, Patrick praises the true "light" of Christianity compared with the worship of the sun. Patrick says those who believe in Christ worship "the true sun who will never perish, nor will anyone who does His will". It is interesting that both *Muirchú* and *Tíreachán* record a fire-ordeal where Patrick showed the superiority of his faith over a pagan druid. According to the story, a servant of Patrick emerged

unscathed from the ordeal, being untouched by the fires of paganism, whereas his opponent was totally consumed by the fire of the Christian faith.

Fearless Missionary

The most striking story from these early biographies describes Patrick as lighting the first paschal fire in Ireland. As an account, it is full of high drama. We are told that the High King *Laoghaire* had the custom of lighting a fire at the royal center of Tara on a certain night and that nobody else should kindle theirs before he did so. Patrick had come to the Hill of Slane nearby, however, and when *Laoghaire* saw a fire burning there he was outraged and ordered that the transgressor appear before him. Then Patrick came to Tara as a great Christian hero, and the High King and all the royal forces were confounded by his miraculous powers.

Miracle Worker

Patrick and his pagan druid opponents are recorded as having several great contests using miracles and magic to change the climate and natural environment. These took place in front of the High King at Tara and his court. The saint won each time. Such accounts potray Patrick almost as a "new" Moses challenging the temporal and spiritual powers of Ireland's rulers just as the leader of the Hebrews

challenged the Egyptian Pharaoh. Indeed, just as Moses caused water to spring from rock at a stroke of his staff, so Patrick is said to have caused holy wells to spring up at different places so as to facilitate the baptism of converts.

The Early Church

The earliest biographies described the mission of Patrick as taking place in the northern half of the country, but around the 9th Century a third account of him was written which extended his mission to the south. In addition to establishing the bishopric at Armagh, it claimed that he founded the bishopric at Cashel, which rivalled the former in prestige. Such claims and counter-claims are closely connected with the rivalry between the *Uí Néill* dynasty in the north and the *Eoghanacht* dynasty in the south. These were the two leading power groups of the period.

The Great Fast

Literature concerning Patrick written in the 9th Century contains the first references to the saint spending 40 days and nights fasting on top of the mountain of Croagh Patrick in County Mayo. God, worried that Patrick might die and thereby leave his mission unaccomplished, asked him to abandon his fast. It is said that Patrick would only do so on three conditions: that the Irish people would not live permanently under oppression, that the country would be

submerged seven years before the end of the world and so be spared the final devastation, and that he would be allowed to judge all the Irish people on the last day. This tradition, which has Patrick as the special champion of the Irish, has given consolation to the people in times of misery and distress.

Banishing the Serpents

The belief that the saint banished snakes from Ireland emerged in various biographies about him in the 11th Century. The indications are that this idea was suggested by the many accounts of how the saint banished the "demons of paganism", and that it was borrowed specifically from a similar motif in the biography of St. Honoratus, founder of the island-monastery of Lérins in France where Patrick is said to have studied. The fact that there were no snakes in Ireland was well known from antiquity, and indeed was referred to by the Graeco-Roman writer Solinus 200 years before Patrick was born.

Explaining the Trinity

Patrick is also closely associated with the shamrock. It is said that Patrick used the plant to explain the mystery of the Trinity by explaining that just as three leaves can spring from one stem, so there are also three persons in one God. Today shamrock is traditionally worn on St. Patrick's

Day by Irish men and women around the world. It is now one of Ireland's national symbols.

Many other stories of a curious and sometimes humorous nature have been passed down the centuries. He is said, for instance, to have met survivors of the legendary *Fianna* warriors, and to have obtained baptism posthumously for their fellows. It is also claimed that he blessed and cursed various parts of the country, depending on the preferences of the storytellers.

Patron Saint

Veneration of Patrick gradually assumed the status of a local cult. By the 8th Century homage to Patrick as Ireland's saint was already apparent. At this time Patrick's status of national apostle was made independently of Rome; he was claimed locally as a saint before the practice of canonization was introduced by the Vatican. The veneration in which the Irish have held St. Patrick is evidenced by the salutation, still common today, "May God, Mary and Patrick bless you." Within the Christian calendar Patrick has long been remembered with fondness. This began as early as the 9th Century with the Feast of St. Patrick's "falling asleep"—in other words his passing on March 17. Patrick, Columba, and Brigid are Ireland's three patron saints.

Patrick, the slave-boy forcibly brought to Ireland, has become an inspirational figure to many generations of Irish

people. He is remembered as a courageous and protective figure, proficient in miracles, scrupulous in teaching, but full of human kindness and humour.

There are numerous places in Ireland connected with St. Patrick. Lough Derg (red lake), County Donegal, contains an island shrine to the saint. Legend says he killed the lake monster there. The annual three-day pilgrimage begins on June 1.

The Downpatrick Shrine, Downpatrick, is located in the Cathedral church of the Holy Trinity. This is where St. Patrick, St. Brigid, and St. Columba are believed to be buried. A bell, tooth, and hand from St. Patrick were discovered in the 12th Century. St. Patrick's hand was enshrined in silver and placed in the high altar of the Abbey church. Water was poured through it to heal sores.

According to tradition, Patrick built a stone church at *Ard Macha* or Armagh (Macha's height) in 445. In 447 St. Patrick ordained that Armagh should have pre-eminence over all the churches of Ireland, a position which it holds to this day. Armagh remains the seat of both the Protestant and Catholic primates.

St. Patrick's Shrine, County Down is dominated by a 12.5m (41ft high) statue of the saint erected in 1938. Finally, Croagh Patrick, County Mayo, is the mountain where Patrick is said to have stayed during his great fast. Pilgrims climb to the summit every year on the last Sunday in July.

ABOVE: *The Papal Cross in Phoenix Park, Dublin, marks the site where Pope John Paul II celebrated Mass for 1.25 million people in 1979.*

Prayers and Blessings

◆ ◆ ◆

These ancient words of praise are translated from Irish.

◆ ◆ ◆

Christ with me,
Christ before me,
Christ within me,
Christ below me,
Christ above me,
Christ on my right hand,
Christ on my left hand,
Christ in my sleeping,
Christ in my waking,
Christ in the heart of all who think of me,
Christ in the mouth of all
who speak of me,
Christ in every eye that looks at me,
Christ in every ear that listens to me.

— *ascribed to St. Patrick*

May your blessings outnumber the shamrocks that grow,
And may trouble avoid you wherever you go.

This day God gives me Strength of high heaven
Sun and Moon shining, Flame in my hearth
Flashing of lightning, Wind in its swiftness,
Deeps of the ocean, Firmness of earth.

This day God sends me Strength as my guardian,
Might to uphold me, Wisdom as guide.
Your eyes are watchful, your ears are list'ning,
Your lips are speaking, Friend at my side.

God's way is my way, God's shield is 'round me,
God's host defends me, Saving from ill.
Angels of heaven, Drive from me always
All that would harm me, Stand by me still.

Rising I thank you, Mighty and Strong One
King of creation, Giver of rest.
Firmly confessing Threeness of Persons
Oneness of Godhead, Trinity blest.

— *ascribed to St. Patrick*

Prayer to St. Brigid

Brigid. You were a woman of peace.
You brought harmony where there was conflict.
You brought light to the darkness.
You brought hope to the downcast.
May the mantle of your peace cover those who are troubled and anxious, and may peace be firmly rooted in our hearts and in our world.
Inspire us to act justly and to reverence all God has made.
Brigid you were a voice for the wounded and the weary.
Strengthen what is weak within us.
Calm us into a quietness that heals and listens.
May we grow each day into greater wholeness in mind, body and spirit. Amen

O Lord, grant us that love which can never die, which will enkindle our lamps but not extinguish them, so that they may shine in us and bring light to others. Most dear Savior, enkindle our lamps that they may shine forever in your temple. May we receive unquenchable light from you so that our darkness will be illuminated and the darkness of the world will be made less. Amen.

— *ascribed to St. Columba*

A. Fort
Erected by Tyrone against Terlogh Lenogh
Donaillee
TIE
Dromglas ecclesia perochialis Dungano
Temple Stokan
Temp: Deserderigh
Terowen fl.
Dungannon
T: Clo-ne
Tullogh oge, On this hill the Irish Create their O Neale.
CLAN
Fort Bundernon
Enish Dargell

FOLKLORE

Ireland is filled with legends and myths surrounding its natural features, saints, and heroic leaders.

Irish folklore has a rich heritage of mythic and historical stories. The adventures of the famous warrior *Fionn Mac Cumhaill* are still known to, and related by, many Irish people. These include how he gained his wisdom as a boy by tasting the "salmon of knowledge", how he triumphed over miscellaneous giants and magicians, and how he had the truths of life explained to him in a strange allegorical house. The champion *Lugh*, originally a god of the continental Celts, is also remembered and especially how he slew his tyrant-grandfather who had a horrific eye which destroyed all on which it gazed.

Warriors and Saints

The adventures of the super-warrior *Cuchulainn* are spoken of and tales are also told of more true to life characters, such as the quasi-historical High King *Cormac Mac Airt* and

LEFT: *A depiction of the inauguration of the O'Neill chief. Many legends surround the great Irish leaders of history.*

the historical though much romanticized *Conall Gulban*, son of the great King Niall.

Irish folklore also chronicles many legends associated with the land's saints. While it is undoubtedly true that these holy men and women did have spiritual powers, many fantastic legends have grown up around their lives from the early centuries of Irish Christianity. Holy wells, dedicated to individual saints, are still frequented on their feast days in many areas, and people pray at these wells for relief from different kinds of physical and mental distress.

Fairy-lore

Ireland is famous for its fairy-lore, which also contains vestiges of pre-Christian tradition. The fairies are known in Irish as the people of the *sí* (pronounced "she"). This word originally designated a mound or tumulus. Irish fairies can be connected with early Celtic beliefs of how the dead live on as a dazzling community in their burial chambers. Through their identification in the medieval literature with the *Tuatha Dé Danann* (People of the Goddess Danu) they may also be connected directly to the early pantheon of Celtic deities. In folk belief thousands of raths (ancient earthenwork structures which dot the landscape) are claimed to be inhabited still by the *sí*-people. Many stories are told of humans being brought into these hidden palaces at night as guests at wondrous banquets.

Over many centuries various versions of international folk tales have been incorporated into Irish folklore. The simplest of these are tales concerning the fauna, which deal with such matters as the fox and wolf, or the eagle and wren, pitting their wits against each other. Most popular of all are the "wonder tales", which are long and lend themselves to very imaginative events and to highly stylized descriptions, and are therefore very suitable to storytelling in the Irish language. The plots of these stories are situated in a never-never land long ago, and they introduce the audience to the overthrow of wizards and giants, and many other kinds of amazing events.

The novelle-type tales are based on other international plots concerning tricks and coincidences, but in a more true to life setting—many of these have, in fact, come to be told of leading Irish social figures such as Jonathan Swift and Daniel O'Connell. There is, of course, a large variety of humorous stories in Ireland.

Afterlife

There has always been a great respect for the dead in Irish culture. Indeed, a very special female spirit, the *bean sí* is often heard to announce by her wailing the impending death of a member of a family. People not only prayed, but also sang, told stories, and even played games at the wake of a departed relative or friend who had enjoyed a long and

fulfilling life.

Songs in Irish focus on the expression of feeling but also historical events. Ballads were introduced from England and Scotland in the course of the 18th and 19th Centuries. They were often printed on broadsheets and sold at fairs and other gatherings, and thus formed the basis of Irish folklore in the English language.

Festivals

There was also a great taste for posing and solving riddles, for tongue-twisters, divination games, and of course for practical jokes. The indigenous festivals of the Irish calendar—such as *Imbolc* (St. Brigid's Day, February 1), Bealtaine (May 1), the festival of *Lughnasa* (August 1), and *Samhain* (All Hallows, November 1)—all had their own special forms of amusements and preserved vestiges of earlier rituals. In the Celtic way of measuring time the day began at sunset and hence the best-known internationally of these festivals, Hallowe'en, is on October 31.

The realm of folk-belief is well represented in Irish traditional culture. Folk-belief provides a good illustration of how realistic knowledge, derived from observation and experience, combines with fanciful ideas which are borne of curiosity and lively imagination. In Ireland, as elsewhere, popular lore testifies to the fusion of the practical and the poetic.

Leprechauns

One of the most famous creations of Irish folklore are the leprechauns. These "little people" are solitary creatures, avoiding contact with mortals and other leprechauns. The leprechaun pours all of his passion into the concentration of carefully making shoes. A leprechaun can always be found with a shoe in one hand and a hammer in the other.

Most leprechauns are ugly, stunted creatures, not taller than boys of the age of 10 or 12. But they are broad and bulky. Leprechauns have a mischievous light in their eyes and their bodies, despite their stubbiness, usually move gracefully. They usually dress in grey or green colored coats, wear a sturdy pocket-studded apron, and a hat.

They have been known to be foul-mouthed and they smoke ill-smelling pipes called *dudeens*. Leprechauns guard the fairies' treasures. They must prevent them being stolen by mortals. When the marauding Vikings landed in Ireland they hid this treasure. Although they hide the treasures well, the presence of a rainbow alerts mortals to the whereabouts of gold hordes. If a mortal catches a leprechaun and sternly demands his treasure, he will give it to the mortal. Female leprechauns do not exist.

Merrows

Good or bad weather, the male merrow sits on a rock, scanning the sea for cases of brandy lost from wrecked

ships. He is a friendly fellow with a red nose, possibly from too much drink. He is a bringer of good luck. He wears a red cocked hat and has a green body, with green hair and teeth. He has the eyes of a pig, scaly legs, arms like fins and wears no clothes.

Mulrruhgach Maidens

The female merrow (*mulrruhgach*), also called a mermaid (*murúch*) or a sea-maiden (*maighdean mhara*), is lovely and graceful. She has the tail of a fish and web-like scales between her fingers. She sometimes wears a white gown. The gown is trimmed with red and purple seaweeds. The sea water on her hair glistens like dew when the rays of the sun's morning light shines upon it. She also wears a red hat which suits her alluring face with its mocking eyes. In legends the singing of a mermaid, or her sirensong, is described as irresistible. As she lounges upon the rocks, she attempts to attract fishermen to her. But if he comes too near, she dives into the sea, laughing at them. Her presence always ensures a storm or a disaster at sea. When a sailor fails to come home from the sea it is sometimes said he "married a mermaid". She upsets the waves and causes rain to fall from the sky.

Irish Dancing

◆ ◆ ◆

Traditional Irish dancing is popular throughout the country. You will also see jigs and reels being performed in many social events and competitions across the world.

◆ ◆ ◆

The early history of Irish dance reveals a constant shifting of population through migration and invasions. Each of these peoples brought their preferred types of dance and music. There are only vague references to the early history of Irish dancing, but there is evidence that among its first practitioners were the ancient pre-Christian peoples, who danced in religious rituals honoring the oak tree and the sun. Traces of their circular dances survive in the ring dances of today.

During the Celtic period new forms of dance emerged. Even after Christianity arrived, pre-Christian styles of music and dance were retained. The Anglo-Norman occupation of the 12th Century brought Norman dance forms into Irish towns. During the mid-16th Century, dances were performed in the great halls of the great castles. Some of these dances were adapted by the English invaders of the 16th Century. They in turn brought them back to the courts of England. Royalty were welcomed to Ireland by

young women performing dances. The landing of King James at Kinsale, County Cork, in 1780, was marked by dancers on the shore.

A prominent feature of dance in the 18th Century was the dance master. These wandering, flamboyant teachers developed group dances to hold the interest of less gifted pupils. The dance masters would challenge each other to public dancing competitions when they met at fairs.

Various versions of the same dance could be found in different parts of the country. In this way a rich heritage of Irish dances was assembled and adapted over the centuries. Today, jigs, reels, hornpipes, sets, half sets, polkas, and step dances are all performed. Solo dancing or step dancing first appeared at the end of the 18th Century.

The costumes worn by Irish dancers today reflect the clothing of the past. Dresses are based on peasant dress but have been adorned with hand-embroidered designs. A Tara brooch is often used to attach a cape. Male dress is less embellished. This may include a plain kilt and jacket. Male and female dancers wear hornpipe shoes, except for reels or jigs when they wear soft shoes.

Today there are many organizations promoting Irish dance. Children, teenagers, and adults compete in separate competitions for titles and prizes. There are group and solo competitions where dancers are graded by age from 6 to 17 and then into the senior categories.

There are dancing championships in all four provinces, and winners of these provincial competitions qualify for the All-Ireland Championships. The World Championships are held in Dublin at Easter where dancers from England, Ireland, the United States, Canada, Australia, and New Zealand compete for the World title.

The Irish word *céilidh* originally referred to a gathering of neighbors to enjoy music, dance and stories. Today it refers to an informal dance evening. These are held in many districts across Ireland or wherever the Irish are to be found. Irish dancing has received international attention through the popular *Riverdance* show. This was originally conceived as an interval act during the 1994 Eurovision Song Contest in Ireland. Michael Flatley and Jean Butler led a chorus of world champion dancers. The routine was so successful it became a two-hour show that continues to tour the world. Offshoots have also emerged, such as Flatley's *Lord of the Dance*. The dancing schools in Ireland today are filled with pupils keen to learn the dancing styles which brought the original *Riverdance* performers international acclaim.

Quotes and Sayings

In many ways, words are the lifeblood of the nation. These witty words of wisdom, many translated from Irish, reflect the nation's love and mastery of language.

On Drink

Good as drink is, it ends in thirst.

Women do not drink liquor but it disappears when they are present.

It is sweet to drink but bitter to pay for.

When the drop is inside the sense is outside.

What butter or whiskey does not cure cannot be cured.

Beware of the public house or limpets will be your food.

Left: *According to one Irish saying, "A narrow neck keeps the bottle from being emptied in one swig!"*

Work and Idleness

If you do not sow in the spring, you will not reap in the autumn.

Little as a wren needs, it must gather it.

He who gets a name for early rising can stay in bed until midday.

It is a bad hen that does not scratch for itself.

Work without end is housewife's work.

Two-thirds of the work is the semblance.

A handful of skill is better than a bagful of gold.

One does not tire of a profitable occupation.

The back must slave to feed the belly.

A long stitch, a lazy tailor.

The work praises the man.

Youth and Old Age

Be good to the child and he will come to you tomorrow.
Youth does not mind where it sets its foot.

The skin of the old sheep is on the rafter no sooner than the skin of the young sheep.

Many a ragged colt made a noble horse.

You cannot put an old head on the young.

Nobody knows where his sod of death is.

Romance and Marriage

Empty and cold is the house without a woman.

From the day you marry your heart will be in your mouth and your hand in your pocket.

The only cure for love is marriage.

It is a lonely washing that has no man's shirt in it.

Your son is your son until he marries, but your daughter is your daughter until you die.

Character and Honor

A bad egg, a bad bird.

A hole is more honourable than a patch.

Fortune and Wealth

A little, often, leaves wrinkles in the purse.

The well-fed does not understand the lean.

Quotations on Ireland

The Irish are a very fair people, they never speak well of one another. – *James Boswell*

In Ireland the inevitable never happens and the unexpected constantly occurs. – *Sir John Pentland Mahaffy*

What's the use of being Irish if the world doesn't break your heart? – *John Fitzgerald Kennedy*

Ireland is rich in literature that understands a soul's yearnings, and dancing that understands a happy heart.
– *Margaret Jackson*

This is one race of people for whom psychoanalysis is of no use whatsoever. – *Sigmund Freud* (about the Irish)

TOASTS

These toasts reflect the humor and wordplay associated with the Irish.

◆ ◆ ◆

May your glass be ever full.
May the roof over your head be always strong.
And may you be in heaven
half an hour before the devil knows you're dead.

Here's to me, and here's to you,
And here's to love and laughter.
I'll be true as long as you,
And not one moment after.

Here's to you and yours
And to mine and ours.
And if mine and ours
Ever come across to you and yours,
I hope you and yours will do
As much for mine and ours
As mine and ours have done
For you and yours!

BELOW: *A pint of stout awaits a toast from its drinker at Tierney's bar in Clonmel, County Tipperary.*

Health and life to you;
The mate of your choice to you;
Land without rent to you,
And death in Eirinn.

Here's a toast to your enemies' enemies!

When we drink, we get drunk.
When we get drunk, we fall asleep.
When we fall asleep, we commit no sin.
When we commit no sin, we go to heaven.
So, let's all get drunk, and go to heaven!

Here's to a long life and a merry one.
A quick death and an easy one.
A pretty girl and an honest one.
A cold beer—and another one!

Here's to our wives and girlfriends:
May they never meet!

I have known many, liked not a few,
loved only one, I drink to you.

May you live as long as you want,
and never want as long as you live.

May the grass grow long
on the road to hell for want of use.

May you live to be a 100 years,
with one extra year to repent.

As you slide down the banisters of life
may the splinters never point the wrong way.

May your troubles be as few and as far apart
as my Grandmother's teeth.

May the roof above us never fall in,
and may we friends gathered below never fall out.

May there be a generation of children
on the children of your children.

May the Lord keep you in his hand
and never close his fist too tight.

May your neighbors respect you,
Trouble neglect you, The angels protect you,
And heaven accept you.

May your pockets be heavy and your heart be light,
may good luck pursue you each morning and night.

May the strength of three be in your journey.

In the New Year, may your right hand always
be stretched out in friendship and never in want.

Here's that we may always have a clean shirt,
a clean conscience, and a guinea in our pocket.

May I see you grey and combing your children's hair.

WEDDING TRADITIONS

◆ ◆ ◆

The ancient Brehon laws set the rules for marriage. On the wedding day itself many signs and portents were observed.

◆ ◆ ◆

Before the arrival of the Normans in the 12th Century, the rules regarding the marriage ritual came under the Brehon laws. These evolved from the customs of the early tribes. Under the law, marriage seemed to be a somewhat casual affair. For instance, a couple could marry "for one year certain" and either one could withdraw after one year if they wished. The regulations surrounding the marriage contract, however, showed it to be far more complex. The laws determined exactly those who could contract a proper marriage and under what conditions. Various people were not allowed to enter into a contract, including impotent men and churchmen.

Once it was determined that a prospective husband and wife could make a contract, their families then addressed the business aspects of the union. The prospective husband paid a *coibche* (marriage portion) to the girl's father, who then divided it with the head of the tribe. The *coibche* was paid each year for a total of 21 years, if the marriage lasted that long. In the second year, the wife kept a third of the

amount for herself, while her father and the head of the tribe divided the remainder. As the years went by, the wife kept a larger part. *Tinol* was a wedding present to the bride from her friends and acquaintances and consisted of cattle, the chief wealth of the time. It was divided between the bride and her father, the father getting one-third and his daughter the rest. Marriage contracts were often made at the great fairs.

Ceremonies

Before marriages were held in church they were often conducted outdoors in a place of mystical significance. On the island of Cape Clear, located off the west coast of County Cork, there are four gallawns (pillarstones). One stone is known as *Cloch na Geallúna* (the trysting stone). It has a hole right through it and in pre-Christian times, a couple would join hands through the stone, and would wed in the presence of the local king.

Equal Rights

Under the Brehon laws, a marriage between two equal partners was looked upon with great favor because it simplified the relationship. The wife is described as *comthigeran* (co-lord), and both she and her husband were required to jointly provide food for the great festivals and collaborate equally on other tasks. In fact, all the details of

life were cared for meticulously by the Brehon laws so as to protect the rights of the wife against any exploitation by her husband or his family. Over the years, and especially after Christianity came to Ireland, other customs developed. In County Donegal, when a man wanted to marry a particular girl, he and a friend went to her house and when the door was opened, he would throw his cap into the house. If the cap was thrown back out, it meant she was not interested.

Other Customs

The main season for marrying used to be from Christmas to Lent, so that by Shrovetide (the three days preceding Ash Wednesday), a great deal of persuasion and pressure was brought to bear on single people to take the plunge. Many signs and portents were observed on the wedding day. A man, not a woman, was always the first to wish joy to the bride.

It was lucky to hear a cuckoo on the wedding morning, or to see three magpies. To meet a funeral on the road meant bad luck and if there was a funeral procession planned for that day, the wedding party always took a different road. The wedding party would always take the longest road home from the church. It was bad luck if a glass or cup was broken on the wedding day.

SPORT

Ireland's role in world sport has in recent years been disproportionate to the size of the population.

Sport, in all its forms, is a year-round national obsession. Hardly a week passes that some sporting event is not the focus of everyday conversation.

Soccer

This is a popular sport across the island. The Republic of Ireland's ambitious and inspirational performance at the 2002 World Cup signalled that the days of Ireland being content with simply qualifying for a World Cup competition are over. Ireland gave the World Cup some memorable moments on the pitch until they crashed out during an exciting last 16 game against Spain.

Many of Ireland's international soccer players make significant contributions to clubs throughout Europe. These include Niall Quinn, Roy Keane, Robbie Keane, and Ian Harte.

LEFT: *Matthew Holland celebrates after scoring Ireland's equalizer in the 1-1 draw against Cameroon in the 2002 World Cup.*

Golf

There are nearly 200 golf courses in Ireland. The island's golf courses are as varied as the landscape itself. Some courses wind around mountains or along rivers; others overlook valleys, or lie under palm trees, and many are within the confines of cities or at farflung resorts. Lahinch, nestled near the Cliffs of Moher on the Atlantic coast of County Clare, has two courses, one of which is considered to be the Irish circuit's most challenging championship layout. One of Ireland's longest courses is on the scenic ring of Kerry at Waterville. It is laid out on lofty sand dunes and bounded on three sides by the Atlantic. Other noted golf courses include Ballybunion in County Kerry and Portmarnock, located just north of Dublin.

There are a number of celebrated Irish golfers. These include Padraig Harrington, Paul McGinley, Darren Clarke, and Christy O'Connor Junior.

Gaelic Games

Hurling, Gaelic football, handball, and rounders are amateur sports administered by *Cumann Lúthchleas Gael*, the Gaelic Athletic Association. Hurling and camogie, which is played by women, are high scoring and exciting field games. Played with stick and ball, there are 15 players on each team. Scores can be either points, with the ball going between the posts and over the bar, or goals with the ball going under

the bar. One goal is equivalent to three points. Gaelic football, also played by two teams of 15, is a field game in which players can pass it in any direction by kicking or hand passing it.

Rugby

Ireland's rugby team consists of players from both sides of the border. The main competitions are the All-Ireland League, the Provincial Cups, and the Inter-Provincial Championship. The provinces also participate in European Rugby Cup competitions. Ulster won the European Rugby Cup in 1999 and Munster were runners-up in 2000.

Equestrian Sports

All forms of equestrian sport are popular. Horse racing attracts large attendances at Ireland's many race courses and there is a large business in off-course betting. Classic flat races are run at the Curragh, County Kildare.

Events such as the Irish Derby are among the most prestigious in Europe and the Irish bloodstock industry is considered one of the finest in the world. Hurdle racing and steeple-chasing are also popular.

Athletics

In the past Ireland has enjoyed success in both the Olympic and Paralympic Games. Sonia O'Sullivan's performance at

the 2000 Olympic games in Sydney, where she won a track and field Silver medal in the 5,000m race, was one of the most outstanding Irish sporting achievements in 2000. In winning the silver medal, Sonia became the first Irish female athlete to win an Olympic Medal in track and field.

Other Sports

Ireland has over 3,000km (1,864 miles) of coastline and sailing is a long-established sport. The Royal Cork Yacht Club, founded in 1720, is the world's oldest sailing club.

The country is superb for angling. Freshwater fish are found in every stream, lough and river. Anglers can also fish at sea. Competitions are held across the island.

In motor racing Eddie Irvine from Northern Ireland has become a champion Formula I Grand Prix driver. Jordan Grand Prix, founded by Dubliner Eddie Jordan, has also become a major name in the sport.

Finally, road "bowling" is quite a unique attraction which is played in well defined areas in Counties Cork, Armagh, Limerick, and Waterford. The game consists of flinging a weighty iron ball in the shortest number of "flings" over a set course of public roads that are sealed off.

FLORA AND FAUNA

◆ ◆ ◆

Ireland was separated from the European mainland after the last Ice Age. As a result the island has a smaller range of flora and fauna than is found elsewhere in Europe.

◆ ◆ ◆

Flora

There are two obvious aspects of the vegetation cover in Ireland. The first is an impression of intense greenness, the result of the abundant grasses responding to the mild moist air. The second is the relative absence of trees, especially along the western seaboard where strong winds are the main limiting factor to growth. The once extensive oak woodlands of the midlands were cleared over most of the country by the 17th Century and remain today only as remnants in remote areas. In recent decades a re-forestation program has favored Sitka spruce, Scots, contorta and other pines, larches, Norway spruce, and Douglas fir.

The flora is of more limited variety than elsewhere in Europe but it has some interesting features. In the extreme

FOLLOWING PAGE: *Gortin Glen Forest Park, County Tyrone, is planted with conifers and contains a herd of Japanese sika deer.*

southwest there is a vegetation with Mediterranean affinities which includes the Arbutus. The numerous bryophytes reflect the mildness and high humidity of this part of Ireland.

The Burren Landscape

The unique Burren country of County Clare is swathed with barren sheets of rock but is surprisingly and wondrously ablaze with wildflowers in May and June. Forcing their way out of the shallow soil through a maze of crevices and fissures, these stubborn plants, thought to be of Arctic-Alpine origin, range from deep blue spring gentians and small mustard-colored rock roses to sprawling snow-white mountain avens, and the unique dense-flowered orchid, a lime-and-cream-colored, upright cluster of blooms.

Fauna

Ireland has 27 species of mammal. These include the red deer, pine marten, badger, otter, hare, and stoat which are native to the country. There are also introduced species such as the fallow deer, rabbit, and other rodents. Ireland's only reptile is a small lizard and there are three amphibia, the newt, the frog, and the toad.

The rivers and lakes have salmon, trout, char, pollan, perch, pike, and eels. Amphibians are represented by a single native species each of frog, toad (natterjack), and newt.

ABOVE: *The National Botanic Gardens in Dublin was founded in 1795.*

LEFT: *Otters are a native species. The animals are rarely seen but live along riverbanks and beside lakes all around the country.*

Bird Life

Of some 380 species of wild birds recorded in Ireland, 135 breed in the country. There is considerable migration of birds to Ireland in spring and autumn, while several species arrive from Greenland and Iceland in winter; 75 per cent of the world's population of the Greenland Whitefronted Goose winter in Ireland. Inland waters support colonies of swans, geese, waders, duck, tern, and gulls. Game shooting is strictly controlled and state-assisted restocking programs augment stocks of wild game birds. Among the more unusual species of bird are merlin, peregrine falcons, corncrake, and chough.

The Peat Bogs

Ireland's bogland has long been an intriguing facet of many parts of the countryside.

Bogs are among some of the most ancient Irish habitats, with some of the oldest examples dating back more than 10,000 years. The bogland of Ireland is spread over the central plain in counties such as Offaly and Laois, as well as throughout the coastal lowlands and highlands of Counties Kerry, Donegal, and Mayo. There is an abundance of bogland around Connemara in County Galway, where over a third of the land is bog.

A Priceless Resource

Climatologists, archaeologists, and biologists all value the peat as essential to research, and naturalists cherish the living carpet that covers the peat. Bogs help to maintain reliable supplies of clean water to rivers. In Europe they also have a cultural importance as some of the last true wilderness areas and are enjoyed by thousands of people.

The boglands are a "living archive" and contain an unparalleled record of our past. A rich archive of information lies preserved in bogs. Much of this is organic

Above: *A landscape in County Offaly transformed by peat cutting.*

and has a capacity to expand our understanding of people, culture, economy, and climate far back into prehistory.

Pollen, plants, evidence for the use of wood and woodland management, boats, weapons, lines of communication and indications of human impact on surrounding landscape, and ecology all contribute to modern knowledge in ways which are seldom approached on dry land. Peat bogs have produced some of the most spectacular finds of Irish archaeology, including remarkably well-preserved bodies.

Peat is rich in fossil carbon, removed from the atmosphere by plants and accumulated over thousands of years. The drainage and destruction of raised bogs results in the rapid loss of the stored carbon in the form of greenhouse gases (carbon dioxide and methane), as the peat decomposes.

Uses

Bogs vary in size from a few hectares to a few square kilometers of land. Usually a former lake basin or shallow pond, it has been filled in over the centuries by parts of decaying trees, plants, mosses, stones, and water. A bog can be like quicksand, swallowing up whatever lies in its path.

Following Page: *19th-Century workers stacking peat ready to be used for fuel. This was a common sight across Ireland.*

When the bog is settled it can be walked upon, small pieces of sod can be sliced from the ground, and stacked. Many bog plants were traditionally used in folk medicine and brewing. Its main purpose, however, has been for fuel. Today new uses are also emerging for bog plants such as biofilters. The most common use of bogs in the west of Ireland has been to provide year-round grazing for animals.

A Unique Habitat

Many rare and protected species of plant and animal are found on bogs. The Greenland Whitefronted Goose relies on wet bogs with pools for feeding and roosting. The invertebrates found on bogs contain many rare species.

The disappearance of the bogs would have serious consequences. For various flora and fauna the last western European refuge would be destroyed. Several species of birds would lose important wintering grounds. A type of landscape which was once found in large parts of Western Europe would no longer exist. It would also mean the destruction of archaeological remains preserved in bogs. An ecosystem which has so far been studied incompletely only, and which has been providing important ecological insights into hydrology, carbon fixation, and environmental change would be lost for further research.

RIGHT: *A peat-burning power station in County Longford.*

ABOVE: *A woodcut from 1581 showing a dog enjoying a bone from the table of a great Irish chieftain.*

NATIVE DOG BREEDS

◆ ◆ ◆

Ireland has produced several native dog breeds. The Irish Wolfhound was once reserved for nobility; commoners had to be content with terriers. Now, of course, Irish breeds of all types are exceedingly popular.

◆ ◆ ◆

Irish Wolfhound

Continental Celts were known to keep greyhounds and the Irish Celts were interested in breeding large hounds. The origin of the breed is lost in antiquity, but there are references to the "Great Hound of Ireland" in many ancient classics. The first written account of these dogs was made by a Roman consul in A.D. 391 Irish hounds formed the basis of the Scottish Deerhound. Pairs of Irish hounds were prized as gifts by the royal houses of Europe and elsewhere from the Middle Ages to the 17th Century. Up until the end of the 1600s the dogs were used for hunting wolves and deer both in Ireland and Europe. In 1652 the export of Wolfhounds was prohibited. This helped preserve their number for a time, but the gradual disappearance of the wolf and the continued demand overseas led to a reduction in their numbers almost to the point of extinction by the end of the 17th Century. The growth in Irish nationalism in

the late 19th Century was accompanied by the revival in Irish traditions, including native dog breeds. The Irish wolfhound became a living symbol of Irish culture. At this time one determined enthusiast began to collect the few Wolfhounds remaining in Ireland. With the help of Deerhound blood and the occasional outcross of Borzoi and Great Dane, he eventually achieved a type of dog that bred true in every generation and was accepted as the legitimate revival of the breed. The Irish Wolfhound is strong but gracefully built, it is very muscular, and its movements are easy and active. The dog's head and neck are carried high and its tail is carried with an upward sweep with a slight curve towards the extremity. The dog's head is long and level. Its muzzle is long and moderately pointed. Its body is long and well ribbed up, its eyes are dark, and its ears are small. They have a distinctive rough grey coat. Its minimum height is a remarkable 79cm (31in).

Kerry Beagle

This dog is one of the most ancient breeds. It is reputed to have descended from a dog vaguely known as "The old southern hound". The dog referred to as *Gadhar* in old Irish literature may be the direct ancestor of the present-day

Right: *Irish Wolfhounds were prized as gifts by the royal houses of Europe and elsewhere from the Middle Ages until the 1600s.*

breed. During the Middle Ages and in later centuries this dog was mixed through breeding experiments with hounds from the continent to produce a very efficient hunting dog. Their fortunes suffered during the Famine in Ireland in 1847 when they were decimated by starvation.

The name Beagle is thought to be derived from the Irish word *beag* (small) and certainly the Beagle is a small hound used to hunt small game like hares, whereas the Kerry Beagle was often used to hunt stag. The present-day word for the Beagle in Irish is *pocadán* which refers to its use as a hunting dog rather than its size.

The Kerry Beagle is a vibrant hound built for speed and endurance. The breed has a moderately long, broad skull with oval eyes. Its eyes are large, bright and vary from bright yellow to deep buff, and deeper brownish yellow. They have long muzzles, their noses are fine in texture and slightly tapering with large nostrils.

Kerry Beagles have large, pendulous ears falling below the neck. The dog has a muscular, fairly thickset body of moderate length. The chest is deep, their shoulders are strong, and they have short but strong legs. The tail is long and it is carried upwards from the loins. Their coat is hard, close, and smooth. It can be black and tan; blue mottled and tan; black, tan, and white; or tan and white. They are approximately 61cm (24in) high. There are a number of Kerry Beagle packs in Ireland today. They are mainly used

for hunting hares.

Irish Red and White Setter

It is believed the Irish Setter came into its own at the end of the 17th Century. When the Irish Setters first appeared at dog shows in the mid-1800s there was confusion about their proper color. By the end of the 19th Century the Red Setter had virtually eclipsed the Red and White Setter. This breed had become so rare that many thought it was extinct. Efforts were made to revive the breed during the 1920s. The Irish Red and White Setter is a strong, well-balanced and proportioned dog. It is athletic rather than racy. They are keen, intelligent, and friendly. The dog's head is broad in proportion to its body. Its skull is domed and its muzzle is square. Their eyes are dark hazel or brown, and their ears are set level with the eyes.

The breed has a strong, muscular body with a deep chest and its legs are well muscled. Their tails are of moderate length, tapering to a fine point, and carried level with or below the back. When moving at the trot their movement is lively and graceful. They have long, silky fine hair called "feathering" on the back of the fore and hind legs, and on the outer ear flap. On most other parts of the body the hair is short and flat. The base color of the breed is white with solid red patches. Dogs are at least 62cm (26in) and bitches are slightly smaller.

Irish Red Setter

This breed was developed for hunting and is derived from the Irish Red and White Setter and an unknown solid red colored dog. The type was identifiable by the 1700s. The Irish Red Setter is racy, athletic, and affectionate. They have long, lean heads, an oval skull, and a moderately long neck. Their eyes are dark hazel or dark brown. Their hindlegs are long and muscular and their forelegs are straight. Their distinctive coats are rich chestnut. Bitches are at least 55cm (21.5in) and dogs are at least 58cm (23in) high.

Irish Water Spaniel

It is thought that Water Spaniels evolved from dogs that came to Ireland from Persia via Spain. Reference is made in 1600 to Irish "water doges that pursue water fowl". Its peculiar "rat tail" suggests the breed had an indigenous ancestor. They are strongly built and intelligent dogs. Long loose curls grow down into a well defined peak between the eyes. Their face is perfectly smooth, their nose is large, and their eyes are small and colored dark amber or dark hazel. The Irish Water Spaniel has very long ears and a fairly long neck. The body is barrel-shaped and their chest is deep. The breed has a smooth tail which gradually tapers. They move with a distinctive rolling motion and the curly coat is rich puce liver. Dogs are at least 53cm (21in) and bitches are at least 51cm (20in) high.

Irish Terrier

The Irish Terrier is one of the oldest of Ireland's terrier breeds. Before the 1880s they were sometimes red, or black and tan, or brindle. By the 20th Century all the breed showed the red coat. The breed displayed bravery and intelligence as messenger dogs during World War I. The Irish Terrier is active and wiry in appearance. Their heads are long, the skull flat, and their nose is black. Their eyes are dark and small. The breed has small, V-shaped ears. They have a symmetrical body with a deep chest. Their fore and hindlegs are carried straight forward and parallel. Their hair is red, dense, and wiry in texture. The breed stands at least 45.5cm (18in) high. They are versatile farmyard dogs, pets, gundogs, or guard dogs.

Kerry Blue Terrier

There are few references to this breed before the 20th Century. It originated as a rat catcher and farmyard dog, and was supposed to be prevalent in Kerry, but it has been developed in other counties. The breed became a mascot for Irish patriots. By 1928 this upstanding and alert breed had become popular worldwide. Their heads show plenty of hair, and their nostrils are large and wide. Their eyes are dark or hazel, and their ears are thin and not large. The breed has a level body, a deep chest, and a thin tail carried upwards. Their "blue" hair is soft and wavy. Bitches stand at least 44.5cm

(17.5in) and dogs stand at least 46cm (18in) high.

Irish Glen of Imaal Terrier
This hardy breed suited the harsh environment of the Glen of Imaal. They are incredibly strong but affectionate. Their bodies are longer than high and low to the ground. Their eyes are medium-sized and brown. They have small ears, their tails are normally docked, and their coats are blue brindle or wheaten and of harsh texture. Dogs stand at least 35.5cm (14in) high and bitches slightly less.

Irish Soft Coated Wheaten Terrier
Wheaten Terriers were always used by small farmers to kill vermin or help with the work about the farm. They were used for a long time in the difficult job of hunting badgers and otters. The breed is hardy, active, and good-tempered. They have a long head and a flat skull. Their dark eyes are not too large and their ears are small to medium.
Their body is compact and their tails are normally docked. Their coats are a good clear wheaten of shades from light wheaten to a golden reddish hue. Dogs stand at least 46cm (18in) high and bitches somewhat less.

IRELAND'S ISLANDS

◆ ◆ ◆

The islands of Ireland are scattered like jewels around the coast. Each island is unique in character and all possess a rich heritage, although many are now abandoned.

◆ ◆ ◆

Most of Ireland's islands are on the southwest and northwest coast, and lie only a few kilometers off the mainland. Their shapes vary from the Skelligs, which have been called "the most dramatic structures in Western Europe", to the boomerang of cliffs that is Rathlin, and the dozens of small drumlin islands, flat as playing cards, that are scattered over Clew Bay. The limestone pavements of the Arans contrast with the tranquil fields of Inishbofin, and the great headlands and cliffs of Tory and Achill.

Small Nations

For thousands of years most islands that could offer some kind of living were inhabited. Each was home to a tribe that was really a small nation. There was a sense of nationhood, of absolute containment. Significantly, one or two, like Tory and Inishmurray, even elected their own kings. Isolation caused each community to differ from others in the way finches differ among the Galapagos Islands.

PREVIOUS PAGE: *Achill Island, off the coast of County Mayo, has been visited by several great writers, including Graham Greene.*

When an island becomes linked with the mainland, these differences are soon dissipated. Great Island has been merged into County Cork for many centuries. The individual nature of the people of Achill has dwindled since a bridge was constructed in 1888. It has been said that Valentia's long history falls neatly into two parts: before the bridge and after it. In 1969, at about the same time Valentia was linked to Portmagee, a cable car was built between Dursey Island and the tip of the Beara Peninsula, too late to keep the old community which, with its current population of under 10, is on life support.

Intrepid Islanders

Today, observing people who are proud of their isolated community and its rich cultural inheritance and who continue to struggle for its survival, we can unravel some of the mystery of why even the most inaccessible islands attracted inhabitants from prehistoric times. Those ancient settlers who have left behind kitchen middens, Megalithic tombs, stone circles, cashels (usually a fort with stone banks), promontory forts, and ancient field systems must have felt a similar sense of close identity.

They had sailed over in the frailest of craft to create

their lonely settlements. They found fertile soil, abundant fishing, and perhaps a sense of security, provided by the surrounding sea, which prevailed until the arrival of the Vikings with their superior seamanship.

Holy Hermits

The seeking out of so many islands by early Christian hermits derived from the austerities of the Desert Fathers and the discipline of the Culdees. The physical discomforts were not much greater than those suffered by Neolithic men and women. But the passion for lonely contemplation of the Divine Spirit manifest in the trackless wastes of the sea and the cry of the sea birds was a Celtic obsession that made this form of isolation a unique display of sanctity.

For some time during the Dark Ages, Christianity depended on the prayers and meditations of the various saints who inhabited the islands. It is hard to believe the saints performed greater miracles than those who supervised the erection of beehive huts on the summit of Skellig Michael or designed the maze on Inishmurray.

By the late Medieval period, the Franciscan friars on Sherkin in West Cork were living in less extreme monastic surroundings. By then Vikings, pirates, clan chieftains looking for fishing dues, and formidable personalities like Grace O'Malley had played their part in island history. Later came the unpalatable fact that islands and their inhabitants

RIGHT: *Garinish Island, off the coast of County Cork, has a remarkable Italianate garden and can be reached by ferry in 20 minutes.*

became spoils of conquest. At different times the Arans were in the hands of the Digby and Guinness families, while Valentia belonged to the benevolent Knight of Kerry.

British Assistance

A defining moment came when the Congested Districts Board took over from the old landlords. Since the board, established in 1891 to dispense assistance to poverty-stricken "congested districts", was an imperial creation during the period of British policy known as "Killing Home Rule with Kindness", its work in distributing land and giving grants for building houses, piers, and fishing has never been fully appreciated.

These islands have a long history of shipwrecks. The lighthouses, some built and rebuilt with enormous difficulty, are still in the control of the body which in 1867 became the Commissioners of Irish Lights. Computers have now replaced the keepers who for so long lived their lonely lives apart from the islanders.

Survival

For island people life was unremittingly hard. On the smaller islands there were no pubs or shops; supplies,

including fuel, were carried over in frail boats. Not only were many communities cut off from the mainland by bad weather for weeks during the winter, but they had to endure a life without doctors or midwives. Those who got sick had to cure themselves with remedies like seal oil.

The majority had to do without churches or priests. Religion, however, was of the greatest importance for those who lived close to nature and to God.

Poverty

There were shortages that took place almost every winter, when people would be reduced to eating cockles, periwinkles, and even seaweed. There were problems with livestock: how to tie down a struggling cow and manoeuver it into a frail currach in order to take it over the waves to the mainland to be sold. When pigs were carried, their feet were muffled in sacks in case their trotters ripped the canvas. On islands near enough to the mainland, like those in Roaring Water Bay, animals would be swum across with a halter around their horns.

There was the constant lack of money. Fishing was a mainstay for most communities, but throughout the 20th Century fishing had been in decline. Although farming, lobstering, and the collection of gulls' eggs might provide seasonal income, there was little money for clothes or cigarettes or the penny to put on the plate when Mass on

the mainland was attended. Mackerel and herring nets had to be bought, as had creosote and paint for the boats. British and US money became essential as sons and daughters emigrated and sent a share of their earnings back to their families.

Island Life

It was not all misery and deprivation. The joys of summer ranged from the hens beginning to lay, to the fish coming in, and the hay and potatoes growing. In winter there would be dancing to the fiddle and mouth organ, storytelling, and card games to the accompaniment of tea, poteen, and porter. A native from an island in Roaring Water Bay felt: "Living on an island makes a person apart. He has different values from the person on the mainland... The dependence of the island people on one another can never be appreciated by outsiders."

By the time the Irish Free State took over the role of the Congested Districts Board, the inhabitants of Irish-speaking islands like the Arans and the Blaskets had taken on a romantic image that brought them an extraordinary fame not only in Ireland but overseas. They had a mythic appeal because they preserved a way of life that was seen to be unsullied by outside influences, in particular by the Anglo-Saxon tongue.

Tory Island may have escaped this image of purity

PREVIOUS PAGE: *Ireland's Eye, off the coast of County Dublin, is 1.6km (1 mile) north of the Howth Peninsula.*

because it was too far offshore for a regular stream of visitors and scholars to visit and admire. Perhaps a literature might have been coaxed out of the Tory islanders in the same way as the men and women of the Blaskets were urged to create their marvellous books. Instead, on Tory it was painting that was encouraged by a discerning visitor to the island.

The old ways that have survived on the islands but had vanished from the mainland—the use of the flail, fishing from traditional currachs and coracles, booleying on Achill, and farming by the Rundale system on Tory—were sources of fascination for outsiders. Robert Flaherty's flim *Man of Aran* confirmed the romantic stereotype. In the years to come, islanders resented tourist interest in "aboriginal Irishness" and the things that were archaic and picturesque. Visitors continue to admire the Arans as the last bastion of Gaelic culture and can now reach the islands by air.

Famous Visitors

The long list of 20th-Century travellers captivated by island life includes artists like Augustus John, Seán Keating, and Paul Henry, and writers and personalities as diverse as Orson Welles and Brendan Behan. They all sought a world

where traditional pastimes of singing, dancing and storytelling survived, along with good conversation—described as "largely medieval, vigorous, direct, rich in oaths and assertions".

Popular tourism waited in the wings. Writing in 1936, the Dublin photographer Thomas Mason gave advice to any intending visitor. It was permissible to offer cigarettes to an islander, but never money; above all else the stranger must eschew any sense of superiority. Mason was addressing a select few. He observed: "I cannot visualize the type who enjoys Blackpool or the Isle of Man forsaking these resorts and vulgarizing the Blaskets." Today, however, boatloads of tourists descend on the Irish islands during the summer.

Abandoned Islands

Meanwhile nothing could stop the decline in numbers. The failure of the fishing industry, the effects of isolation and monotony, and the consequences of wholesale emigration, have depleted island populations. Today only a handful of islands are still inhabited.

Between 1956 and 1966, five islands off the coast of Mayo were abandoned. Gola, off the Donegal coast, Inishmurray off Sligo, and Scattery at the mouth of the River Shannon were abandoned. In 1954 the 20 people remaining on the Great Blasket left their home and took up residence on the mainland.

PREVIOUS PAGE: *Gorumna Island, off the coast of County Galway, is a bleak land mass but fish farming is big business. Some of the bays are filled with salmon cages.*

A Dying World

Not everyone grieved. The young went first, eager to abandon their simple and beautiful lives, and leave a dying world inhabited by old people. And often the old, after a lifetime of hardship, departed without regret. A newspaper report from October 27, 1960, describing the exodus of the last six families and their assorted livestock from Inishark, the island beside Inishbofin, quoted Thomas, 73, grandfather of baby Ann Lacey and father of the island as saying: 'I'll not be grieving for it. I've wanted to leave for years."

Revival

Today on many islands the decline in population has been stemmed to some extent as lifestyles change. The factors that have come to the aid of more distant islands include proper communication—a decent ferry service and a helicopter link with the mainland. Today islanders enjoy enhanced living conditions where most of the old drudgery has gone. Electricity and running water, backed by *Gaeltacht* grants and other subsidies, have helped to alleviate the people's lives. There is now the ability to commute to and

from the mainland. The "Janus-headed" amenity of television has become essential during the long winters; card-playing, dancing, and other community activities have given way to watching soap operas and football games.

Where once you were lucky to find a bed, there are hotels, guesthouses, and hostels. The term "sustainable tourism" is increasingly being applied to Ireland's islands.

Enduring Enchantment

In the face of all the changes, much remains that is marvelous and enchanting. There is the evidence of a rich and varied past, such as the magnificent complexes of Christian ruins on Inishmurray and Scattery.

If people have gone, the birds flourish. Today many of Ireland's islands are officially recognized as wildlife sanctuaries. There are the ghosts. Landing on the deserted Blaskets, one hears the voice of the writer *Tomás Ó Criomhthainn*: "I have written minutely of much that we did, for it was my wish that somewhere there should be a memorial of it all, and I have done my best to set it down—the character of the people about me—so that some record of it might live after us, for the likes of us will never be seen again."

FOOD AND DRINK

◆ ◆ ◆

Ireland has a great agricultural base and it is not surprising that the country has a reputation for good food.

◆ ◆ ◆

Dairy Produce

The dairy economy in Ireland was once extensive and today it still remains a crucial part of the agricultural sector. The country's mild climate and lush green pastures produce some of the finest milk, cheese, and butter in the world. In recent years small, specialist cheese-makers have been an important factor in underpinning the contemporary revolution in Irish food. These "farmhouse" producers offer consumers a fantastic array of soft and hard cheeses, and highlight the potential for producing even more varieties in the future. Notable are cheeses from Clare and west Cork, especially Gubbeen, a soft cheese from Schull, and spicy Mileens. Dunbarra, made in County Dublin, is like French Brie. Cashel Blue and Cooleeny from County Tipperary are also superb cheeses.

LEFT: *Cattle grazing at the foot of the famous Mourne Mountains in County Down. Dairy farming is an important industry on both sides of the Irish border today.*

RIGHT: *The English Market, Cork city, sells fish, fruit, vegetables, and meat. The market traces its origins back to 1610.*

Cereals and Bakery

Cereals were first introduced to Ireland at the same time that farming began in Ireland. It is thought that the first farmers began cultivating crops about 6,000 years ago in 4000 B.C. The first farmers kept livestock and primarily grew wheat and barley. The earliest dated cereal grains from Ireland were found in Tankardstown, County Limerick, but the crops they produced were not like present-day wheat and barley.

Oaten cakes were almost a staple food until the widespread adoption of the potato. The varieties of bread multiplied dramatically during the 19th Century. These included soda bread, and maize breads. By the end of the century white baker's bread becomes increasingly more accessible to a large part of the population.

Poultry and Eggs

Domestic chickens are derived from southeast Asia. They were then introduced into the Roman empire and were brought to Ireland in the first few centuries A.D. The domesticated goose appeared at this time and the domesticated duck probably arrived during the period of Anglo-Norman occupation. By the 18th Century the turkey

had become popular and appeared in the diets of many sectors of society. It was now a farmyard fowl alongside hens, ducks, and geese. The turkey eventually usurped the goose as the festive bird. The emergence of the grocery store in Ireland during the 19th Century enabled women to use their eggs and birds as items of barter and exchange. Seabirds were often a staple diet for those living on the islands around the coast of mainland Ireland. The most popular ones were gannets and puffins. Other less commonly eaten were guillemots, shearwater and cormorant.

Cattle, Sheep, and Pigs

Ireland's green pastureland is ideal for raising fine beef cattle and sheep. The wealth of Ireland's ancient kings was measured according to the number of cattle in their herds. The daily consumption of meat is a relatively recent phenomenon in Ireland. In the past, fresh meat was considered a luxury that was largely enjoyed by the most affluent strata of society. Many people could only afford salted or preserved meat and fresh meat was a delicacy. If fresh meat was served it was normally a piece of farmyard fowl or mutton.

LEFT: *Sheep are kept on farms throughout Ireland. These flocks provide mutton, lamb, and also wool.*

Today the Irish people enjoy a wide variety of meat produce. The nation produces some of the world's finest free range beef and lamb. Despite the meat industry's strong position in Irish agriculture, the variety of cattle continues to diminish and eating habits are changing with the ever growing demand for "fat free" meat. Ireland continues to have a great reputation for producing sausages, and also white or black puddings that were common fare in early Celtic society.

Fish and Shellfish

Ireland's geographical location means it can readily exploit the fish of the North Atlantic. Numerous inland waterways provide abundant stocks of freshwater fish. Fish has always been most popular in coastal areas. Archaeological discoveries from the Mesolithic period, around 7000 and 4000 B.C., reveal that Ireland's earliest inhabitants went along the shoreline picking limpets, periwinkles, and welks off the rocks. Mounds of empty shells left by these ancient people have been found in areas such as County Sligo.

The Vikings introduced a greater sophistication to sea fishing techniques, with long boats, fishing nets and tackle. The indigenous people, however, were used to a more

RIGHT: *These boats in County Kerry are part of the country's fishing fleet and make a valuable contribution to the national economy.*

limited variety of fish, particularly river salmon and eels which were taken from weirs with nets or spears.

The Anglo-Normans were great fish eaters and they imported new species. The earliest recorded import from England was the pike. Fish was the usual alternative to meat on "days of abstinence" and during Lent. The less well off and those inland made do with salted fish. The more affluent elements of society, with access to markets, new cooking styles, and ingredients favored by the Normans, could enjoy more elaborate fish dishes.

Salmon was an export item by the 14th Century. It could be cured in brine and was ideal for curing by smoking. Wild salmon, however, was ideally eaten freshly cooked over an open fire, and was regarded as the king of all fish. The distinction between fish and meat dishes began to blur, with oysters and meat being cooked together.

Ireland now has an important fishing industry. It has a world-wide reputation for quality and freshness. Ireland's fish restaurants have boomed with many dynamic chefs creating amazing dishes. Large numbers of people attend Galway's annual International Oyster festival.

Wild Food

Ireland's woodlands, hedgerows, boglands, and wetlands have all been exploited for the food they have to offer. Some 9,000 years ago the earliest inhabitants of Ireland

survived by hunting, fishing, and gathering before the coming of agriculture. Animals were hunted, berries were gathered, and fish or eels were caught. Even in early urban settings, such as Cork or Waterford, wild food continued to play an important part in the diet. Excavations in Viking Dublin showed how much wild food, such as fruits, contributed to that early diet. Men hunted and women gathered foods, including those suitable for medicinal purposes.

Wild foods were often used when conventional foods were in short supply. Seaweed was collected on the coast. It has been used for preserving foods and also stewing. Honey has been greatly valued for its cooking and medicinal uses. It has been used for basting meats, fermenting drinks, and preserving fruits.

Deer, a native animal, has always been a high status food. The Normans created deer parks for hunting that were enclosed by palisades or ditches. Wild birds, such as woodcock and snipe, were always popular targets for hunters. The communities on Ireland's islands hunted birds, rabbits, fish, seals and porpoises.

The rural nature of Irish society and the self-sufficient nature of many families meant that the knowledge of and need to collect wild foods remained a feature of Irish life until well into the 20th Century. Today game remains a delicacy, shooting game remains popular, and some people will still gather wild foods in rural areas of the country.

The Potato

The potato, often associated with Ireland, was actually unknown to the country until it was introduced in Elizabethan times by Sir Walter Raleigh, when he was Mayor of Youghal in County Cork. It soon became a staple food. The great potato famines of the 1840s and 1850s were a man-made tragedy; Ireland was bursting with food, but the cereals and dairy produce were for export only, and so the peasants starved in their millions when their staple food, the potato, failed in a series of disastrous harvests.

Despite the catastrophe of the Famine, potatoes maintained a stronghold. Their status, however, was changing. They became less important as diets became more varied with more grain, including maize, becoming available. These remained quite popular until the end of the 19th Century. In the 20th Century Ireland gained a reputation for the development of new varieties of potatoes. Floury potatoes remained popular for a whole range of dishes and the chip was introduced.

The Guinness Story

Irish drinks are numerous and invariably alcoholic. There are a great many lagers, ales, and spirits all made and

LEFT: *Coopers at the Guinness Brewery in Dublin in 1890. Their task of making barrels was once a vital trade in the brewing industry.*

consumed in Ireland. The most recognized of Irish brands is of course Guinness. This black, yeasty stout with a foamy head was first produced in Dublin by Arthur Guinness in 1759. The brewery made its first export of stout to England a decade later. Arthur Guinness eventually came to dominate the domestic market for "porter" (or stout) and began to take a leading share of the trade on mainland Britain.

Arthur Guinness had originally brewed ale in addition to stout. In 1799, however, he stopped his ale production in order to concentrate on stout.

Guinness made its first export overseas in 1803 with a consignment of the stout being sent to British possessions in the Caribbean. The medicinal qualities of Guinness were promoted by the story of a wounded cavalry officer at the Battle of Waterloo in 1815 claiming that the drink helped him regain his health.

In 1821 the Guinness brewery produced the Extra Superior porter. This was stronger than the company's ordinary brew and had a higher hopping. By 1840 this brew accounted for some 82 per cent of the company's production and eventually became the standard brew familiar to today's drinkers.

The incredible demand for Arthur Guiness's product led to the expansion of his premises at St James's Gate. By 1833 it had become the largest brewery in Ireland. In 1858

McMullens' of New York took over the Guinness franchise in the United States. Speakman Brothers in Melbourne were then given the franchise in Australia in 1869.

The commercial success of the Guinness empire led to the company being floated on the London Stock Exchange in 1886, by which time St James's Gate had become the world's biggest brewery.

By the second decade of the 20th Century there were three million barrels of Guinness being produced annually and in 1932 a brewery was being built in west London.

Draught Guinness was launched in 1961 and the British canned version appeared in 1989. To give the canned version a creamy head the company pioneered the Widget, a plastic ring inside the can which releases nitrogen into the beer when opened.

The Guinness brand is now known throughout the world. Its success is not only due to the distinctive taste of the stout but also the highly innovative advertising campaigns it has launched. The first press advertisement for Guinness appeared in 1929. The firm then developed the phrases "Guinness is good for you" and "Guinness for strength", and about the same time the artist John Gilroy joined the team. He created some of the most widely

FOLLOWING PAGE: *The Guinness Brewery in Dublin, around 1867. The works at St James's Gate employed hundreds of workers by this time.*

RIGHT: *Bewley's Oriental Café is a Dublin institution and a popular destination for visitors to the capital.*

recognized graphic art of the century.

In 1935 he started the animal posters that appeared in Guinness advertising from the 1930s to the 1950s. The Toucan first appeared as a Guinness character in 1935. The Toucan became a bird that was to be closely identified with Guinness for almost fifty years! In 1999 the company launched its first-ever global enterprise when it sponsored the Rugby World Cup.

Irish Hospitality

Today, as always, the tradition of hospitality in food and in drink continues in Ireland. Visitors can enjoy unpretentious but delicious cooking. Fresh ingredients simply prepared and served without fuss makes eating in Ireland a real pleasure. Ireland's chefs are also creating stunning, contemporary menus using the finest Irish ingredients. Pubs remain an ideal place to enjoy good food, drink and great company. In addition to traditional pubs you will also find smart bars in city centers.

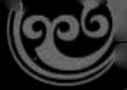

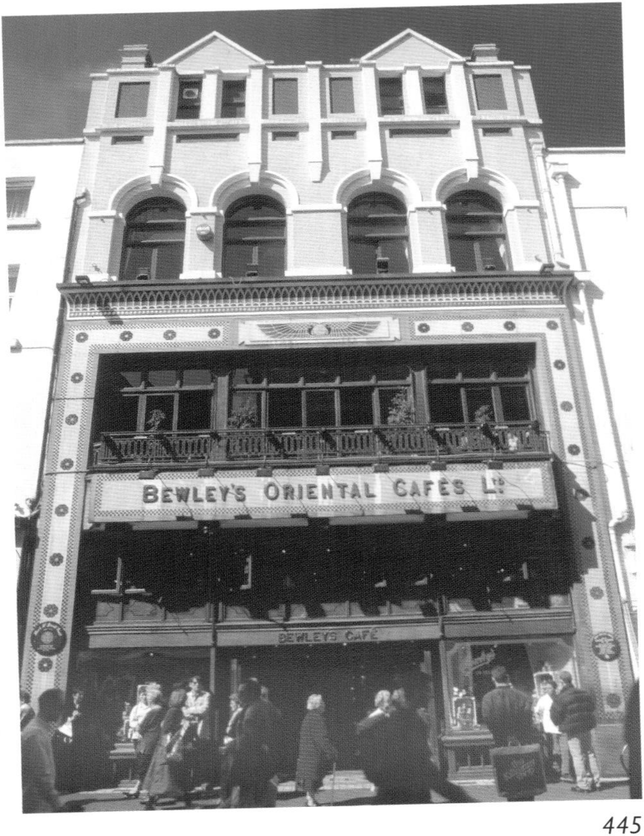
BEWLEY'S ORIENTAL CAFÉS LD
BEWLEY'S CAFÉ

FAVORITE DISHES

Ireland has a wealth of authentic dishes, from the sophisticated to the simple.

The essential spirit of Ireland is reflected in many of the traditional dishes in this chapter. Dishes such as delicious Broiled Trout with Almonds and mouth-watering Guinness Cake appear alongside more humble but traditional selections, including Nettle Soup and Soda Bread.

Other traditional recipes include Crubeens, best eaten with a pint of stout, and potato "staples" such as Champ which is best served with salty farmhouse butter. Folklore decrees that Colcannon should hide a ring for a bride, a button for a bachelor, a thimble for a spinster, and in former times sixpence for wealth!

In addition to these traditional dishes, the culinary experiences of the Irish abroad and a growing appreciation of the versatility of the country's great produce have combined to produce what is now called by some, "new Irish cuisine".

LEFT: *A pub sign advertising food. Many of Ireland's traditional dishes can still be ordered from bars around the country.*

Potato Soup

- 2 lb potatoes, sliced
- 1/4 cup butter
- 2 onions, sliced
- 1 small carrot, sliced
- bouquet garni
- salt and freshly ground black pepper
- 5 cups chicken or vegetable stock
- 2 1/2 cups milk
- freshly chopped chives

Melt the butter in a large pan and add the prepared vegetables. Slowly cook the vegetables until they are soft, but not browned. Stir in the seasonings and stock and bring to the boil.

Cover and simmer slowly for 30 minutes, or until the vegetables are tender. Press the soup through a sieve or blend it in a liquidizer or food processor until smooth.

Return the soup to the pan and add the milk, then heat the mixture gently until it is almost boiling. Season to taste and serve garnished with a few freshly chopped chives.
Serves 8

Nettle Soup

- $3\frac{3}{4}$ pints stock
- $1\frac{1}{4}$ pints milk
- $2\frac{1}{2}$ cups nettles
- $\frac{1}{3}$ cup oatmeal
- $\frac{1}{4}$ cup butter

Wear gloves when collecting the nettles. Only use young, green leaves. Remove any stalks and chop up the leaves using a food processor.

Melt the butter in a large saucepan. Add the oatmeal and cook until the mixture is a golden brown.

Remove the pan from the heat and add the stock. Bring it to the boil and add the milk. When it is boiling again, add the chopped nettles and cook for another few minutes. Season to taste.

Serves 6–8

Colcannon (right)

- 1lb cooked mashed potato
- 1 1/2 cups cooked cabbage
- 1/4 cup butter
- 1/4 cup milk
- 1/2 cup finely chopped onion, leak or scallion

Gently fry the onion in melted butter until soft. Add the milk and the well-mashed potatoes and stir until heated through. Chop the cabbage finely and beat into the mixture over a low heat until all the mixture is pale green and fluffy. This dish is an excellent accompaniment for boiled ham.
Serves 4

Champ

- 1 1/2 lb cooked potatoes
- 4 oz scallions
- 1/2 cup milk
- salt and pepper
- 4 large pats butter

Peel the potatoes and boil them in salted water. Drain them well and allow to dry out completely. Meanwhile, trim and wash the scallions. Slice them finely, including the green part, and put them in a saucepan with the milk to simmer gently until soft. Drain the scallions, reserving the milk, and

beat them into the potato, gradually adding the hot milk until you have a nice fluffy mixture. Season well with salt and pepper and divide between 4 bowls, shaping each serving into a mound with a dent in the top into which you put the butter. It is eaten by dipping the potato into the melted butter.

Serves 4

Crubeens

- 1 pig's trotter (per person)
- 1 onion
- 1 carrot
- pinch of salt
- few peppercorns
- 1 bay leaf
- chopped parsley and thyme
- lettuce and tomato for garnish

Put the trotter in a pan with the other ingredients. Cover with cold water, bring to the boil, and simmer for 3 hours. Serve surrounded by lettuce and tomatoes.

BREAD

Soda Bread

- 2 cups plain white flour
- 4 cups wholewheat flour
- 1 tsp salt
- 1 tsp sugar
- 1 heaped tsp cream of tartar
- 1 heaped tsp bicarbonate of soda
- 1 tbsp baking powder
- 1 tsp vegetable oil
- 2 cups sour milk or fresh milk mixed with 1tbsp yoghurt

Add salt, sugar, cream of tartar, and baking soda to the all-purpose flour. Sift into a large mixing bowl. Add wholewheat flour and mix thoroughly with a round-ended knife, using a lifting motion to aerate the mixture. Make a well in the center and add milk, mixing until the dough leaves the sides of the bowl clean. Knead into a ball, flatten slightly and place on a greased cookie tray. Cut a cross into the top of the loaf. Brush the top with a little milk and bake in the oven, 400°F, for 40 minutes. Remove from the oven, turn loaf upside down and return to the oven for a further 5 minutes. The loaf is done when it sounds hollow when tapped on the base. Wrap it in a slightly dampened cloth and stand on its side to cool. Cut into quarters, slice and butter generously.

Coddle

- 8 oz thick bacon slices
- 1 lb pork sausages
- 1 1/2 lb potatoes
- 1 lb onions
- salt and pepper

Place the bacon and the sausages in a saucepan. Cover with boiling water. Bring back to a boil and simmer for 5 minutes. Drain off the liquid into a bowl and reserve. Peel and slice the potatoes and onions, and place them, with the meat, in a heavy saucepan or greased casserole dish. Cover with the reserved stock, season with salt and pepper before putting on the lid. Simmer on top of the stove or in a moderate oven, 350°F for about half an hour.

Serves 4

Boxty Pancakes

- 1/2 lb raw potatoes
- 8 oz mashed potatoes
- 1 tsp salt
- 1 tsp baking soda
- 2 cups all-purpose flour
- pepper
- 1/4 cup butter, margarine or bacon fat
- milk

Peel and grate the raw potatoes. Wrap them tightly in a cloth and squeeze over a bowl to extract as much of the starch liquid as possible. Thoroughly blend the grated raw potato into the cooked mashed potato. Pour the liquid off the bowl of potato starch and the starch into the potato mixture. Sift the salt and baking soda with flour and add to the potatoes. Mix well. Add the melted fat and mix again. Add as much milk as necessary to make the mixture into a batter of dropping consistency, season with pepper, and cook in spoonfuls on a greased griddle or heavy pan until crispy and golden on both sides.

Serves 6

Boiled Ham and Cabbage

- piece of uncooked ham about 3 lb
- 1 1/2–2 lb green cabbage
- 1/2 medium-sized onion or one small onion cut in half

Parsley Sauce

- 1 1/4 cups stock
- 1/4 cup butter or margarine
- 3 tbsps all-purpose flour
- 1 1/4 cups milk
- 1/2 cup chopped parsley

Soak the ham for several hours or cover it with cold water, bring to the boil, discard water, and cover meat with more boiling water. Bring it back to the boil, skim, and simmer for 20 minutes to the pound and 20 minutes extra. Reserve the stock. Meanwhile, cut the cabbage in half and cut out a V in the stalk end of both halves to remove the fibrous end of the stalk. Cut the two halves down through the V and rinse the quarters in salted water. Place in a large saucepan with the cut onion. When the ham is cooked add 3–4 ladles of the stock to the cabbage, cover tightly and cook for about 20 minutes. Meanwhile, skim the ham, cut the lattice pattern in the fat, coat it with brown sugar, and stud it with cloves. Brown it in a hot oven while the cabbage is cooking. Drain the cabbage and remove the onion.

Measure out 1 1/4 cups of the stock in which the

cabbage was cooked to use for the parsley sauce. Melt the butter or margarine in a saucepan, stir in the flour, and make a roux. Cook without browning for a minute or two. Gradually add the stock and then the milk. Bring to a boil and stir for a few minutes. Add the chopped parsley. Adjust the seasoning. Serve with the ham and cabbage, and potatoes boiled in their jackets.
Serves 6–8

Boiled Chicken and Parsley Sauce

- 2–3 oz chicken fat
- 1 large boiling fowl
- 1 large onion, chopped
- 1 carrot, chopped
- 1 turnip chopped
- 1 stick celery, chopped
- bouquet garni
- salt and pepper
- parsley sauce (see Boiled Ham and Cabbage)

Put the chicken fat in a large pan. Wash and dry the bird, and season well with salt and pepper. Brown slightly in the fat, remove and add the vegetables. Turn them in the fat for a few minutes then add the bird and cover with boiling water. Add salt, pepper, and bouquet garni. Bring back to the boil, skim, then cover the pot, and simmer the contents slowly for about 3 hours or 40 minutes to the pound. When the bird is cooked, remove it from the pot, and keep hot on a serving dish. Measure out 1 1/4 cups of the stock in which the cabbage was cooked to use for the parsley sauce. Melt the butter or margarine in a saucepan, stir in the flour, and make a roux. Cook without browning for a minute or two. Gradually add the stock and then the milk. Bring to a boil and stir for a few minutes. Add the parsley.

Serves 4–6

Guinness Cake

- 1 cup butter or margarine
- 1 cup brown sugar
- 1 1/4 cups Guinness
- 1 1/2 cups raisins
- 1 1/2 cups currants
- 1 1/2 cups golden raisins
- 3/4 cup shredded orange and lemon peel, mixed
- 5 cups all-purpose flour
- 1 tsp allspice
- 1 tsp nutmeg
- 1/2 tsp baking soda
- 3 eggs

Grease and line a 9-in cake pan with wax paper. Place the butter, sugar, and the Guinness in a saucepan and bring slowly to a boil, stirring constantly until the sugar and butter have melted. Mix in the dried fruit and peel, and bring to the boil. Simmer for 5 minutes. Remove from the heat and cook thoroughly. Sift the flour, spice, and baking soda into a large mixing bowl. Stir in the cooled fruit mixture and beaten eggs. Turn into the cake pan and bake in the center of a pre-heated oven, 325°F for 2 hours. Test with a skewer. When done, cool in the pan before removing the cake.

Smoked Mackerel Pâté

- 8 oz skinned, smoked mackerel fillets
- 1/3 cup softened butter
- juice of 1 lemon
- black pepper
- lemon slices for garnish
- parsley for garnish

This takes only seconds to make using a food processor or electric blender, but you can mash up the mackerel in a bowl, and thoroughly mix in the butter and lemon juice. Season with freshly ground black pepper, and either divide between small individual custard cups or arrange mackerel attractively in a serving dish, garnished with lemon slices and parsley. Serve with brown toast or soda bread.
Serves 4

Broiled Trout with Almonds

- 4 fresh trout
- 1 lemon, quartered
- 1/4 cup butter
- 1/4 cup slivered almonds
- parsley for garnish

Clean the trout. Place a lemon wedge in the cavity of each. Line the broiler pan with buttered foil and carefully lay the

fish on it. Smear a little butter on each. Preheat the broiler and cook the trout under it for 5 minutes. Turn them very carefully, put a little more butter on top and broil for another 5 minutes. Keep the fish warm on plates while you toss the almonds in the butter in the broiler pan and brown them under the broiler. Sprinkle them over the fish. Serve with garnish of lemon slices and parsley.
Serves 4

Boiled Lobster

- salt or seaweed
- 4 1-lb lobsters
- lemon wedges
- parsley sprigs
- 1 cup melted butter

Fill a large stock pot with water and add salt or a piece of seaweed. Bring the water to the boil and then turn off the heat. Place the live lobsters into the pot, keeping your hand well away from the claws if they are not secured. Lower them in claws first. Bring the water slowly back to a boil and cook the lobster for about 15 minutes, or until they turn bright red. Remove them from the water and drain briefly on paper towels. Place on a plate, and garnish with lemon wedges, and parsley sprigs.
Serves 4

Irish Stew

- 2 lb boned lamb or 3lbs rib chops
- 2 lb potatoes
- 2 large onions
- salt and pepper
- a bouquet garni
- 1 1/2 cups water
- chopped parsley for garnish

Trim the meat, leaving a little of the fat on. Peel and slice the potatoes and onions. Season the meat and vegetables with salt, pepper and herbs. Then, starting and finishing with a layer of potatoes, layer the potatoes, meat, and onions in a large saucepan or casserole. Add the water and cover tightly. Either simmer on a very low heat on the top of the stove for 2–2 1/2 hours or cook in a slow oven, 275°F, for the same length of time.

The pot or casserole should be shaken occasionally to prevent the potatoes from sticking and you should check that the liquid has not dried out. The finished stew should not be too runny. The potatoes should thicken it sufficiently. Brown the top potato layer under a hot broiler and serve sprinkled with chopped parsley.

Serves 4

Potato Cakes

- 1 cup all-purpose flour
- 1/2 tsp salt
- 1/2 tsp baking powder
- 2 tbsp butter
- 2 3/4 cups mashed potato
- bacon fat or dripping

Sift flour, salt, and baking powder. Cut in the butter. Mix in the potatoes and knead into a ball. Cut this in two and roll half out on a floured board or work surface into a circle half an inch thick. Divide into 4 segments. Cook them for 2–3 minutes each side, on a very hot pan or griddle greased with bacon fat or dripping. Repeat the process with the other half.

Serves 8

INDEX

Page numbers in *italic* refer to illustrations

Achill Island 25, 411–14
Act of Union 63, 90
Adams, Gerry 99
Adare 149
agriculture 29, 429–34
Ahern, Bertie 11, 99
Aherne family 224
Aidan, St. 343
Alexander, Harold, Earl of Tunis 100
Allen family 224
angling 388
Anglo-Normans 38–45, 81
Antrim, Co. 9, 24, 28, 153
Aragh 168
Aran Islands 179, 411, 419, 422
Ardmore *332–3*
Armagh 154, 357
Armagh, Co. 9, 24, 154
arts and crafts 325–9
Athenry 179
athletics 387–8
Athlone 178
Australia 139–40
Austria 142–3

Bacon, Francis 100
Balfe, Michael William 100
Ballybunion 148
Ballycastle 153
Banim brothers 299–301, 305
Bann, River 25
Bantry House 147
Barnardo, Thomas John 101
Barrett family 225
Barrow, River 164, 166
Barry, John 101
Barry family 227
Beckett, Samuel 303, 305
Beenkeragh, Mount 21
Behan, Brendan 287, 422
Belfast 9, 25, 65, 188–90
Berkeley, George 101
Best, George 102
Big Bow Meel Island 20
Binchy, Maeve 303, 306
birds 394, 400, 427, 433
Birr Castle Demesne 177
Blackwater River 154
Blanchflower, Danny 102
Blarney Castle 147
Blaskets 419, 422, 423
Bloody Sunday 98
bogs 167, 395–400
Boland, Eavan 303, 306
Bono 102
Book of Kells 35, 173, *300*
Boru, Brian 38–9, 81, 103
Boycott, Charles 103
Boyd family 228
Boyle, Robert 104
Boyle family 228
Boyne, Battle of 57, 88
Boyne, Palace of 173

Boyne Valley 29
Boyzone 323–4
Brady family 231
bread 430, 457
Breen family 231
Brendan, St. *342*, 343
Brennan family 232
Brigid, St. 344, 361
Brontë, Patrick 161
Bronze Age 32, 162
Browne family 234
Browne's Hill Dolmen 164
Bunratty Castle 146
Burke, Edmund 104, 299
Burke, John 105
Burke, Robert O'Hara 105
Burke family 235
Burr Point 20
Burren 146, 392
Bushmills 205
Butler, James 54, 55, 88
Butler family 43, 44, 217, 235
Butt, Isaac 66, 105
Butterstream Gardens 173
Byrne, Gay 106
Byrne family 237

Cahir Castle 152
Canada 138–9
Cape Clear 382
Carleton, William 299, 306
Carlow 164
Carlow, Co. 9, 24, 164
Carrauntuohill, Mount 21
Carrickfergus Castle 41, 153
Carroll family 238
Carrowmore 159, 183
Casement, Sir Roger 106
Cashel, Rock of *220*, 221
Castleisland 148
Cavan, Co. 9, 155
Céide Fields 181
céilidh 371
Celts 32–4, 80
ceramics 328–9
Champ 452
Charles I 51–2, 86
Charles II 55, 88
cheese 429
Chicken, Boiled 465
Chieftains, The 322
Childers, Erskine 106
Christianity 34–5, 80, 337–41, 415
cities 24, 184–93
Clare, Co. 10, 146
climate 26, 27
Clonmacnoise 35, 177, 338, *348*
Clontarf, Battle of 38, 81
Coddle 458
Colcannon 453
Collins, Michael 71–4, 107
Collins Barracks *108*
Colman/Columbanus, St 344
Columba, St. 80–1, 173, 192, 344
Comeragh Mountains 150, *151*
Connacht 10, 39, 43
Connolly, James 107, 218
Connolly family 238
Cooley Peninsula 169
Cork 25, 36, 190–2, *431*
Cork, Co. 10, 24, 28, 147
Corkery, Daniel 303, 306
Corlea Trackway 168
Corrs, The 324

Cosgrave, William 74
counties 9–10, 24, 145–83
Cranberries, The 323
crannogs 79
Crean, Tom 109
Croagh Patrick 354, 357
Croaghaun 21
Cromwell, Oliver 54, 86–8
Crubeens 454
Cuchulainn 298, 363
Cullen family 240

Davitt, Michael 109
Delaney family 241
Derry 25, 55, 98, 192, *193*
Derry, Co. 9, 156, *203*
Desmond, Earls of 44, 48
De Valera, Éamon 71, 74–5, 93, 109, *111*
dishes, traditional 447–71
dogs 403–10
Donegal, Co. 9, 17, 159, *288*
Down, Co. 9, 18, 60, 161, *197*
Downhill Strand *157*
Downpatrick 357
Doyle, Roddy 303, 307
Doyle family 241
Drogheda 54
drumlins 155, 411
Dublin *8*, 24, 26, 36, 70, 184–8, *393*
  cathedral 222, *223*, *340*
  townhouses 212, *213*
Dublin, Co. 9, 24, 165
Dublin Bay 165
Dún Eoghanachta *30–1*
Dún Laoghaire 25
Dunamase, Rock of 167
Dungarvan 150
Dunluce Castle 153
Dunwoody, Richard 110

Earhart, Amelia 156
Easter Rising 70–1, 72–3, 93, *94–5*
Eddery, Pat 110
Edgeworth, Maria 299, 307
Edward the Bruce 112
Elizabeth I 48–9, *50*, 83
emigration 65, 135–42
Emmet, Robert 62, 90
English Civil War 53–4
Enniskillen 55, 158
Enya 323
Europe 142–3
European Union 75, 76, 98

fairies 364
family names 224–63
Famine 64–5, 90–1, 439
Famine Museum 182
Farquhar, George 298, 307
Farrell family 243
Fastnet Rock 20
Fenians 65, 68, 92, 142
Ferguson, Sir Samuel 112
Fermanagh, Co. 9, 158
ferry routes 16
festivals 366
Fiacre, St. 345
Field, John 320
first names 265–81
fish 434–6
Fitzgeralds 43–8, 244
Fitzgibbon, John 59
Fitzmaurice, James 112

Flaherty family 244
food and drink 429–71
French, Percy 182, 319

Gaels 32–4, 37–43, 49, 80
Gaeltacht *282*, 285–7
Gall, St 346
Galway 25, 43, 193, *201*
Galway, Co. 10, 17, 24, 179
Garinish Island *417*
Garraun Point 21
Gearóid Mór 45, 83
geology 17–18
Giant's Causeway 205, *206–7*
Gladstone, William 67, 92
glass 327–8
Glebe House 159
Glen of Imaal Terrier 410
Glendalough 35, 176
Glundubh, Niall 112
Goldsmith, Oliver 307
golf 386
Gonne, Maud 113
Gortin Glen Forest *390–1*
Gorumna Island *424–5*
government 9, 10–12
Gregory, Lady 302, 308
Griffith, Arthur 68, 74, 113
Guinness 439–44
Guinness, Arthur 113, 440
Guinness Cake 466

Ham and Cabbage 462
Hamilton, Hugo 303, 308
Handel, George F. 320
Haughey, Charles 114, *115*
Healy Pass *22–23*
Heaney, Seamus 303, 308
Henry II 39–40, 82
Henry VII 45
Henry VIII 46–8, 83, 341
hermits 415
Herzog, Chaim 114
Higgins, Alex 116
Hillery, Patrick 116
Hoban, James 116
Holland, John Philip 117
Holland, Matthew *384*
Home Rule 66–70, 74, 92–3
horse racing 170, 387
Hume, John 117
hurling 386
Hyde, Douglas 117

Inishmore *30–1*
Inishtrahull Island 20
IRA 71, 74, 76, 93, 97–8
Ireland's Eye *420–1*
Irish-Americans 135–8, 163
Irish Citizen Army 70, *72–3*
Irish dancing 369–71
Irish language 283–95
Irish National Stud 170
Irish Republic 74–5, 93
Irish Sea 17
Irish Setter 407–8
Irish Stew 470
Irish Terrier 409
Irish Volunteers 70, 71
Irish Water Spaniel 408
Irish Wolfhound 403–4, *405*
Irvine, Eddie 118, 388
islands 20, 25, 411–27
Ita/Ida, St. 346

James I 51–2, 83
James II 55, 57, 88
Jerpoint Abbey *42*, *210*, 211
jewelry 329
Jordan, Eddie 118, 388
Joyce, James 302, 308–10

Kavanagh, Patrick 162, 310
Keane, Robbie 118
Keane, Roy 119
Kearney family 246
Kells 35, 173
Kelly family 246
Kennedy, John F. *134*, *175*
Kennedys 138, 174, 247
Kennelly, Brendan 311
Kerry, Co. 10, 148
Kerry Beagle 404–7
Kerry Blue Terrier 409–10
Kevin, St. 34, 176, 347
Kieran/Ciaran, St 348
Kildare, Co. 9, 60, 70, 170
Kildare, Earls of 44–8, 83
Kilkenny, Co. 9, 166
Kilkenny Castle 166, *216*, 217
Killary Harbor *6*, *282*
Kilmainham Jail 218, *219*
Kinsale 49, 83, 147
Kinsella, Thomas 303, 311
Kitchener, Lord 119, *121*
knitwear 327
Knock 181

Lahinch 386
lakes 25
languages 14, 283–95
Laois, Co. 9, 167
legal system 10, 12
Leinster 9, 33, 38–40, 60
Leitrim, Co. 10, 24, 180
leprechauns 367
Letterkenny *288*
Lewis, C.S. 303, 311
lighthouses 416
Limavady 156
Limerick 25, 36, 38, 81
Limerick, Co. 10, 149
linen 327
Lisburn 25
Lismore 150
Listowel 148
literature 287, 297–317
Littleton Bog 152
Lobster, boiled 469
Longford, Co. 9, 168
Lough Beg 153
Lough Derg 146, 152, 357
Lough Erne 158
Loug Gur 149
Lough Key Forest 182
Lough Neagh 25, 153
Louth, Co. 9, 24, *26*, 169
Lynch family 249
Lyons family 250

Malachy, St. 349
Malin Head 20
Markievicz, Countess Constance120, *122*
Mary I 48, 83
Massey, William 120
Maynooth *171*
Mayo, Co. 10, 17, *144*, 181
McAleese, Mary 10, 120

McCabe, Patrick 303, 311
McMahon, Marshal 143
MacMurrough, Diarmuid 39–40
Meagher, Thomas 123
meat 433–4
Meath, Co. 9, 173
Mellifont Abbey 169
mermaids/merrows 367–8
Middle Ages 41–4
Mitchel, John 123
Mitchelstown Caves 152
Moher, Cliffs of 146
Monaghan, Co. 9, 162
Monasterboice 169, *330*
monasteries 34, 36–7, 48, 80, 337–41
Montague, John 303, 312
Moore, George 301, 312
Moore, Thomas 124, 299, 312, 319
Moore family 250
motor racing 388
Mount Sandel 28
mountains 21
Mourne Mountains *160*, 161, *428*
Muckross House 148
Muldoon, Paul 303, 312
Mumba, Samantha *318*, 324
Munro, Gen. George 53–4
Munster 10, 38, 39
Murphy family 251
Murray family 252
music 319–24, 366
myths/legends 297–8, 363–8

Navan 154
Neeson, Liam 124
Nettle Soup 451
New Zealand 140–1
Newgrange *78*, 79, 208, *209*
Newtownabbey 25
Nine Years War 48–9
Nolan family 254
Northcliffe, Viscount 114
Northern Ireland 75–6, *96*, 97–8

O'Brien, Aidan 124
O'Brien, Edna 303, 312
O'Brien, Edward 303, 313
O'Brien, Kate 303, 313
O'Brien, Vincent 125
O'Brien, William 91, *91*, 218
O'Brien family 39
Ó Ceallaigh, Séan 125
O'Connell, Daniel 62–4, 89–90, 125
O'Connor, Frank 303, 313
O'Connor, Sinead 323
O'Conor family 39, *84–5*
Ó Dálaigh, Cearbhall 126
O'Donnell, Daniel 324
O'Donnells 41, 51, 143
O'Faolain, Sean 303, 313
Offaly, Co. 9, 177, *396*
O'Flaherty, Liam 314
Ogham 297
O'Grady, Standish 314
O'Higgins, Bernardo 141
Omagh 26
O'Malley, Grace 415
O'Neill, Hugh 49, 51, 83, 126, 163
O'Neill, Owen Roe 53–4
O'Neill family 33, 38, 39, 41, 143, 163, *362*
O'Rourke family 180
O'Shea, Kitty 67
O'Sullivan, Sonia 387–8

Pale 41–2, 43, 44, 46
Palladius 34, 80, 337
Parliament 11
Parnell, Charles S. 66–7, 92, 127, *128*, 218
Patrick, St. 34, 80, 154, *336*, 351–7
Pearse, Patrick 70, 127, *129*, 218, 287
peat bog 167, 168, 395–400
Petty, William 54, 127
Phoenix Park *133*, 165, 218, *358*
placenames 194
plants 389–92, 400
Plunkett, St. Oliver 55, 349
pop music 323
population 12–13, 24, 88, 91
Portarlington 167
potato 64, 439
    recipes 448, 461, 471
Poulnabrone 29
Powerscourt 26, 214
prayers 359–61
Protestants 51, 53–9
provinces 9–10, 145

Quinn family 255
quotes and sayings 373–6

Raleigh, Sir Walter 439
recipes 447–71
Redmond, John 68, 70, 129
Reid family 255
Reilly family 257
religion 13–14, 337–61
restaurants 444
Restoration 55–6
Richard II 43–4, 82, 193
Riverdance 321, 371
rivers 25
road bowling 388
Robinson, Mary 77, 130
Roe Valley 156
Rogers family 258
Roscommon 10, 21, 182
Rosslare 26
round towers 37, 331–5
rugby 387
Ryan family 258

sailing 388
St. Patrick's Day 10, 136
saints 343–7, 366, 415
Shackleton, Ernest 130
shamrock 355–6
Shannon, River 25, 146, 155
Shannon Estuary 148, 149
Shaw, G.B. 302, 314
Sheridan, Richard 315
Sinn Féin 68, 71, 74, 93, 98
Skelligs 35, *264*, 411
Slane, Hill of *336*, 353
Slane Castle *172*
Slieve Donard 21
Sligo, Co. 10, 183, *200*
Sligo Abbey *84–5*, 159
Sloane, Hans 131
Smoked Mackerel Pâté 468
soccer *384*, 385
Soda Bread 457
South America 140
Sperrin Mountains 163
sport 68, 385–8
Steele, Richard 298, 315
Stephens, James 65, 91–2

Stone Age 28–9, *78*, 79, 208
Strangford Lough 161
Strokestown Park House 182
Strongbow 40, 81–2, 167, 222
Stuarts 51–3
Swift, Jonathan 298, 315
Synge, John M. 302, 315

Taaffe, Viscount 143
Talbot, Richard 55
Taoiseach 11
Tara 33, 80, 173, 353
Tearaght Island 21
Thurles 152
time zone 14
Tipperary, Co. 10, 152
toasts 377–80
Tone, Wolfe 60, 89, *89*, 131, 147
Torr Head 25
Tory Island 411, 419–22
Tralee 148
transport 15–16
Trimble, David 12
Trinity College *187*, *300*
Trout with Almonds 468
Tudors 46–8
Tullynally Castle 178
tweed 325–7
Tyrone, Co. 9, 24, 163

U2 323
Ulster 9, 33, 41, 43, 64, 65–6
  Plantation 49–51
Ulster America Folk Park 163
United Irishmen 60, 62, 142
United Nations 76–7, 97
United States 135–8, 163

Vikings 36–9, 81

Walsh family 259
War of Independence 71, 93
Ward family 261
waterfalls 26
Waterford 36, 81
Waterford, Co. 10, 150, *151*
weddings 381–3
Wellington, Duke of 132, *133*
Wentworth, Thomas 52, 86
Westlife 324
Westmeath, Co. 9, 178
Wexford 36, 54, 174
Wexford, Co. 9, 60, 174
Wheaten Terrier 410
Whelan family 262
White family 262
Wicklow, Co. 9, 18, 60, 176
Wicklow Mountains 214, *215*
Wild Geese 57, 88, 143
Wilde, Oscar 302, 315–17
wildlife 392–3, 400
William of Orange 55–7, *56*, 88

Yeats, W.B. 183, 301–2, 317
Young Ireland 63, 65, 91

ACKNOWLEDGEMENTS

All pictures Chrysalis Images except
page 315 Action Press/Rex FeaturesRex Images and
page 318 Andrew Milligan/Rex Features.

Special thanks to Paul Brewer, Stella Caldwell,
Noel Cullen, Katherine Edelston, Terry Forshaw, Colin Gower,
Brian Shaw, and Dr. Mark Waugh for their support and
contributions to the production of this book.